Reclaiming Personalized Learning

My grandma Helen Walla France was the first person to tell me I was a writer. She simply loved when I wrote her e-mails. She told me I had a way with words and I was "quite the writer." And just like that, I became one.

For all the people who have seen things in me that I was unable to see in myself—this is for you. I wouldn't be me without you.

Reclaiming Personalized Learning

Learning

A Pedagogy for Restoring
Equity and Humanity in Our Classrooms

Paul Emerich France

Foreword by Carol Ann Tomlinson

FOR INFORMATION:

Corwin

A SAGE Company

2455 Teller Road

Thousand Oaks, California 91320

(800) 233-9936

www.corwin.com

SAGE Publications Ltd.

1 Oliver's Yard

55 City Road

London EC1Y 1SP

United Kingdom

SAGE Publications India Pvt. Ltd.

B 1/I 1 Mohan Cooperative Industrial Area

Mathura Road, New Delhi 110 044

India

SAGE Publications Asia-Pacific Pte. Ltd.

18 Cross Street #10-10/11/12

China Square Central

Singapore 048423

Program Director and Publisher: Dan Alpert

Content Development Editor: Lucas Schleicher

Senior Editorial Assistant: Mia Rodriguez

Production Editor: Tori Mirsadjadi

Copy Editor: Megan Granger

Typesetter: C&M Digitals (P) Ltd.

Proofreader: Victoria Reed-Castro

Indexer: Jean Casalegno

Cover and Interior Designer: Scott Van Atta

Marketing Manager: Sharon Pendergast

Printed in the United States of America

Library of Congress Cataloging-in-Publication Data

Names: France, Paul Emerich, author.

Title: Reclaiming personalized learning : a pedagogy for restoring equity and humanity in our classrooms / Paul Emerich France.

Description: First edition. | Thousand Oaks, California : Corwin, [2020] | Includes bibliographical references and index.

Identifiers: LCCN 2019020896 | ISBN 9781544360669 (paperback)

Subjects: LCSH: Individualized instruction. | Educational equalization. | Critical pedagogy.

Classification: LCC LB1031 .F72 2020 | DDC 371.39/4—dc23 LC record available at https://lccn.loc.gov/2019020896

This book is printed on acid-free paper.

Certified Chain of Custody
SUSTAINABLE Promoting Sustainable Forestry
FORESTRY www.sfiprogram.org
INITIATIVE SFI-01268
SFI label applies to text stock

19 20 21 22 23 10 9 8 7 6 5 4 3 2 1

DISCLAIMER: This book may direct you to access third-party content via web links, QR codes, or other scannable technologies, which are provided for your reference by the author(s). Corwin makes no guarantee that such third-party content will be available for your use and encourages you to review the terms and conditions of such third-party content. Corwin takes no responsibility and assumes no liability for your use of any third-party content, nor does Corwin approve, sponsor, endorse, verify, or certify such third-party content.

CONTENTS

FOREWORD

By Carol Ann Tomlinson

Early in this book, the author gives himself—and me—permission to tell a story. Stories, he reminds us, are what remain when we've forgotten most of the daily details of life. Here's the story of my first teaching experience. What I remember of that fragile time is one of the reasons I am captivated by Paul France's ideas, experiences, language, and wisdom.

My first experience as a public school teacher was—to be generous—chaotic, untethered, and terrifying. I had not majored in education in college (although that might not have improved my prospects much). I landed my first teaching job at the end of the first marking period in a K–12 school in rural North Carolina during the first year of mandated segregation—a second reality for which I was fully unprepared. The central office person who hired me (I never learned his role), and who was doubtless looking for a warm body to put in a classroom that was about to be lacking a teacher, didn't quite know what I would be teaching but did caution me to try to find the school before I showed up to teach, because, in his words, "It's way out there—a little tough to locate."

I spent most of that weekend trying to figure out how to make my way from the small city in which I lived to the unremarkable school building that looked at once both aged and ageless. The principal was not at school when I arrived ninety minutes before the bell that seemed to warn of the day to come. Neither was he there when the bell sounded. As I grew more nervous, the secretary summoned the assistant principal, who was teaching a class at the time, and he loped in front of me down the long corridor that led to the room that would mark the beginning of my fifty-year career in education. An elderly and slightly frail-looking man answered the door when the assistant principal knocked. "Mr. Melton," the assistant principal said, then paused. Pointing to me, he continued, "This is your replacement. You're fired."

Mr. Melton was enraged. I was mortified, and fighting a powerful instinct to run out of the nearby exit. Mr. Melton also had a keen desire to exit the room, but he was in a carpool and it was not his day to drive. He had no transportation of his own. He turned to me and snarled, "Okay, if they think you're better than I am, you see what you can do to get these fine young people to listen to you."

I was shy, generally voiceless, devoid of self-confidence, but apparently had in me a survival instinct that had not previously emerged in my twenty-three years. "I'm sorry," I lied, "but I was told I could observe for a day before I began teaching. I'm not prepared to teach today"—that part was as true as any words ever spoken—"and so I think I'll sit in the back of the room and watch."

Mr. Melton sat in the front of the room—and watched. And what we watched was five classes of high school sophomores (in two world history classes) and three periods of high school juniors (in English classes) spar, shout, and generally entertain themselves by climbing in and out of the first-story windows. The one exception was sixth period, when it had gotten beastly hot outside, so those students sparred, shouted, and tried with little success to set the freestanding bulletin board on fire.

It would have been wise, of course, to focus my attention on creating some sort of lesson plan(s) for the next day. My brain, at a DEFCON-1 level of anxiety, generated only one sound loop that played and rewound and replayed for seven hours, nonstop. "I don't need a job this badly."

The truth was, though, that I was desperate for a job, so at the risk of annihilation by humiliation, I returned the following day.

The story is long after that—and funny and tragic and enlightening and humbling—and unpredictably gratifying. When the year ended, I knew with certainty two things: I was a mighty poor teacher, and teaching was the most amazing job on the planet.

I survived the year, of course, and occasionally thrived. Because I didn't know how to teach, I relied on the only source I had to help me figure out how to get those "fine young people to listen" to me. I began my long journey as an educator with one instinct that I now understand saved me. I was captivated by the young human beings who showed up in our blank, bleak room every day. I was curious to know who they were and what their lives were like. I wanted to know what their dreams were and how our seemingly divergent lives intersected. I wanted to help them experience important ideas together and, despite the palpable animosities that swirled around their community, our state, and the country that year, learn to see one another's common humanity. I wanted them to know that learning was marked with joy, as well as productive struggle. And I counted on the students to help me understand how to accomplish those things.

I discovered on my first day as their teacher (rather than the previous day, when I was an unnamed accessory in the back of the room) that no tenth grader in my two history classes could tell me the name of the country we lived in. That was followed by two interlocking decisions, informed only by what I suppose was instinct or common sense. First, it made no sense to me to try to "cover" the world history textbook with them in the remaining twenty-four weeks of school when they had so little sense of historical time and place in the world. Second, I would begin with some moment in history that seemed in some way connected to their knowledge and experience. Through a series of conversations and questionnaires, I learned of two elements of significance in most of their lives: stock car racing and a sort of fundamentalist religion. It was beyond me to draw on stock car racing to enter the study of the history of (Western) mankind, so we began rambling around at the time when the Reformation gave rise to Protestantism—which I never succeeded in helping them accept as connected in any way at all to the churches they attended or the traditions they practiced.

Nonetheless, we traveled about three hours on a questionable school bus to visit the Hillel House and the Newman Center in a "nearby" college town. The students had not heard of Catholics or Jews. We talked about the music the high schoolers sang in their services and compared it with music in the Jewish tradition and the Catholic liturgy. We talked about the time in which these young people lived, when daily headlines (largely beyond their awareness) reflected a world about to boil over with tension and the drive to make change, comparing the unrest of current times with discontent in the Reformation. Both periods seemed new and interesting to adolescents, who by nature are restless. And so we proceeded with the study of world history.

In English class, it took little time or probing to realize that a few students were proficient and thoughtful readers and that many had access neither to books nor the fundamentals of reading. So I read to the students, and they loved the music of the words. We talked about their lives reflected in the themes of the stories we shared. I often gave different ones of them different things to read in a class period as I came to know their interests and developing skills. And we talked about the people and problems and wisdom and folly they encountered on the printed page and in their world. They wrote their stories early on—and later stories of the important people in their lives, and we related those stories to the literature, working as a class, individually, and as partners and in small groups.

I would not have gotten passing marks on fidelity to the textbooks, or adherence to a curriculum guide had there been one. I lacked critical knowledge about teaching reading. My feedback on student writing was often flimsy or formulaic. And, of course, there were times when the students became restless because I checked attendance aloud or returned papers student by student or didn't stop our work in time to ready them for a peaceful exit from the class.

But on the plus side, our time together was what Paul France would call "humanized." We developed what he terms a "collective conscious"—a sense of shared belonging, mutual respect, and foundational knowledge from which we could move forward both together and in small groups. And we grew in both group and individual reflection, developing both shared and personal identities. We began to believe in ourselves and in the power of learning to help us make meaning of our own lives and the world we inhabited.

I moved to another state at the end of that year, but I took with me as a gift from young people who were, in fact, quite fine a nascent understanding of the art of teaching that would guide me in developing, with like-minded public school colleagues, the concept of differentiation that allowed us to teach the full range of learners in rhythms that brought students together to explore rich ideas, and also allowed us to divide them into a great range of fluid groupings so they could explore and develop in a more granular way. It led me to understand that learning had to happen *in* my students, not *to* them. It reminded me that young people of all ages (and I would assert adults, as well) need to find joy in learning often enough to propel them to take the next step, and the next.

Later, in my second life at the University of Virginia, what I took away from my first year in the classroom shaped the way I presented the role of the teacher to both the undergraduate and graduate students I taught. It also has caused me to chafe against and mourn for nearly three decades our increasing tendencies to "cover curriculum," focus nearly all our efforts on test preparation, and measure the worth of both teachers and students by standardized test scores—even as our students become less standardized and as it has become clearer by the day that challenges in both the present and future of our students have no standard answers.

Reclaiming Personalized Learning: A Pedagogy for Restoring Equity and Humanity in Our Classrooms is both wise and smart, both visionary and sane. It is both poetic and approachable, both challenging and affirming. Its author is deeply knowledgeable about technology and deeply skeptical of the likelihood that technology-centered pedagogy will better teaching and learning in today's schools. He is wary of adopting "personalization" as the next new thing, and yet offers a vision of personalization that is restorative.

It has been a long, long time since I have read a book that has challenged me as often or energized me as deeply as this book has. I wish that same experience for legions of other educators who care to create schools and classrooms that make us all more fully human.

ACKNOWLEDGMENTS

I am both a teacher and a storyteller. All teachers are. I am grateful to all my courageous students for sharing pieces of themselves with me, for bravely sharing their stories and allowing their inner dialogues to be molded by my words. Without their stories, I would have very little to say, and for that I am indebted to them.

This book would not have happened if not for Jim Knight, who connected me with my now friend, editor, and thought-partner, Dan Alpert. Thank you to both of them for giving me the opportunity to make a dream of mine come true.

Teaching is not a solitary practice, and for this reason, I want to thank my friends and colleagues who have helped me become the teacher I am. When I began teaching, I was on a team called the Voyagers, and that team—Courtney, Monica, Andrea, Katy, Markus, and Amanda—is responsible for who I am as a teacher today.

Markus is one of the greatest LGBTQ allies I've ever known. My story would be incomplete without sharing my experiences as an openly gay teacher. Markus was an ally before it was cool—and before it was safe. "A good friend would bail you out of jail," he once said to me. "But a best friend is the one sitting there in the cell with you saying, '*Damn*, that was fun!'" Thanks for being a best friend when I needed it.

Finally, for loving me unconditionally and giving up Saturday morning cuddles so I could go and write, I want to express deepest gratitude to my husband, David. With your love and support, I've uncovered pieces of myself that I've grown to love. Those pieces have helped me tell these stories.

PUBLISHER'S ACKNOWLEDGMENTS

Corwin gratefully acknowledges the contributions of the following reviewers:

Sammie Cervantez
Principal
Shell Beach Elementary School
Pismo Beach, CA

Tamara Daugherty
Third Grade Instructor
Zellwood Elementary
Zellwood, FL

Amanda McKee
Mathematics Instructor
Johnsonville High School
Johnsonville, SC

Kendra Simmons
Educational Consultant
Center for the Advancement of Transformative Education (CATE)
Evergreen Park, IL

Janice Wyatt-Ross
Program Director
Success Academy of Fayette County Public Schools
Lexington, KY

ABOUT THE AUTHOR

Paul Emerich France is a National Board Certified Teacher, dedicated to helping all learners feel seen, heard, and valued in the classroom. Paul writes for a number of prominent education publications, such as *Educational Leadership*, Edutopia, EdSurge, and the International Literacy Association's *Literacy Today*.

Paul has taught in multiple settings, ranging from transitional kindergarten to fifth grade. He has taught in both public and independent schools, even spending a bit of time in Silicon Valley working for an education technology company, founding three microschools, and building personalized learning software for the classroom. It was this experience that secured Paul's understanding of human-centered pedagogy that prioritizes humanity over technology.

Now Paul is a sought-after writer and speaker, having presented at SXSW EDU and serving as keynote speaker at regional and national conferences. His teaching and thought leadership have been featured in the *Atlantic*, *WIRED*, and the *New Yorker*. Above all else, he enjoys connecting with his students and fellow teachers, encouraging all to have courageous conversations about identity to make learning personal for adults and children alike.

INTRODUCTION

The Paradox of Personalized Learning

"Stories are data with a soul," says Brené Brown, vulnerability and shame scholar. Too often, we forget this. We forget that our own education is defined by the stories we tell about it, not by the bits of information we gathered along the way. Albert Einstein went as far as to say that education is not "what is learned" but, instead, "what remains after one has forgotten what one has learned."

It's simple, really, and maybe its simplicity is what makes it so hard for us to understand: what remains from our time in school is our stories.

In the modern, postindustrial era, the stories that define our schools are slipping away. They're becoming lost, buried underneath what feels like insurmountable initiative after insurmountable initiative, the latest of which is *personalized learning.*

I spent nearly three years, from July 2014 to June 2017, in personalized learning classrooms in Silicon Valley, working for an education technology start-up company and network of personalized learning microschools created and funded by the technology elites of Silicon Valley. I founded three microschools with three different teams of teachers, spoke with reporters around the country, and even traveled to China to contribute to this nascent philosophy of technology-powered personalized learning.

To say the least, it was invigorating. Never before had I been given so much autonomy, a blank slate on which to design schools and classrooms, or the opportunity to bring my ideas for the classroom to life.

At first, the premise of technology-powered personalized learning seemed like a panacea. Through meticulously crafted algorithms that paired children with individualized content, Silicon Valley's brand of personalized learning aimed to minimize the complexity of individualizing education and, in effect, make individual teachers more powerful. It surmised that the technology would take the load off us, the educators, so we would have more time for what mattered most: face-to-face interaction with our children.

It all took place on a *playlist*. Each individual child's playlist housed unique sets of activity cards containing individualized learning activities. The design and selection of each activity card accounted for the child's academic level, learning preferences, and interests. And while it sounded like a great idea at first, it didn't take long for the challenges associated with this brand of personalized learning to set in.

I probably don't need to tell you that the workload was immense and unsustainable. When I began teaching in Silicon Valley, I had a mere twelve students, all of whom I shared with a co-teacher. By the end of the year, we had almost twenty, and I swear I aged a year for each of them. While we hypothesized that the workload would become more sustainable with time, it never did. I relearned very quickly that for a curriculum to be individualized, a person—not a computer—had to do the individualizing. While digital technology could organize the activity cards and the data, it was my responsibility to *know* the students, understand their needs, and curate learning experiences for them. What I did not yet know was that this degree of individualization was unnecessary to personalize learning. And over the course of this book, we will discuss why.

Alas, this individualized brand of personalization prevailed due to its appeal to investors and parents. After all, the parents and investors were the primary groups we were trying to please. They were the ones paying for this unique brand of teaching and learning. Their money and support were keeping the company and the ideology alive, when in reality, it should have been its inherent value to children and educators that kept it alive. As a result, I soon realized that the brand of personalized learning we were selling was not based in evidentiary need; it instead grew from economic demand, fueled by privilege.

We live in a culture that values self-interest and competitiveness. It comes as no surprise, then, that a highly individualized brand of personalized learning would move to the forefront of the educational conversation, especially in affluent circles. Through misinformation disseminated via social media and a corporate-driven agenda that prioritizes instant gratification and self-interest, parents all over the country have begun to believe that in order for their children to have a high-quality education, it must be tailored specifically to them.

John Dewey (1938) once said that "any movement that thinks and acts in terms of an 'ism becomes so involved in reaction against other 'isms that it is unwittingly controlled by them. For it then forms its principles by reaction against them instead of by a comprehensive, constructive survey of actual needs, problems, and possibilities."

Our principles were, indeed, formed out of reaction to some of the failures of mainstream education. They were also built off of an economic demand for individualized learning that so many had yet to realize would provide no better an education than offered in most public schools that weren't individualizing curriculum. I know because I *was* a public school teacher beforehand. I've experienced public school in direct juxtaposition with this seductive, technology-powered brand of personalized learning. I saw no increases in test scores (as determined by the Northwest Evaluation Association's Measures of Academic Progress, or MAP) between the two different settings; I noticed no qualitative differences in my students' writing; I observed no significant differences in their ability to think critically or solve problems on their own; I felt no difference in their ability to empathize with others. And it was because in public school, I was employing many of the practices that I will unpack over the course of this book—practices that embody a personalized pedagogy that *humanizes* the learning experience, as opposed to *dehumanizing* learning through digitized and industrialized models for individualizing curriculum.

This stark differentiation between *humanized* personalization and *dehumanized* personalization is what lies at the center of my criticism of technology-powered personalized learning. Technology-powered individualization is just as industrialized as the standardized practices of the late 20th and early 21st centuries. It still encompasses a one-size-fits-all approach to teaching and learning; the only difference is that it's delivered digitally. It's still tracking children even if they are allowed to "go at their own pace." This isn't learning that's inherently meaningful and personal; it's learning that *dehumanizes*, serving only economic and utilitarian purposes.

It's true that education must serve a utilitarian purpose, but only in part. Meaningful education helps children grow into adults who secure jobs; it teaches children to communicate with one another; it even has the capacity to help learners push boundaries and move our country forward. But as we look at modern history and move through this precarious time in our country, it's more important than ever that education serves the purpose of restoring humanity and human connection. It must help all individuals find their purpose within a collective society.

Not only does restoring humanity in schools—and, in turn, humanizing personalization—include ensuring that our children are learning from other human beings; it means ensuring that *all* children are able to do so. This cannot happen if we do not bring equity and justice to the center of our conversations about personalized learning. Many assume that Silicon Valley's brand of personalized learning supports and promotes equity, but this reveals a gross misunderstanding of the true meaning of *equity*. Equity is not about giving all children the *same* experience or tool; it's not about providing each child a unique playlist of activities. We promote equity when we differentiate the supports given to each child, supports based on individual needs that remove barriers and help them gain access to the same high-quality education as their peers.

In essence, personalization becomes humanized when equity, justice, and inclusion are at the center of our intentions for personalization. By building inclusive learning environments, specifically engineered for the education of diverse groups of learners, learning becomes personal through student empowerment, self-awareness, and the intimate personal connections students build through authentic learning experiences. Not only is this more meaningful than Silicon Valley's dehumanizing brand of technology-powered personalized learning, it's more sustainable for educators, as well.

This isn't just a matter of classroom practice. We cannot possibly make learning personal for diverse groups of students if we do not address the socioeconomic and cultural barriers experienced by students of color, students from low-income households, and LGBTQ students. This problem can't be solved through individualized curricula, either; instead, it necessitates a foundational change in our pedagogy, the systems we build to support a *humanized* pedagogy, and the way our schools are funded.

While the intentions were good, this technology-powered, hyper-individualized brand of personalized learning has gotten us further away from the democratic principles on which our education system was founded. But that's not to say that everything happening in schools in Silicon Valley is ineffective. I've met and worked with countless skilled, talented, and creative educators who would do anything to help their children feel seen, heard, and valued in their classrooms. I've witnessed innovative projects and empathetic classroom practices that make learning feel *personal*. But I've also seen the detrimental effects of putting technology at the center of a school system, at the expense of turning away from the very people who have the capacity to make learning personal in the first place—the teachers and the children.

It's ironic, really. In our quest to personalize learning in Silicon Valley—in our quest to individualize curriculum using technology—we made our classrooms and the culture of the school all the more *impersonal*. We chose to individualize in an effort to personalize, when in reality, we needed to focus on equity, sustainable pedagogy, and collective school culture. We should have begun by investing in collective experiences and practices. We should have put our energy toward building collectivist classroom cultures that would eventually nurture individual learners in their agency and autonomy. It was a wild realization—at least for me—that these two seemingly opposed ideas, *individualism* and *collectivism*, could sit in the same space and actually support each other.

When two ideas sit in the same space, seemingly working in opposition, we call it a paradox. When more closely examined, a paradox reveals its uniquely comforting power to bring order, balance, and harmony through uncertainty, chaos, and disorder. The very idea of humanizing personalization by focusing on equity, pedagogy, and school culture does that for me.

F. Scott Fitzgerald (1936/2017) once said, "The test of a first-rate intelligence is the ability to hold two opposed ideas in mind at the same time and still retain the ability to function." Education is filled with situations like this: paradoxes that tempt us to lose our ability to function. But we must continue to function because of and in spite of them.

As we move forward into an era that beckons us to personalize learning, I hope we can all remember that the most personal mementos we take with us from school are our stories. It's true that stories are filled with conflict, opposing ideas, and dissonance. But they are also filled with heroic tales of courage, vulnerability, and humanity, none of which would exist without the main characters' willingness to sit in dissonance and be vulnerable. When we do, we see that the complexities of learning can shine in colorful abundance.

Personalized learning is no different. There are countless conflicts, dissonances, and paradoxes that make the classroom a beautifully complex place to teach and learn. It is these paradoxes and the dissonance that accompanies them that make our schools inherently personal places to restore humanity and engage in the human experience of learning.

This book is filled with stories; these stories are *my* data. They come directly from my heart and soul. In the first section, we will explore the foundations of *humanized personalization*. In the second section, we'll explore pedagogy that supports a culture of personalized learning. It's important to note that this section is not intended to be a playbook of rigidly structured processes; instead, you'll see that the pedagogy that supports a culture of personalized learning is multifaceted and will begin to take shape only if we act with vulnerability and embrace the many paradoxes that dominate the class-room. In the final section, we'll explore equity, an oftentimes overlooked but incredibly critical piece of the conversation around personalized learn-ing. After reflecting on your school's practices in the first two sections, it is my hope that you'll see the degree to which a humanized approach to personalized learning is lacking in the schools that need it most.

The truth is this: there isn't any one framework or tool that makes learning personal, as personalized learning companies with a vested interest in profits might tempt you to believe. *People* personalize learning. And for learning to feel personal, people, not technology, need to be at the center of education.

It's time we reclaim the term *personalized learning*. The education technology industry has claimed it as its own, exploiting it for profits and reducing it to individualized tracks for learning, further isolating our children when they need to be working together. The work of making learning personal resides with educators and learners. It blossoms within the relationships we build and withers when those intimate human connections are broken.

By the end of our time together, I hope to leave you with the message that personalized learning is more about culture and pedagogy than it is about individualization; I hope to leave you feeling inspired to walk into your learning space with the vulnerability and courage to navigate the many paradoxes that make the classroom feel uncertain. But most of all, I hope to leave you with the knowledge that personalized learning is a feeling more than anything else—one that helps us connect to one another through the ubiquitous human experience of learning.

FOUNDATIONS

CHAPTER ONE

PERSONALIZATION MYTHS

Every movement is a response—a rebuttal in an ongoing ideological debate. These movements sometimes manifest as responses to lessons learned from past movements or perhaps even as swift reactions to them. Personalized learning is no different. Its inception is an emphatic response to the late 20th and early 21st centuries.

In the early 1980s, the Reagan administration's *A Nation at Risk* (National Commission on Excellence in Education, 1983) became a catalyst for subsequent decades of conflict and dissonance in education, couched as sweeping educational reform. This era valued both the standardization of content and the industrialization of curriculum delivery, all for the purpose of controlling and predicting test scores. Now, after years of standardizing and the painfully palpable failure of No Child Left Behind, it's clear that one-size-fits-all curriculum isn't quite making the cut. As a result, the standardization movement has been met with a new movement: one that values differentiation, individualization, and personalization.

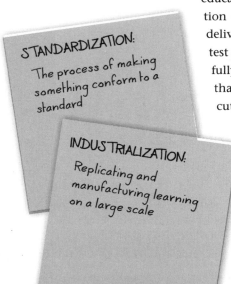

STANDARDIZATION:
The process of making something conform to a standard

INDUSTRIALIZATION:
Replicating and manufacturing learning on a large scale

What's ironic about this response, however, is that it maintains some of the educational hallmarks of the late 20th and early 21st centuries. One might think that a response to standardization—a response intended to address the shortcomings of the industrialized mindset—would signal a deindustrialization of education. But that's not what is happening. Instead, the industrialized model for education has merely been reborn in a new form. Enabled by technology, industrialized learning is now actualized on an individualized basis. Instead of a lecture-based, didactic style of teaching consumed by a class of twenty or more students, didactic instruction is now enacted through digital means, plodding children through educational videos and accompanying activities, mirroring the same passive consumption that a one-size-fits-all curriculum might. It's just now done in an individualized manner, euphemistically labeled as *personalized learning*.

This digitized response to standardization and industrialization has not been designed after "a comprehensive, constructive survey of actual needs, problems, and possibilities," as John Dewey would beckon us to do; it has not rebuilt the faulty ideological foundation on which the standardized era was built; it has neither analyzed nor evaluated the many systemic and cultural barriers that prohibit so many students from accessing an equitable education.

Instead, this response has taken the flawed large-scale practices of industrialized education and made them all the more complex by individualizing the tracks on which our students are sent. As a result, the foundation of the personalized learning movement is faulty, as well. This flawed ideology is grounded in neither equity nor humanity but, instead, is implemented with technology at the center, when in actuality *people* need to be at the center of the education system. Before personalizing learning, we must build a strong ideological foundation to avoid the mistakes of past initiatives.

When we examine these two eras closely—the standardized era of the late 20th and early 21st centuries and this current era of technology-powered personalization—we see that they're not that different at all. Both are defined by an obsession with controlling, predicting, and comparing the outcomes of our education system with those in countries around the world. This is not done with an intrinsic purpose of truly bettering our education system; it is, instead, typically enacted with fear—a fear of losing our perceived standing as the world's primary hegemonic power. We equate our success in educational outcomes with our success as a nation. This need to control, predict, and compare has engendered a toxic culture of achievement that plagues the education system. It adds pressure, generates anxiety, and counterintuitively stunts our growth as a society.

Despite our fervor to measure, control, and predict every aspect of our students, classrooms, and schools, there are some aspects of education that defy quantification. Take a moment to reflect on the ephemeral nature of a classroom's tender moments: the quizzical conversations that bubble among engaged and curious learners, the moment a child's insightful comment changes the direction of a lesson, or even the frustrating interactions where you and your students struggle to understand one another. These cannot be controlled; in fact, the power of these moments lies within their ephemerality. They are powerful because they are unpredictable and undeniably *student-driven.*

Our perceived need to control and predict is what has most heavily influenced the technology-powered personalized learning movement. I saw it firsthand when I worked in Silicon Valley. I moved there with high hopes of making monumental change in education. At first, I was enamored with the company's philosophy on personalized learning. Our hypothesis was that, by rigorously collecting data on our children, we would be able to curate individualized playlists of activities, tailored to individual needs. Theoretically, one could have as many curricula in the classroom as there were children—and all simultaneously through the technology-powered individualization of content.

Over the course of my three years there, I learned just how flawed this hypothesis was. If it had worked, it would have meant that every child would have the opportunity to work at their "just-right" level and on content that was suited to their interests. If it had worked, it would have meant that all learning could be interest-based and that all children could experience optimal engagement every moment of every day.

But these expectations and visions for personalized learning were drowned in major myths related to personalized learning (see Figure 1.1). I hope to clarify these misconceptions and share a more nuanced vision for a brand of personalization that's *humanized,* actualized by helping individuals witness their agency and autonomy, all while still connected to a collective community of learners.

Figure 1.1: Five Personalization Myths

1	2	3	4	5
MYTH	**MYTH**	**MYTH**	**MYTH**	**MYTH**
Personalizing learning means that curriculum must be individualized.	Personalizing learning means that curriculum must be interest-based.	Personalizing learning lies within the teacher's locus of control.	Technology is necessary when personalizing learning.	Digitally driven personalization paves a path to equity.
REALITY	**REALITY**	**REALITY**	**REALITY**	**REALITY**
Curriculum must be designed so all learners can access it.	Interest and engagement are not synonymous.	Personalizing learning is a partnership between educators and learners.	It can help, but only in a way that humanizes the classroom and preserves human connection.	To restore equity, we must focus on inclusive practices that remove barriers to learning.

© Paul Emerich France, 2018 www.paulemerich.com, Twitter: @paul_emerich

MYTH 1: PERSONALIZING LEARNING MEANS THAT CURRICULUM MUST BE INDIVIDUALIZED

It's intuitive to conflate personalized learning with individualized learning. But if personalization and individualization were synonymous, it would imply a linear relationship between the degree to which a curriculum is individualized and the quality of the learning itself.

John Hattie's *Visible Learning* has become somewhat of a bible for best practices in the modern classroom. Hattie conducted a meta-analysis of more than 800 studies and published the first edition in 2008. In it, he substantiates his conclusions on the effectiveness of classroom practices using *effect sizes*. An effect size, measured on a scale of 0 to 1, illustrates the effectiveness of various classroom practices by relating them to student achievement. Practices with effect sizes above .40 are considered within the "zone of desired effects," meaning the research suggests that by incorporating these practices, pedagogy can be improved beyond the range of "typical" teacher effects or even "developmental" effects, as described by Hattie.

Not only do Hattie's effect sizes show that individualized instruction has an effect size of .23, which is beneath the zone of desired effects; they show that there are a number of negative effects to individualizing instruction. It robs children of the opportunity to serendipitously collide with like- and unlike-minded peers; it strips learning of its social and emotional elements; it removes the need for the child to build self-efficacy, autonomy, and independence. The latter is of utmost importance. Learning is most meaningful when it builds autonomy, but too often, personalized learning models that focus on individualization do so *on behalf* of the child, as opposed to *in partnership* with the child. These models rely on adaptive technology that assigns lesson after lesson to children, making learning experiences no more mindful or student-driven than the one-size-fits-all lessons from a textbook or whole-class lecture. Instead, this approach to personalization creates learners who are dependent on a device, acting in direct opposition to learning experiences that build agency and autonomy (Hammond, 2014).

Degrees of individualization can, of course, improve the classroom. However, as I learned during my time in Silicon Valley, individualized learning eventually reaches a point where its returns diminish. Instead of depicting this relationship between individualization and personalization as a linear graph, I prefer to display it as an inverted U, illustrating that, in many cases, the magnitude or intensity of any single input—in this case, individualization—actually has diminishing returns (see Figure 1.2). In layman's terms, it is possible to have "too much of a good thing" (Gladwell, 2013; Yerkes & Dodson, 1908).

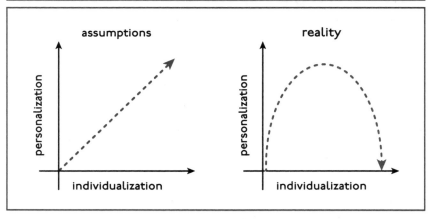

Figure I.2: Assumptions Versus Reality

© Paul Emerich France, 2018 www.paulemerich.com, Twitter: @paul_emerich

In this case, it's possible to over-individualize, resulting in the aforementioned negative effects: social isolationism that removes natural opportunities for social interaction and building emotional intelligence, as well as the erosion of a child's sense of self, autonomy, and agency in the learning journey, engendering *dependence* as opposed to *independence*. In essence, this heightened level of individualization has the potential to *depersonalize* the visceral human experience of learning. This is especially true for technology-driven personalization.

Some argue that technology-driven personalization could allow for more opportunities for individualized feedback and an increased responsiveness to the child. However, these benefits come with the aforementioned social and emotional costs, as well as engendering dependence in students due to the didactic nature of digitized curriculum. By stepping back and giving our students space to spread their wings, we create opportunities for self-reflection and productive struggle, both of which are critical to inherently personal learning. It's not the individualization of curriculum that provides this productive struggle; it is, instead, the complexity and depth of any given task that provides it, as complex tasks create challenge and provoke dissonance in children.

James Nottingham (2017), author of *The Learning Challenge*, refers to this productive struggle as the "learning pit" (see Figure 1.3). In the first step of his process, children encounter a *concept*. Afterward, they fall "into a pit" through cognitive *conflict* and internal dissonance. This is where the productive struggle begins. To climb out of the pit, students *construct* knowledge through feedback and autonomous problem solving, and by the end of the four-step process, they are able to *consider* the stages they've just gone through and the strategies they've used. They are able to reflect. Should we foster dependence in children, as many automated personalized learning

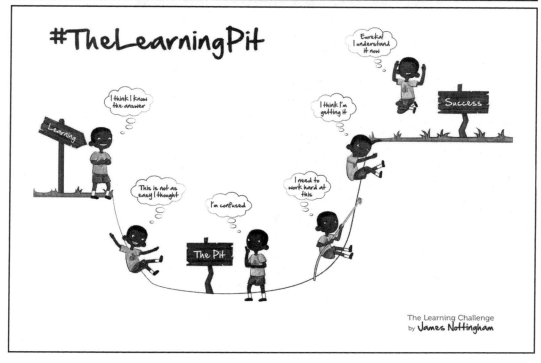

Source: James Nottingham, *The Learning Challenge* (Corwin, 2017). © James Nottingham

tools do, we rob them of this valuable process, and by proxy, we take away opportunities for autonomous learning.

In the next few chapters, we'll delve more deeply into the differences between individualized learning and personalized learning. Creating a sustainable model for personalized learning necessitates engineering a learning environment where there are opportunities for children to *converge* around a common task or provocation, as well as *diverge* into small groups or work individually. In all three of these cases, inherently *personal* learning can take place. I call these the *three dimensions of personalized learning.*

In the first dimension, we shape the collective conscious of the classroom through practices that unite an entire group of students. The second dimension of personalized learning urges us to leverage small-group and partnered instruction. It is here that we can group students strategically or allow them to learn from one another through dialogue and discourse. In the third dimension, we nurture a child's inner dialogue, as opposed to individualizing the curriculum. While some argue that individualization necessitates an individualized and interest-based curriculum, this further engenders social isolationism, bringing me to our next myth.

MYTH 2: PERSONALIZED LEARNING MUST BE INTEREST-BASED

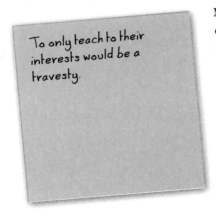

To only teach to their interests would be a travesty.

Many believe that meaningful learning must be linked to a child's interests. This simply is not true. When children start school, they are five years old and have hardly scratched the surface of the world's many languages and literacies. In fact, they have hardly begun to get to know themselves, their senses of self budding along with the rest of them. To only teach to their interests would be a travesty. It would rob them of the opportunity to learn about unfamiliar topics; to build a diverse schema for later learning; to see the value in learning about such unfamiliar, seemingly uninteresting topics. This is true for older students, too.

Meaningful engagement is defined by an investment and participation that grows out of an intrinsic motivation, not a curriculum that aligns only with student interests. In Daniel Pink's (2009) book *Drive: The Surprising Truth About What Motivates Us*, he identifies three major inputs to intrinsic motivation: *autonomy, mastery*, and *purpose*. People who are intrinsically motivated will be meaningfully engaged even if the topic isn't of highest interest. They feel a sense of *autonomy*, meaning they can exercise their freedom to make decisions within socially defined constraints; they have the sense that they are continuously *mastering*, or getting better, at a given skill or competency; and they understand the *purpose* behind learning and growing.

In turn, the personalized classroom need not be tailored to the interests of every single child; it need not be a place where children simply decide what they're going to learn. The personalized classroom, instead, needs to be designed to help children witness their agency and autonomy; to help them see, understand, and verbalize their performance and progress; to help them understand how learning is *relevant* to their lives. When we view personalized learning in this way, we begin to see that it is a partnership—a responsibility shared with the child, for the child will be the writer, narrator, and protagonist of their learning journey.

MYTH 3: PERSONALIZED LEARNING IS ONLY THE TEACHER'S RESPONSIBILITY

It makes sense to think that personalizing learning is entirely the teacher's responsibility. However, in a personalized classroom, our role as teachers changes quite a bit. Sure, we're still responsible for planning lessons and providing students with material to spark learning, but instead of the educators being the ones who are giving students the gift of learning, the children themselves are doing the hard work of writing their own learning narratives.

I'm a firm believer that if you're doing more work than the twenty or more students in your class, then you're doing too much. Your kids should be working harder than you during the school day. It is, after all, *their* education. By sharing the responsibility of personalizing learning with our children, we suddenly see the engagement, investment, and intrinsic motivation we hope for in our kids. Our duty, then, becomes less about *making* the children learn and more about *partnering* with students to create environments and build curricula that allow children to ask questions, construct ideas autonomously, and engage with peers in conversations around learning.

Instead of planning twenty or more sets of curricula, we construct multiability provocations that allow diverse groups of students to converge around common content so they may learn *with* one another. This allows all children access to rigorous tasks, granting each individual child the opportunity to integrate provocations into a preexisting schema in a manner that's meaningful for them. When personalization is achieved in this manner— through multi-ability curricula with students as partners—it's suddenly more sustainable for the teacher.

A CLOSER LOOK

DIFFERENTIATION, INDIVIDUALIZATION, AND PERSONALIZATION

Barbara Bray and Kathleen McClaskey, authors of *Make Learning Personal* and *How to Personalize Learning*, illustrate differences between personalization, differentiation, and individualization through their PDI chart. "[Personalization] is learner-centered," the chart says. "The others are teacher-centered."

I have a slightly different opinion. To me, personalization, differentiation, and individualization are interrelated; they all play a critical role in the

(Continued)

(Continued)

classroom. Teachers must engage in the process of differentiation to engineer learning environments where all learners can access learning experiences. "Differentiation is a teacher's response to a learner's needs," says Carol Tomlinson (1999), author of *The Differentiated Classroom*. This definition of differentiation, from the source herself, illustrates that differentiation is likewise learner-centered and only unlocked when educators engage in a cycle of inquiry to constantly know and understand students in more sophisticated and intimate ways.

Individualization is similar. When reduced to its most basic definition, individualizing is *the process of giving an entity unique or individual character*. In our case, it means giving a unique character to learning. While it's true that individualization can be teacher-centered, especially when adaptive technologies get involved, individualization can also be learner-centered. For instance, children can individualize their own learning through autonomous decision-making that allows them to personalize a learning experience for themselves.

But this doesn't have to mean that the curriculum is individualized. It can be much simpler and more sustainable than that. By using open-ended and project-based tasks, engineered for diverse groups of learners, curriculum becomes individualized through a child's unique interpretation of a provocation or approach to a complex problem. It is in this way we see that personalization, differentiation, and individualization are not orthogonal. Differentiation can support students in their agency, helping them individualize content through their unique interpretations of and approaches to it. It is this process—not the process of individualizing curriculum—that humanizes personalization in our classrooms (see Figure I.4).

Figure I.4: Differentiation, Individualization, and Personalization

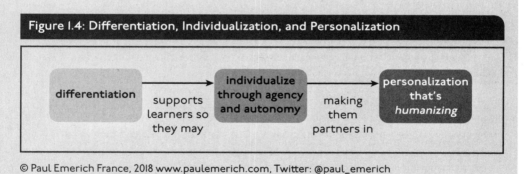

© Paul Emerich France, 2018 www.paulemerich.com, Twitter: @paul_emerich

Because you've begun to share responsibility with the students, seeing them as partners in the process of personalization, you will also see that clearly defined standards help create a vision for learning, allowing you to hone your understanding of what to look for when your kids are off constructing knowledge on their own; you will see that formative assessment and meaningful feedback are far more important than grades and gradebooks, as formative feedback will aid you in building trusting relationships with your students; you will see that meaningful conversations about a child's obstacles will help you get to know them on a personal level, empathize with them, and help them better understand how to conquer those same obstacles in the future; you'll start to see that your children are hardwired to encounter these obstacles with grace and resilience, and that all you needed to do all along was give them a bit more credit and invest more of your faith in them.

Later on, we'll talk about what it looks like to plan for a personalized environment, but I assure you it's within your reach. Through abiding by the tenets of backward design, mindfully constructing assessments that align with your outcomes, and allowing students to shape your daily lessons and reveal the places where they need the most feedback, you'll find this way of planning to be more sustainable in the long-term.

MYTH 4: DIGITAL TECHNOLOGY IS NECESSARY TO PERSONALIZE LEARNING

Personalized learning is often conflated with technology-driven education, but given my experience working in Silicon Valley, I argue that personalization needn't hinge on technology use. When influenced by the first three myths about personalized learning, technology can actually create more complexity when personalizing learning—complexity that becomes unmanageable, unsustainable, and dehumanizing, turning both educators and learners off to the concept entirely.

I should make it clear that I am a technology advocate—that is, when technology is used in a way that humanizes the learning process. Too many digital learning technologies dehumanize the learning process by reinforcing toxic achievement cultures and over-individualizing to the point of isolation.

There isn't a formula for ensuring effective technology use, but having the courage to take mindful risks with technology will help you hone your use of education technology over time. You'll quickly learn which technology works and which doesn't. We'll touch on this more in Chapter 11, which includes more detailed recommendations for technology that humanizes personalization. But what's most important is that technology allows us to preserve, enhance, or even restore equity and humanity to our classrooms.

MYTH 5: DIGITALLY DRIVEN PERSONALIZATION PAVES A PATH TO EQUITY

Advocates for digitally driven personalization—solutions that generally rely on web-based, adaptive technologies to personalize *on behalf of* the student and *in place of* the teacher—often argue that web-based, adaptive tools offer a sustainable solution for personalizing learning. Many even argue that they pave a path to equity, due to the fact that technology provides academic content at a level determined by the programs' assessments. While it's true that the programs are capable of doing this, make no mistake: this is not a path to equity.

Equity can be defined as *fairness* or *impartiality*, and in the final section of this book, we'll further discuss its implications for humanized personalization. Simply providing children with content that is presumed to be within their zone of proximal development does not necessarily ensure fairness and impartiality in the classroom. In fact, using these tools as the main source for personalization is more likely to track students, reinforcing discrepancies in achievement and posing a significant threat to equity.

This assumption that digitally driven technologies can pave a path to equity in the classroom is both reductive and flawed, resting on a narrow-minded view of equity. To create classrooms and schools that are fair, impartial, and equitable, we must remember that students need much more than appropriate academic content to reach their full potential. They need explicit instruction in executive functioning skills; they need to cultivate self-awareness, agency, and autonomy; and above all else, students need *access* and *inclusion*. They need to be afforded the same opportunities as their peers, and in the event that there are barriers standing in their way, preventing them from accessing an inclusive and equitable curriculum, our job as educators is to partner with them to remove those barriers. More often than not, this necessitates providing extra tools that either accommodate differences in ability or scaffold access to content. Using digital technology neither accommodates nor scaffolds access; instead, it creates chasms between students, affording them entirely different learning experiences. This, in turn, creates a classroom culture that is partial to high-achieving students who are able to play by the rules of an industrialized education.

RESPONDING TO INDUSTRIALIZATION

The question stands: How might we respond to the post–*Nation at Risk* era of industrialized learning? To respond in a manner that is truly progressive, we must make a movement toward the deindustrialization of learning while still preserving the structures, boundaries, and points of convergence that foster human connection and build relationships among learners. It is here that we discover another uncomfortable paradox that accompanies personalized learning: the tension that exists between structure and autonomy.

To humanize personalization in partnership with our children, we must be ready for learning to be messy. We have to see the classroom for what it is: an art studio, a science lab, and a workshop for the many languages and literacies that define the human condition. This messy lab where creativity brews and curiosity sparks is not an assembly line where children are filled with knowledge that corresponds with an arbitrary level. It is, instead, an intricate, amorphous, emergent social system that requires structure, management, norms, and boundaries within which children can chart their own paths.

Yes, you heard me correctly: it is possible to move away from industrialization and toward messy, creative, and student-driven learning—even with structure, boundaries, and high expectations. When we do, we personalize learning in a humanizing way, maintaining healthy structures that help us teach large classrooms of children. When we settle into the discomfort and uncertainty that oftentimes accompanies messiness, we find balance, allowing learning to feel *personal*, despite the fact that it may not be entirely individualized or interest-based.

THE FIRST DIMENSION

Shaping the Collective Conscious

In the summer of 2016, I found myself in Beijing, China. Yinuo Li, the director of the Gates Foundation in China, had an idea: she wanted to create a school for personalized learning. Her intentions were twofold: to benefit the children in the school she was building and to scale personalized learning to rural areas of China in an effort to make a dent in the educational inequity that currently plagues the country. I was humbled when she invited me to work with her group of founding teachers and engineers. Not only did we talk pedagogical and technological vision; I was even able to teach a bit.

One of the first questions I get when telling this story is, If you were teaching in China, did the kids speak English? My answer is generally: Well, sort of. A sizable number of the children were fluent in English, but a number of them were not. But there was something that posed an even bigger challenge than the language barrier: I had a classroom of forty-five fourth-graders in front of me.

You heard me correctly. There I was at Tsinghua University Primary School, at one of the best universities in the People's Republic of China, and due to unfortunate economies of scale, I was teaching a class of forty-five children. On top of that, I was asked to demonstrate my philosophy around personalized learning. To many, teaching forty-five children simultaneously is the epitome of industrialized learning. Further, all I had was a document camera and a projector in front of me: no adaptive technology, iPads, flexible seating, or playlists. Just me, a projector, and forty-five kids in forty-five desks. If it sounds intimidating, it was. In fact, it was one of the biggest tests of my own vulnerability to date.

I had arrived earlier that morning in Tsinghua, welcomed with open arms by two warm and kind children named Derek* and Julia. They told me about their school, gave me some of its history, and walked with me to the place I would be teaching.

The classroom was as big as a cafeteria might be in the United States. There were almost fifty desks situated in the center of the room, with rows and rows of chairs lined up around the perimeter. Soon enough, an ocean of educators flowed into the classroom. More than a hundred people had their eyes on me, watching me share this humanized brand of personalized learning, in quite possibly one of the most industrial learning environments I'd ever experienced.

My nerves were paralyzing. Impostor syndrome had set in, and I was unsure that I had what it took to pull this off. It felt as though there was so much stacked against me: so many children didn't speak fluent English, and I hardly knew anything about them. Knowing children on a personal level is critical to humanizing and, in effect, personalizing the classroom. I wasn't sure how I'd be able to convey that in one sixty-minute lesson.

It wasn't long, though, before the children came in. I connected with them, learned with and from them, and concluded the sixty-minute lesson. And much to my pleasant surprise, the teachers in the room erupted in applause, asking me questions and reflecting on the stark differences in pedagogy.

A couple of hours later, as I was reflecting on the lesson with the team and looking through photos, I came across a picture of me next to a group of students. Both of my knees were touching the tile floor, and my elbows rested on a child's desk. To many educators in the United States, this image would seem unremarkable. To the educators in China, however, it was quite the opposite.

"A teacher in China would never get down to a child's level like that," a team member said to me. "Many people here have never seen that before."

It was then that I realized just how potent and powerful this humanized brand of personalized learning truly is. It became clear that personalizing learning is not about an individualized pedagogy; it is, instead, about building a learning environment where teachers partner with children in the learning process. It is about human connection. This image (see Figure 2.1) will forever remind me of that.

Figure 2.1: Kneeling Image

Credit: ETU Education

*All names are pseudonyms.

You need not travel to China for an experience like this. In schools across the United States, large class sizes and under-resourced classrooms are commonplace. In fact, they are quite similar to this fourth-grade class I traveled halfway around the world to teach. The idea of personalizing learning for thirty or more students seems near impossible—that is, if one conflates personalization with individualization. To individualize learning for a group of thirty or more children seems belaboring and unsustainable—and that's because it is. Alas, modern thinking around the intersection of technology and education has led us to believe that adaptive tools will solve our individualization woes. But we need not look that far or invest our resources into expensive technology to reach our kids on a personal level. We instead need to focus on the place where we all converge—in the collective conscious of the classroom.

SHAPING THE COLLECTIVE CONSCIOUS

In 1893, Emile Durkheim, one of the founding thinkers of sociology, first introduced the concept of collective conscious, which referred to the shared values, beliefs, ideas, and knowledge within a social group. The collective conscious impacts behaviors and identities; it impacts our ability to feel as though we belong. In the classroom, the collective conscious not only includes shared values, beliefs, and knowledge; it also includes the learning environment itself. To sustainably actualize a vision for humanized personalization, it is essential that we converge on shared values and beliefs. It is paramount that we build learning environments that allow learners to converge often enough to contribute to and benefit from the collective conscious, meanwhile allowing the collective conscious to act as a foundation on which individuals can diverge and get in touch with their agency and autonomy.

> In the first dimension of personalized learning, we shape the collective conscious of the classroom.

When I was teaching in China, there was no choice but to intentionally structure the collective conscious of the classroom. While I was able to circulate, provide individualized feedback, and even pull groups of children to the front board, there was no way I would have been able to offer an appropriate level of individualization without knowing them better.

It was there in Beijing where I truly realized the power of this first dimension of personalized learning. The first dimension of personalization is arguably the most important part of this framework because it builds the foundation for the second and third dimensions (see Figure 2.2).

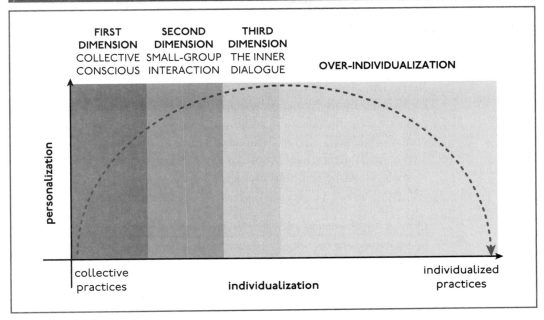

Figure 2.2: A Continuum of Individualization

FIRST DIMENSION COLLECTIVE CONSCIOUS

SECOND DIMENSION SMALL-GROUP INTERACTION

THIRD DIMENSION THE INNER DIALOGUE

OVER-INDIVIDUALIZATION

personalization

collective practices

individualization

individualized practices

© Paul Emerich France, 2018 www.paulemerich.com, Twitter: @paul_emerich

Within the collective conscious of the classroom, we focus our energy toward collective practices and universal knowledge that will later support small-group interactions in the second dimension and nurturing the child's inner dialogue in the third dimension. While shaping the collective conscious may at first seem to act in opposition to personalizing learning, it doesn't. The collective conscious, mediated by the learning environment, is the only place where every individual within a diverse group of learners will *converge*.

At the heart of this model for humanized personalization lies equity. To continuously work toward equity in our classrooms—to ensure that all children get what they need—we must help children operate within the collective conscious of the classroom, for it is within the collective conscious that they will be able to learn through human connection and find a sense of belonging. Oftentimes, our conversations about equity are limited to giving all children what they need in terms of academic content and instructional resources. In the process, we forget that all children *need* to connect with other human beings; they need to know that they belong.

Because the collective conscious accounts for the places in our classrooms where all learners converge, it includes sociocultural factors within the classroom, as well as structures that support multi-ability curricula. When I say sociocultural factors, I'm referring to classroom norms, routines, and management practices that lay the foundation for collaboration and autonomy. Not only do these factors contextualize a child's agency; they contextualize the learning relationships children will have in the classroom, which, in effect, build the classroom culture itself.

Herein lies the essence of the collective conscious: it is critical to building classroom culture. Human connection and healthy interpersonal relationships are critical to building a strong classroom culture and a healthy first dimension. These relationships are essential if we strive for an equitable, active, and student-driven learning environment where students and teachers are connecting with one another to learn.

CONNECTING WITH CHILDREN

In Rita Pierson's (2013) TED Talk, "Every Kid Needs a Champion," she reminds us that kids "don't learn from people they don't like." But I'd argue it goes further than just liking you. They have to be able to *humanize* you, too. It helps if they can see that you, too, are a human being who's imperfect and vulnerable—or even just a real person who experiences joy, struggle, and pain. We are united by all these within the collective conscious: our obstacles, our pain, and our unequivocal, purposeless joy.

Knowing this, I began my lesson at Tsinghua with an energizer in an effort to connect with the children personally before trying to reach them academically. I taught the children a series of handclap patterns I had picked up while working at a summer camp in college (see Figure 2.3).

Figure 2.3: Handclaps

Credit: ETU Education

These handclap patterns were my first step in establishing a collective conscious in the classroom. They engaged the children kinesthetically and allowed them to have a little bit of fun before the lesson started. They also served as a means for managing the classroom and getting their attention later. Finally, they helped me introduce my minilesson, focused purely on making mistakes, being persistent, and taking risks. The handclap patterns, due to their complexity, made mistakes inevitable, serving as a fun yet low-risk example for what they were about to learn.

After we concluded the energizer, I jumped into the lesson itself. For many of my lessons, regardless of content, I use the workshop model because it supports student autonomy within multi-ability curricula. The workshop model consists of three components: the minilesson, the workshop, and the reflection. The workshop model became especially popular in the late 1980s and 1990s with Lucy Calkins's (1986) *The Art of Teaching Writing*. The workshop model is now used for reading and math workshops, as well. In Jo Boaler's (2015) *Mathematical Mindsets*, she shares a pedagogy that incorporates similar points of convergence and divergence—much like Calkins's workshop model—that allow for students to leverage the benefits of working on an open-ended math task with a "low floor, and a high ceiling," intended to create varied entry points for a diverse group of learners.

The workshop model is composed of three key elements: the minilesson, the workshop, and the reflection.

MAINTAINING THE SPIRIT OF THE WORKSHOP MODEL

I use the workshop model for most of my lessons, but not for all. Some days, it makes sense to modify the lesson structure, but the *spirit* of the workshop model is always there because it allows for both convergence and divergence.

To maintain the spirit of the workshop model, one must make space to shape the collective conscious of the classroom (the first dimension), to allow small groups to form based on needs (the second dimension), and to nurture a child's inner dialogue through human connection and interpersonal feedback (the third dimension). In Chapter 9, "Humanizing Instruction to Personalize Learning," I'll go into more depth about different kinds of workshops you might want to explore.

MINILESSON

Despite the caveat above, many of my lessons follow a relatively linear structure, beginning with whole-group convergence around a common provocation. In math, it may look like unpacking a math task, brainstorming different methods for approaching a problem, or discussing habits of mathematicians; in literacy, we may examine a mentor text or model a specific strategy for reading or writing, as recommended by Lucy Calkins; in morning meeting, we discuss feelings or emotions and then role-play. This intentional, but brief, part of the lesson structure, when conducted repeatedly, builds a culture of collaboration and solidifies a common language with which to provide feedback when in small groups or one-to-one conferences. It allows learning to become personal—and paradoxically universal—granting opportunities for developmentally appropriate social interactions with age-alike peers, authentic situations in which children can learn how to emotionally and physically regulate, and moments to collaborate with peers around metacognitive strategies for literacy, numeracy, social learning, and building emotional competencies. This gradually builds the collective conscious of the classroom and paves a path to equity that affords all learners access to the same content.

At Tsinghua in Beijing, our provocation was related to mathematical thinking and necessary socioemotional mindsets for approaching complex math tasks. This included taking risks, making mistakes, and collaborating with peers. I shared with the children the ways mathematicians must approach complex problems to solve them. In this case, the explicit instruction on mathematical mindsets made sense.

For this minilesson, in particular, I chose persistence, making thinking visible, looking for patterns, and attending to precision. I explained what these meant, modeled them briefly using think-alouds, and invited them to think about these and use them during the workshop by referring to them on their own mathematical practice cards (see Figure 2.4).

Figure 2.4: Mathematical Practice Cards

| 坚持不懈 | 写下你的思考过程. | 寻找模式 | 仔细检查 |
| Be persistent. | Make your thinking visible. | Find patterns. | Attend to precision. |

Source: Images courtesy of Pixabay.

Because these lessons about persistence, visible thinking, risk-taking, pattern finding, and attending to precision are universal, they were very appropriately placed in a minilesson that was intended to build the collective conscious of the classroom. But it's important to note that even the content was universal and specifically chosen to address grade-level skills, making it just as crucial to building the collective conscious of the classroom. Universal content is necessary within *complex instruction*, a pedagogy that leverages multi-ability curricula and preserves equity in the classroom. We'll unpack *complex instruction* more in Chapters 9 and 10.

The series of multi-ability tasks allowed all students to wrestle with the same content, preserving equity and convergence among all forty-five students in the classroom. As a result, this minilesson allowed for children to take a universal lesson and shape it to meet their own personal needs when applying it during the workshop.

The tasks were inspired by Jo Boaler's (2015) philosophy of the "low floor" and "high ceiling." I specifically curated four tasks that would increase in complexity as the children completed them (see Figure 2.5). For the children who were still grappling with fundamental math concepts, they could spend as much time as they wanted on the first task. For those who were able to pick up on patterns and apply them easily, they would be able to ascend through the tasks to higher levels of complexity.

Figure 2.5: Math Tasks

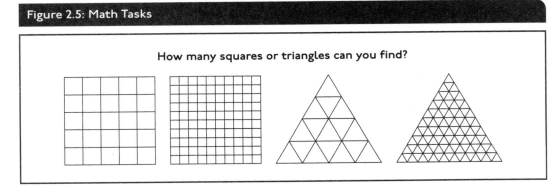

How many squares or triangles can you find?

As a result, by embracing the tension that exists between universal and personal learning, I was able to capitalize on the strengths that a heterogeneous, diverse group of learners brings: it exposes children to different ways of thinking, it allows individual strengths to shine in different contexts, and it engenders a beautifully rigorous and equitable learning environment through learning tasks that possess entry points for all learners.

WORKSHOP

It wasn't long before triumphant noise broke out. The children began working on the tasks, and humanized personalization was able to shine. I saw motivation, joy, frustration, metacognition, and vulnerability—all the universal human experiences that occur when we learn. It was these universal human experiences that built the collective conscious of the classroom. But I also saw a diverse group of learners working diligently, all accessing universal content in different ways. While some counted the squares and rectangles, others used area formulas and patterns of square numbers. Moreover, I was able to toggle between each of the three dimensions for personalized learning, providing feedback to groups of students and individuals when I felt that the scaffolding was appropriate and least restrictive.

REFLECTION

To conclude our time together, we came back from independent and small-group work to reflect on the experience. This is critical when building the collective conscious because it allows for another point of convergence before the lesson concludes, creating a pathway for children's individual experiences to become part of the collective conscious as they share various paths to a conclusion, obstacles, or mistakes they've made. This both normalizes the messy process of learning and helps build a culture of persistence and perpetual growth. It humbles and humanizes the process, personalizing learning and welcoming the discomfort that comes with growth. Most of all, it allows for meaningful connection between learners, through both their successes and their vulnerabilities.

"I need to see some mistakes you made so I can learn something new."

"I'm looking for all sorts of answers. I need right ones, wrong ones, and ones you're not sure about so I can see what we've learned."

In my classroom, I make a concerted effort to praise the mistakes my students share with the group during reflection. I'll say things like, "I need to see some mistakes you made so I can learn something new," or "I'm looking for all sorts of answers. I need right ones, wrong ones, and ones you're not sure about so I can see what we've learned." Too often, we don't emphasize to our children just how much the missteps and mistakes are necessary to the learning process. We forget to teach them to be grateful for them. We've conditioned them to believe that mistakes are high-stakes—moments to avoid, not moments to embrace. By honoring these through daily reflection, we humanize the learning process to an even greater degree, engendering agency, autonomy, and a growth mindset that will compound over time and translate into an even greater capacity for intrinsic motivation. But most of all, it allows the class to come together and contribute their individual experiences and reflections to the collective conscious of the classroom, allowing local knowledge to become global wisdom.

BUILDING ON THE FIRST DIMENSION

Once the first dimension is secured by shaping the collective conscious, it is only natural to find opportunities to create a more intimate setting for learning in smaller groups. This paves the way for the second dimension of personalized learning, which entails encouraging partnerships and creating small groups of children to enhance personalization.

CHAPTER THREE

THE SECOND DIMENSION

Leveraging Small-Group Interactions

Finland is often regarded as having one of the best educational systems in the world. Some argue that Finland's lack of diversity makes it easier for them to create a large-scale education system that meets the needs of all learners. This rhetoric places Finland's education system in direct juxtaposition with that of the United States, arguing that it might be the United States' diversity that makes large-scale education so challenging. Some posit that if, perhaps, we could control or limit this diversity, large-scale public education might be more successful.

It's seductive to subscribe to this logic, but it is not Finland's homogeneity that makes its education system so great. Never mind the fact that Finland's social policies, such as universal health care, support the collective; the schools in Finland are publicly funded based on the number of pupils in them, instead of by property taxes. What's more, in places where there is a higher concentration of immigrants or other vulnerable populations, Finland offers *more* funding, instead of less. In essence, there are fewer barriers to an equitable education in Finland. It has nothing to do with its relative homogeneity.

We see this flawed logic manifest in classrooms, too. The history of segregation and tracking in U.S. public schools provides ample evidence of our proclivity for homogenous groupings. Perhaps it's seductive or even intuitive to believe that limiting diversity and optimizing for homogeneity would make it easier to reach all learners. But the truth is, it probably wouldn't. If anything, it would get us closer to industrializing the classroom and further from the personalized and humanized education system we so desperately need.

It's the more vulnerable choice to instead subscribe to the notion that the benefits of diversity outweigh the complexity it creates. Granted, making this choice sometimes forces us to sit in the uncertainty and discomfort that oftentimes accompany vulnerability. However, when we do, we remember that diversity only adds to a conversation. Diversity helps us think differently than we once thought; it helps us see perspectives that were once invisible to us. It bolsters empathy and helps us break free of the categories that so painfully confine us as individuals and as a society. To put it simply, diversity helps us learn.

> To create inclusive learning environments, we must promote and protect diversity.

> The second dimension for personalized learning is defined by small-group and partnered interactions.

As a result, we need classrooms where diversity is appreciated, protected, and promoted. In fact, when we are intentional about diversifying our classrooms, we open up another dimension of personalized learning—the second dimension—by expanding the possibilities for productive *partnerships* and meaningful *small-group* learning.

The benefits of diversity with regard to gender, race/ethnicity, language, religion, and sexuality are boundless. On the other hand, diversity with regard to age level has its limits. While we don't want homogenously grouped students with identical skill sets, we also do not want classrooms that span too many age levels, given the vast differences in developmental needs. I've witnessed both ends of the continuum in Figure 3.1. I've taught classes that were specifically designed for homogeneity (classes that were composed by tracking

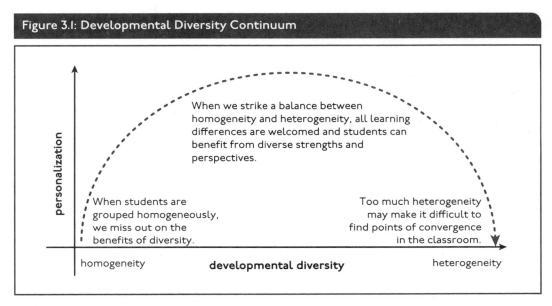

Figure 3.1: Developmental Diversity Continuum

When we strike a balance between homogeneity and heterogeneity, all learning differences are welcomed and students can benefit from diverse strengths and perspectives.

When students are grouped homogeneously, we miss out on the benefits of diversity.

Too much heterogeneity may make it difficult to find points of convergence in the classroom.

personalization

homogeneity   **developmental diversity**   heterogeneity students using test scores), and I've taught in classrooms where an excess of heterogeneity (about twenty children spanning ages six to ten years old or four to seven years old) was believed to be beneficial. The inverted U reminds us that it is possible to have too much—and too little—of a good thing.

To be clear, this continuum applies only to age level, and the tension here is palpable, creating dissonance and uncertainty. It also assumes an inclusion model, given that the proper supports are in place for students with significant needs or learning differences. Too little developmental diversity robs children of opportunities for meaningful social and emotional learning, while too much diversity in terms of age level can pose a threat to equity— which was my experience in the aforementioned multiage classrooms. You'll see what I mean as we continue to unpack both the dangers of homogeneity and the limits of heterogeneity.

THE DANGERS OF HOMOGENEITY

When I was teaching in public school, I was on a team with five other incredible teachers. We had more than 150 children among all six of us, and we were always trying to find ways to differentiate our instruction to best meet the needs of the children.

A CLOSER LOOK

DIFFERENTIATED INSTRUCTION

The term *differentiate* is commonly misinterpreted and misused in schools. Early in my career, I was guilty of this, too. At that time, differentiation meant providing different activities to different children. It meant having four copies of the same text, rated by Lexile or Fountas and Pinnell level; it meant flipping my classroom so I could ability group.

Carol Tomlinson, author of *The Differentiated Classroom* (1999), states that educators can differentiate instruction in four ways: through the content, process, product, and learning environment. At first glance, this may sound like it entails the educator creating different content, processes, products, and learning environments for children, but this view of differentiation is reductive and unsustainable. Instead, differentiating entails broadening the possibilities of the content we use so children have flexibility in how they go about interpreting that content and demonstrating their understanding of it.

Differentiation begins with the materials we choose to use in our classrooms, for our instruction is mediated by the materials we select for learning. By choosing materials that allow for varied entry points into the curriculum, our instruction becomes naturally differentiated because the materials transform our teaching. Lessons that use open-ended tasks with varied entry points nudge teachers toward modeling flexible skills and nurturing strategic thinking, metacognition, and the internal dialogue children need to develop to learn autonomously. Technology that leverages web-based, adaptive programs attempts to personalize in this reductive manner, resulting only in technology-powered tracking. Instead, educators need to provide open-ended tasks that provide varied entry points, as these allow for instruction to become inherently differentiated and for learning to become inherently personal for each child. We'll unpack this more as we continue exploring the second dimension.

One of our methods for "differentiation" was to use standardized assessment scores, coupled with our in-classroom observations of the children, to create what we euphemistically called *flexible groupings* of children for math. (We later saw that these groups were mostly fixed and rarely *flexible*.) We ended up with six groups—from remediation and below average all the way up to high average and accelerated math. We surmised that this would allow educators to focus on a narrower range of needs and reach more children at once in a whole-group setting.

A lack of diversity actually works against us.

What we would soon learn was that this lack of diversity within the whole group actually worked against us. And later, I would realize that what we were doing wasn't differentiation at all; it was *tracking*. In the remediation and low-average groups, there were very few peer models and a disproportionate number of significant needs. Moreover, many students in these groups had not yet developed strong learning habits. They had not yet learned to engage with their own autonomy and, as a result, were constantly crying out with questions or disruptive behaviors.

Conversely, the children in the above-average groups had many peer models for mathematical thinking. Many of them had strong number sense, mathematical persistence, and strong language skills, making it much less taxing for them to grapple with new content. One could argue that this approach benefited these children in some ways, but it's more important to note that the approach was not equitable for the collective, as it did not allow us to close achievement and opportunity gaps. Furthermore, this method of creating math classes based on standardized test scores only perpetuated the factory model, segregating and tracking children based on ability. In some cases, this meant unintentionally segregating by race or socioeconomic status. Almost invariably, children from low-income homes, despite having many valuable assets from their homes, families, and cultures, simply didn't enter with the same *academic* advantages (e.g., early literacy exposure, tutoring, availability of parents to assist with homework) as their more privileged peers. Eventually, we realized that this was neither best for children nor a way to provide an education that was personal and equitable for *all*. It was simply a way to perpetuate privilege and accelerate children through content.

Finally, due to the homogenous grouping of children at the class level, it disincentivized us from becoming creative with our pedagogy and instead incentivized us to standardize our practice, building off of a flawed assumption that, because children fell into the same score band on a standardized test, they could all be reached in the same way.

Fortunately, we now know better. We now know that needs are intersectional and learning differences are multidimensional. We now know that differentiation is much more complex than this and that tracking students (and euphemistically calling it *flexible grouping*) is *not* differentiation. Differentiation instead entails engineering equitable learning environments that meet the needs of all learners, allowing for points of convergence and divergence within a multi-ability curriculum and removing barriers for vulnerable populations without inadvertently creating more. We cannot possibly promote equity by tracking our classes based on test scores. We *can* promote equity by humanizing our pedagogy and creating classrooms where diversity is expected and inclusion is intentional.

I'm often asked, But what about the high achievers? Is it fair for them to be in classes where they're forced to "go more slowly" than they are able to go? In short, the answer is yes. It is fair if the learning environment and curriculum are intentionally designed for agency, autonomy, and humanized pedagogy. By building a curriculum and a classroom environment that allows for varied entry points into the same learning experiences, we allow all learners to get what they need without anyone being excluded.

It's true that designing learning environments and learning experiences that meet the needs of a diverse group of learners is challenging. But it can be done if we change the way we think about curriculum, assessment, and instruction. In Section II, "Pedagogy," we'll discuss ways to humanize curriculum, assessment, and instruction so you can leverage diversity within your classroom and allow all learners to access the curriculum in a rigorous manner.

The following year, my team and I changed our approach, optimizing for greater heterogeneity and challenging ourselves to tap into the unique strengths of all children within the classroom. While we hadn't yet learned to solve all our personalization problems and we still hadn't reached a point where children were fully connecting with their own agency, we had taken an important first step in prioritizing equity and justice, paying homage to the natural diversity in our classrooms.

Increased ability-level diversity allowed for the best of both worlds. It allowed me to capitalize on the serendipity of whole-group learning. This also created the space and time for children to work independently while I worked with small groups. What's more, I showed myself it was, in fact, possible to meet all students' needs, with 90 percent of students meeting their NWEA-MAP (Northwest Evaluation Association Measures of Academic Progress) growth targets in mathematics. I wonder, if not for our decision to change these groupings, would I have chosen to make more time for small groups? Would I have moved away from lecture-based learning? I probably wouldn't have.

By protecting and promoting diversity in our classrooms, we are pushed to become stronger and more innovative with our pedagogy.

As a result, I began developing more structures and processes that would enable autonomy, agency, and personalization in my classroom. While many of these structures and processes were still teacher-directed, it was a step in the right direction. I began to use more formative assessments to strategically group and progress-monitor individual students' growth, and provide more options for learning through math games and other activities on my classroom website.

THE LIMITS OF HETEROGENEITY

In 2014, I began teaching for a personalized learning company and network of microschools based in San Francisco. Our vision was to bring personalized learning to the masses by rebuilding the education system from the ground up. We opened microschools, we built web-based classroom tools, and we curated individualized playlists for each child in an attempt to personalize learning. We optimized for class size and student-to-teacher ratio, with about eight children to one teacher in our first year. Our definition of personalization was conflated with an unsustainable, interest-based individualization of curriculum, leading us to believe that we could have an unlimited amount of heterogeneity in the classroom. Theoretically, due to the individualized nature of each child's curriculum, it wouldn't matter if, for instance, there was a six-year-old in the same classroom as a ten-year-old. In my case, this wasn't just a theoretical scenario. It was reality.

You heard me correctly: it was essentially the one-room schoolhouse. At first, I was excited to try something different, but in hindsight, it was arrogant to think that we could try such an experiment at the expense of the overall classroom environment. It was silly to believe that we could disregard developmental psychology research that states that six-year-olds and ten-year-olds have radically different needs and, therefore, should be in different learning spaces. Alas, our flawed vision for personalized learning made us believe that it was possible.

As you can imagine, I soon began to see the associated problems with this level of heterogeneity. In Chapter 2, I mentioned that when engineering the classroom environment, it is important to intentionally incorporate points of convergence and divergence within a workshop-model lesson structure. These points of convergence, built into the routines of the classroom, lay the foundation for this second dimension of personalization, where children can work with partners and in small groups.

In the "one-room schoolhouse," where my co-teacher and I had about fifteen children ranging from first-grade age to fifth-grade age, there were very few points of convergence. It was virtually impossible to conduct a minilesson that would meaningfully build the collective conscious of the classroom, due to the fact that it was so challenging to find places where all learners could converge. These vastly different age levels required vastly different modes of managing social learning, monitoring emotional competencies, teaching metacognition, and helping navigate differing levels of abstraction.

Additionally, the extreme amount of heterogeneity in the classroom created far too many opportunities for divergence. It was exceedingly difficult to provide all children feedback simultaneously while they worked through individualized playlists and activities, spreading us thin and making the workload unsustainable. We rarely could pause for whole-group teaching points or help students learn from one another's mistakes, because the content varied too greatly, making the first and second dimensions of personalized learning virtually invisible in our classrooms. Finally, children were working in silos, largely unable to collaborate. When we tried to have them collaborate, it was challenging to find tasks to which children of various ages could equitably contribute, due to developmental appropriateness.

It became clear to me that there were some structures, even from the seemingly archaic industrial model of education, that could provide benefits in the modern classroom. Putting mindful limits on the level of heterogeneity in the classroom—in terms of age level—would have allowed us to work within constructive constraints, providing a healthy amount of both convergence and divergence that could still be monitored and regulated by developmentally appropriate classroom routines and norms. This would have allowed children to form mutually beneficial *partnerships* around common provocations, as the children in my classrooms do now.

There are many examples of this throughout the day, but I find examples from math workshop to be the most valuable in illustrating this. During math workshop, there are opportunities for *convergence* through both whole-group and small-group partnerships at their tables. While each child completes their own math journal, they are encouraged to talk with one another about their individual methods on the same open-ended math task. See Figure 3.2 for an example of a task I might use.

"What sorts of questions do you have after looking at this math task?" I ask the children. "Turn and talk to a neighbor."

Children turn their bodies toward one another and begin sharing their wonderings with neighbors. As they do, the second dimension comes to life through discussion.

"I wonder which one is the biggest," one student says.

"I was wondering which one is the smallest," another retorts.

"I was wondering how much they would be if we put them all together!" another child adds.

It's not long before I turn them loose and let them explore these questions in their math journals, using methods that work for them to answer one of the questions they've asked. This task, in particular, is designed to address area (a third-grade standard). Due to the nature of both the workshop model and the open-endedness of the task, children may lend different perspectives about how one might find a plausible answer. Some count the squares individually, while others deconstruct the shapes and use multiplication to calculate the area of pieces of the shapes. Some even subtract the negative space. In Figure 3.3, students respond to a similar problem.

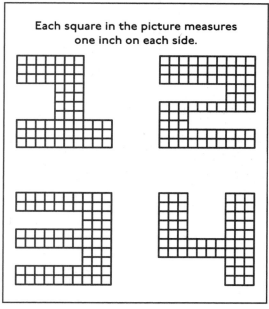

Figure 3.2: Areas of Numbers

Each square in the picture measures one inch on each side.

Source: Adapted from Illustrative Mathematics, https://www.illustrativemathematics.org/contentstandards/3/MD/C/tasks/516

You'll see in the work samples that follow that open-ended tasks such as these allow for the aforementioned points of convergence but also for divergence with regard to methodology. The diversity of methods supports personalization because the children *themselves* personalize the task through their unique interpretation of it. Conversely, the universal yet open-ended nature of the task allows for social learning to thrive through collaboration, dialogue, and discourse, creating forward momentum for student-driven personalized learning.

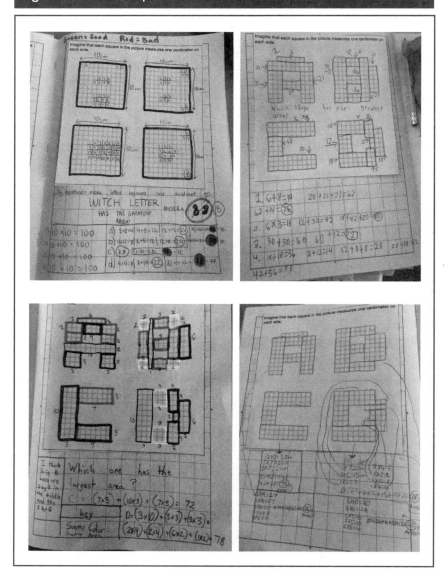

THE HALLMARKS OF A
STRONG SECOND DIMENSION

The second dimension of personalized learning is defined by *partnerships* and *small-group* interactions. It is shaped by the children who weave the cultural fabric of your classroom, it is dependent on the natural diversity of a classroom, and it allows us to shape a collective conscious on a smaller and more intimate scale. This second dimension comes alive through *discussion and discourse* and becomes more intimate when educators use *formative assessment* to capture information on students so they may form strategy- and skill-based groups as needs arise, ensuring that even small groups are sometimes heterogeneous in nature. The second dimension is where we see the returns on increased individualization beginning to slow but not yet to the point of diminishing returns. It is also in the second dimension where the tension between heterogeneity and homogeneity becomes undeniably palpable. In this uncomfortable and dissonant space, we are beckoned to lean one way or the other, but we must remember that truly personal learning lies somewhere in the middle—where all learners are seen, heard, and valued, still united by the collective classroom culture.

> The hallmarks of the second dimension are discussion and discourse, formative assessment, and the strategic grouping of children.

DISCUSSION AND DISCOURSE

Too often, we take too didactic an approach during minilessons or other moments of whole-group convergence. We assume that we need to do all the telling and showing, forgetting that there are twenty or more human beings in front of us who can share in this responsibility of constructing knowledge.

While it's beneficial to have a clearly defined objective for a minilesson, it's also healthy to leverage the background knowledge and contributions of your children in the minilesson. This is why classroom discussion is a hallmark of the second dimension of personalization, due to its importance and its tender complexity. It is through discussion and discourse that children are able to wrestle with ideas, recognize their own misconceptions, and channel background knowledge to communicate distinct ideas with clarity and precision. The only way students can develop this is through constant practice and feedback. The same goes for educators. Nurturing discussion and discourse within the classroom is a tender pedagogy, and we can hone our skills for classroom dialogue and discourse only by allowing ourselves to be vulnerable with our practice. We can get better at this only if we open ourselves up to its uncertainties and give it a try.

Further, discussion and discourse make this second dimension come alive because they allow learning to become personal through *humanized* practices. Discussion and discourse do not necessitate a heavy investment in tools or technology. Instead, they require an investment in human beings, making the act of personalizing learning more sustainable by leveraging student agency and autonomy. Discussion and discourse also make personalization more equitable, as they can be cultivated in far more classrooms than a complex technological infrastructure could.

There are infinite situations in which leveraging discussion and discourse is applicable, but I'll provide just a few here to get you thinking about the degree to which you are already using them in your classroom.

Introducing a New Topic

Students share what they know about a topic based on a guiding question or brainstorming map for a new topic. Children can share what they know with a friend, after which, they can share the results of their conversation with a new partner. Repeating this process many times over creates a free flow of information and ideas that provide energy and momentum to a new topic.

Agree/Disagree

Perhaps you or a child has just shared a controversial idea with the class. Instead of affirming or negating the idea, make some space in between and allow for discourse. Ask the children to use some of the following sentence stems to engage in discourse with peers. Not only is this best practice for humanizing personalization, it's also best practice for educating in a socially just manner, especially when controversial topics arise.

- "I agree because . . ."
- "I disagree because . . ."
- "I'm not sure if I agree because . . ."
- "I have a different idea . . ."

Summarizing

Sometimes didactic, direct instruction has its place. Say you want to share a mathematical property with your children once they've had a chance to explore it on their own, or perhaps you've shared some class-wide feedback on how to correctly punctuate a sentence. An excellent way to unobtrusively assess is to have the children turn and talk to partners, summarizing it in their own words. By scanning the room and listening closely, you can get a quick read on which students convey the ideas fluently and which are still struggling to comprehend the concept. You can also use summarizing to scaffold the processing or rehearsal of multistep directions, a skill critical to building their autonomy and agency. And it's as simple as saying, "Turn to a buddy and summarize what we've just discussed."

There are lots of other ways to have your students engage in discourse in the classroom. At a minimum, it should serve two purposes: creating points of convergence for social learning and creating opportunities for formative assessment.

We'll delve into *interaction* more in the third dimension, when we talk about the internal processes that occur for a child to learn. Interaction is critical to the learning process, as all learning is a conversation, whether it be a literal, *interpersonal* conversation between two individuals or an *internal* dialogue through which a child can make meaning. Discussion and discourse are so critical to the second dimension and to personalizing learning because they provide us with the opportunity to unobtrusively use formative assessment to better understand our students, and they provide learners with the ability to interact with their peers and leverage human connection for learning.

FORMATIVE ASSESSMENT

The three dimensions of personalization are not orthogonal. They cannot be placed neatly into three categories, despite the fact that I'm trying to do so. As we continue to unpack the three dimensions of personalized learning, you'll see that formative assessment is important to all of them. I've chosen to include formative assessment in the second dimension because it is integral to strategically building small groups and partnerships.

In addition to dialogue and discourse, there are other ways to formatively assess children to create small groups for instruction, many of which can be achieved through whole-group instruction.

Seating Chart Documentation

One year, I had the pleasure of working with Dr. Akihiko Takahashi, an expert in Japanese Lesson Study and cocreator of Chicago's Lesson Study Alliance. After working with him, I borrowed an idea to use in my classroom for formative assessment purposes. I noticed that while he was walking around studying the children, he would bring a seating chart with him. This seating chart allowed him to document methods the children were using while solving a problem. While this was done specifically in the context of math, his documentation helped me see each child's varying developmental stages, arming me with helpful data for future lessons.

For instance, children who used number bonds to add multi-digit numbers were communicating that they were in a semi-representational stage of math, breaking up numbers into parts to add partial sums to a larger number. There were other children, however, who were adding multi-digit numbers abstractly, using the standard algorithm with fluency. Others were in a concrete stage, using base-ten blocks and pictures to demonstrate their understanding.

This was excellent data to have because his tool didn't assess the end product, answer, or solution (as assessments so often do);

instead, it gave me clear insight into the *process* by which children were conquering a problem. The process is, after all, the most personal part of learning. It is the part where children exercise their autonomy and mold a curriculum to their own abilities. To continue partnering with learners for the purpose of making learning personal, collecting data on the process is critical.

Self-Selected Intervention

Oftentimes, as I'm concluding a minilesson, I send my children off to begin working on their own. This is especially true in reading and writing workshop, where Lucy Calkins's Units of Study minilessons ask that the children go off and explore lessons and strategies autonomously. All curricula have their limitations—Calkins's Units of Study included—and to ensure students are ready to move on and work independently or in small groups, I sometimes offer self-selected intervention or reinforcement should children feel they need it.

I begin by asking all students to turn and talk to summarize the minilesson or the directions I gave in their own words. Then I do some more probing to figure out who feels confident to apply the minilesson on their own and who feels like they may need extra help.

"If you feel like you know what you're supposed to do, and you don't need any help from a teacher, give me a thumbs-up by your heart."

I wait for students to follow.

"All right, those of you who are ready, you may go and get started."

This simple call-and-response is liberating to children who've processed the directions quickly. It makes them feel seen and heard, but also gives you the reassurance that they feel confident about what they're about to do. It also helps them actualize their agency by making a choice that they feel is best for them.

If the minilesson was effective, this sends most of the class to their seats. When I'm left with a larger group, it is a great opportunity for me to get feedback on the clarity of my lesson. On most occasions, I'm left with only a handful of children: my "usual suspects," if you will, who generally need a little extra TLC.

I first use this time to field any questions the children may have. Generally speaking, one or two children have an extra clarifying question or need help fleshing out an idea before getting started independently. In some cases, they need an extra scaffold, which I can provide right there in the moment. Perhaps another demonstration is needed, or maybe an extra tool is necessary, like a graphic organizer to collect their thoughts before writing. They may even need a bit of guided practice before going off and working on their own. Whatever the scaffold, I can offer it in a small group where the children can have a little more airtime to ask questions and get feedback before I release the responsibility to them entirely.

Exit Slips

Of course, children are not always accurate in their evaluations of themselves or their understanding. They're kids, and we expect them to be wrong. Being "wrong" is good because it provides an opportunity for feedback later on. The exit slip is a classic example of formative assessment that allows us to check for understanding.

I recommend giving exit slips frequently. While it's good to see that the children are confident, it is also important to make sure they're applying the minilesson in a productive way that demonstrates meaningful learning. Frequently, giving exit slips or collecting written work for the purpose of formative assessment provides an opportunity for evaluation and feedback.

But wait, doesn't this mean more grading?

It could mean more grading, but it's important to note that formative assessment is not synonymous with grading. Formative assessment doesn't always mean we provide children with individualized feedback or a score. Sometimes it's perfectly appropriate to look over student work and modify your plans based on your observations.

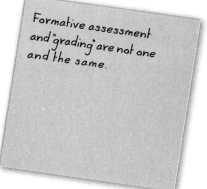
Formative assessment and "grading" are not one and the same.

Below, I've provided two examples of how technology can, in fact, minimize the complexity of assessment collection—and without dehumanizing learning. While formative assessment does not *necessitate* technology use, it can in many cases minimize its complexity. It does so by making assessment relatively unobtrusive and easy to organize.

Google Forms

Google Forms are a great way to aggregate data, especially if your learners can read and type. Collecting the data via Google Forms allows you to provide a variety of assessment questions, or even just one field for reflection, and aggregates the data nicely so you can refer back to them later. You can also link multiple Google Forms to one data spreadsheet so all your data are in one place.

Seesaw

Seesaw is a digital portfolio tool that allows children to submit work in a variety of ways. They can take pictures, make videos, and even type notes. Oftentimes, I have my kids snap a picture of their work and put it on Seesaw so I can look at it later. Most of the time, I simply look for strengths, weaknesses, or misconceptions that I can address in future minilessons or strategically engineered small groups.

STRATEGICALLY GROUPING CHILDREN

The first two hallmarks of the second dimension—discussion/discourse and formative assessment—aid us in forging partnerships serendipitously and collecting data for the purpose of creating small groups. That said, a necessary component of the second dimension is actually enacting small-group instruction. But it's important to remember that small-group instruction isn't conducted simply for the purpose of delivering similar content or lessons to small groups of children; it's also conducted so teachers can build on the collective conscious of the classroom in a smaller and more intimate setting.

Small-group instruction shouldn't be only for ability grouping. It also scaffolds social learning in a more intimate setting.

When humanizing personalization, we must avoid tracking in small-group instruction. Grouping only by ability can be stigmatizing and dehumanizing. It's also a threat to equity. We *must* embrace the diversity in our classrooms, allowing the small-group and partnered interactions to be both heterogeneous and homogeneous.

I suggest making two types of small groups: groups that are designed to address ability-based needs, as well as groups designed to mix levels. I do this with a simple grid. Vertically, I create groups by ability level, while horizontally, the groups are structured heterogeneously based on students I feel would benefit from collaborating with one another in a mixed-ability group (see Figure 3.4). Having them placed in this way allows me to pull two different types of groups. This is just one way I've come up with to balance heterogeneous and homogeneous grouping, to make sure I'm not tracking children in the same groups over and over. Here are some more examples of how to balance heterogeneous grouping and homogeneous grouping:

Host a reading group where students with varied abilities are exploring a similar strategy—for instance, finding the main idea through repeated words—but do so individually with texts they've chosen for their book bins. This allows children of varying ability levels to join together, meanwhile allowing for a diverse group of learners to access a universally meaningful lesson. Keep a list to see which students you've reached and which you haven't, and be sure to get through the whole list before creating new groups.

Figure 3.4: Balancing Homogeneous and Heterogeneous Grouping

	GROUP A	GROUP B	GROUP C	GROUP D	GROUP E
GROUP 1	ALEXA	EMILY	ELLIE	SAM	ALLEN
GROUP 2	ELLEN	MICHAEL	SIMI	ANNIE	
GROUP 3	RALPH		WINNIE	HENRY	ALEX
GROUP 4	SARA	AXEL	LILAH		OWEN
GROUP 5	CHASE	CALVIN	GEORGE	HALLIE	

Invite a heterogeneous group of various students to participate in a small-group peer feedback session during writing workshop. Students can practice providing feedback that's grounded in the rubric, all the while doing so in an intimate setting where you can guide them through the process.

Pull a mixed-ability group to the carpet during math workshop to introduce a new math game. Math games are known to build fluency in a variety of skills, meanwhile serving as a fun way for students with varying abilities to converge around a learning experience. You could even pull a mixed-ability group to share varying methods for the same math task.

With time and enough variance, students become unaware of which groups are ability-based and which are not. In fact, if this is done from the very beginning, it is likely they will have a hard time figuring out that any of the groups are ability-based. This is especially powerful because it removes the stigma of small-group learning, meanwhile giving each child what they need to succeed.

These varied groups also create opportunities for all sorts of connections to occur: children can connect with ability-alike peers and with peers who are very different from them. Such is the beauty of strategically grouping, not only for ability level but also for the purpose of protecting equity and helping kids develop meaningful connections with others.

THE FOUNDATION OF INDIVIDUALIZATION

It is impossible to reach a level of individualization that is humanizing and meaningful if the first two dimensions are not secured with intention. Think of these first two dimensions as the foundation of a house or a building: without a strong foundation, it is impossible to build upward and erect a three-dimensional structure. When personalized learning begins by individualizing curriculum, it does so atop a shaky foundation—a foundation that can actually be a threat to equity and humanity.

Personalized learning that values the individualization of curriculum conflicts too harshly with a classroom that truly values the diversity each child brings. It undermines the collective conscious of the classroom. Individualization is motivated by self-interest and competition, whereas diversity, equity, and inclusion are grounded in the well-being of the collective.

In the third dimension, personalizing learning continues to be a shared responsibility between the teacher and each individual learner. Our role changes slightly, though, as we engage in the delicate process of nurturing a child's inner dialogue to help them become more autonomous and less dependent. In the third dimension, we count on the structures built by the first and second dimensions to support feedback, agency, autonomous decision-making, and goal setting. While technology companies may attempt to persuade you into believing that the individualized dimension is dependent on an individualized curriculum, the evidence base for this is incredibly weak. Instead, this final dimension is defined by an inner dialogue that is constantly unfolding within each of our students, externally manifested by the decisions our learners make each and every day.

THE THIRD DIMENSION

Nurturing a Child's Internal Dialogue

In the third dimension of personalization, we make space for a healthy amount of individualization. But this does not entail individualizing a child's curriculum. Instead, individualization occurs within the internal dialogue of the child, still engaged in the collective conscious of the classroom. In all these situations, a nuanced understanding of motivation and engagement is critical.

> The third dimension of personalized learning is defined by situations where the child is working independently, reflecting independently, or receiving individualized feedback, still engaged in the collective conscious of the classroom.

Learning requires a conversation. Without this conversation—one in which the learner engages and interacts—meaningful learning will not occur. The constant exchange of information and ideas is what makes it possible for all of us to learn. While it's not always a conscious choice to enter into a learning conversation, it can be a conscious choice to avoid the conversation. In fact, our learners with the most significant needs oftentimes choose not to interact. They've learned, time and time again, that interacting comes with making dangerous mistakes that lead to shame. It comes as no surprise when they choose to disengage. It is for this reason—and especially with these students in mind—that we'd be remiss in leaving motivation out of our discussion of personalized learning. Addressing motivation ensures we create learning environments where mistakes are safe, necessary, and *valued* in the learning process.

Motivation is oftentimes categorized in an extrinsic-intrinsic dichotomy, but I don't believe that extrinsic and intrinsic motivation are mutually exclusive. They exist in a relationship; there is tension between them. As is the case with any dichotomous tension, finding a balance between these two extremes is critical.

AUTHENTIC ENGAGEMENT AND INTRINSIC MOTIVATION

In *Shaking Up the Schoolhouse* (2001), Phillip Schlechty identifies myriad ways children engage or disengage in the classroom. His ideal is *authentic engagement*, resulting in learning that has clear meaning and immediate value to the child. Other forms of engagement move away from this ideal. *Ritual engagement* and *passive compliance*, also known as *strategic compliance*, entail the child agreeing to complete any given task, assignment, or direction, not necessarily because it possesses clear meaning or immediate value but, instead, because the extrinsic benefits are clear. These extrinsic benefits may vary for each child: some may value their relationship with their teacher, while others may want to avoid negative consequences at home.

As we move further away from authentic engagement, we move into the territory of outright disengagement. *Retreatism* occurs when a child makes little to no effort to comply with the teacher, and *rebellion* occurs when children disrupt others and/or present off-task behaviors (Schlechty, 2001).

While we strive for authentic engagement, it's not realistic to expect this 100 percent of the time. Our constraints in education are clear, and they're unlikely to go anywhere in the near future. Most of us have twenty or more children in our classrooms, and it is impossible to make them all happy at the same time. School is challenging by design, and we know it won't always be fun. It's supposed to push and stretch us in ways we've never been stretched before. This is uncomfortable, and at times it's downright painful. Sending the implicit message that to be engaged, one must be operating only off of intrinsically motivating factors proliferates the problems of entitlement and instant gratification of our youngest generation.

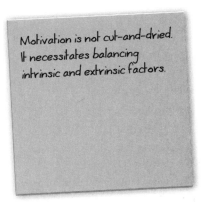

Motivation is not cut-and-dried. It necessitates balancing intrinsic and extrinsic factors.

It's easy to lose sight of what it truly means when an environment is student-driven and personalized. Many believe this means children do whatever they please—that they must be operating off of intrinsic motivation entirely. It's possible, if you are currently in a traditional school or a rigid public school, you've never seen this before. But I have, especially in affluent environments pursuing supposedly progressive pedagogy. It's a toxic symptom of affluence: many children from affluent homes have been conditioned to avoid struggle and instead constantly seek instant gratification. They frequently get what they want, and what's more, little time elapses before their wishes are granted. As a result, any sort of discomfort becomes a trigger for emotional dysregulation, anxiety, retreatism, or rebellion.

Our reality is that we live in a world ruled by extrinsic social norms and expectations. Aiming to create classrooms where children operate entirely off of intrinsic motivation would be unrealistic. Instead, we must strike a balance between extrinsic and intrinsic motivators. One of the purposes of schooling is to socialize children and help them gain an understanding of how to operate in a world filled with other people—to help them "overcome natural inclination," as Dewey (1938) would say. To do this, they must engage with the world around them through both extrinsic and intrinsic means. At times, they will simply want to comply, and at other times, they won't want to. But it won't change the fact that they may have to.

To some, this sounds like an authoritarian approach to classroom management, but I assure you it's not. Conversely, by allowing for extrinsic motivators, it might sound like I'm advocating for sticker charts or meaningless rewards. I'm not doing that, either. Instead, I promote an authoritative approach, one where teachers help children develop an understanding of the benefits of social norms and routines, meanwhile helping children learn to make decisions for themselves that work within healthy boundaries. It is through an authoritative approach that children learn the most powerful extrinsic factor that motivates us: human connection.

THE POWER OF ASKING WHY

During my first year in Silicon Valley, I was paired with Kristen, who would be my co-teacher that year. Our class was especially challenging, not only because we were trying to individualize curricula for almost twenty children but also because we had a number of students with sensory integration needs, symptoms of autism, and severe challenges with emotional regulation.

Kristen's background was in neuropsychology, whereas I was a more traditionally trained teacher—my greatest strengths in curriculum development and research-based pedagogy. Kristen's superpowers shone in moments of emotional and regulatory crisis. She was patient, she was empathetic, and she was consistently kind. Through observing her, I learned one of my most critical lessons over my three years in Silicon Valley.

I remember Timothy, a loving young boy who struggled with emotional awareness and regulation. He was constantly reaching out for validation and attention, generally through explosive physical, emotional, and defiant behaviors. While I generally assumed his defiance could be treated with clear consequences, Kristen saw nuance there that I didn't.

"I don't want to do my playlist right now," Timothy said one day, crossing his arms defiantly with a furrowed brow.

My blood pressure rose; my patience thinned. My experience told me he needed clearer boundaries and that we couldn't let him get out of doing his work. My teacher armor went up, and I planted my feet, so to speak. I braced for a meltdown and an all-out emotional war.

Kristen, on the other hand, took a more vulnerable approach, one that I'm proud to say I now take more often than I used to.

"Why?" she asked, sitting next to him and moving herself into his downward gaze.

"I'm hungry," he said. "I didn't eat breakfast this morning."

Kristen immediately got Timothy a snack, and within minutes, he came back to life—and got back to work. We later found out that Timothy's unique needs—a by-product of his daily medicine and his challenges with emotional regulation—caused his body to require food more frequently than the rest of us. That day, when he refused to do his playlist, he was *hangry*, and he did not yet have the skills to advocate for himself.

After Timothy got his snack, I'm relatively certain that he still didn't *want* to work on his playlist, but I am grateful we were able to get him to a point of compliance, at the very least. For Timothy, school was strenuous, and he would have rather been out playing and running around than sitting and reading or learning new math concepts.

It never hurts to ask a child why.

It's important to note that Timothy was an outlier, with more significant needs than the average child. While not all children who say they are hungry will truly need a snack, what I learned from working with him (and through watching Kristen) is that it never hurts to ask why. It might provide some insight into what's driving a child while also building trust, letting them know that you genuinely want to understand their needs.

At times, strategic compliance is the best we are going to get. Certainly, there were moments when Timothy was authentically engaged—during hands-on, exploratory tasks such as the archaeological dig Kristen created, or when he would get to build new creations with Legos. Inevitably, there were times when Timothy needed to be strategically compliant so he'd learn how to read, write, and compute.

This is, for better or for worse, the way our world works. We live in a world defined by social norms, laws, and systems. To survive in these systems, strategic compliance is necessary, hopefully tempered by authentic engagement, joy, and a passion for something greater than oneself. Kristen intuitively understood this intricate balance between extrinsic and intrinsic motivation, and as a result, she was able to create a truly personal learning environment where all felt seen, heard, and understood.

INTRINSIC MOTIVATION IN THE THIRD DIMENSION

To balance extrinsic and intrinsic factors, I subscribe to Daniel Pink's theory on intrinsic motivation. In *Drive: The Surprising Truth About What Motivates Us* (2009), Pink shares a framework for motivation that is realistic, and while he calls it "intrinsic motivation," it's clear that intrinsic and extrinsic factors are not mutually exclusive, even in his framework. Pink identifies three critical inputs to *intrinsic motivation: autonomy, mastery*, and *purpose* (see Figure 4.1).

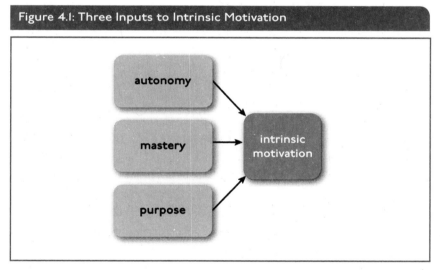

Figure 4.1: Three Inputs to Intrinsic Motivation

Source: Adapted from Pink (2009), *Drive: The Surprising Truth about What Motivates Us*
Published by Riverhead Books.

Conversation is ubiquitous in the personalized classroom. It is necessary for meaningful learning to occur. This conversation can be *interpersonal* (between two individuals) or *intrapersonal* (an inner dialogue that is reflective in nature). For children to enter into either of these two types of conversations, they must *choose* to do so. As Pink tells us, this choice is defined by *autonomy* (the degree to which one can work independently within constraints), *mastery* (the degree to which one feels appropriately challenged and can see one's progress), and *purpose* (the degree to which one understands *why* one is doing something). In all three of these inputs, both extrinsic and intrinsic factors play a role. After all, autonomy must be contextualized by an external learning environment; mastery is mediated by physical materials, tools, and other human beings; and purpose necessitates an understanding of the big picture—of something greater than oneself.

Because all children are different, autonomy, mastery, and purpose will exist in different proportions within different children. This is, again, where educators must use their intuition to understand what, specifically, is driving a child. It's uncertain and sometimes uncomfortable, but this dynamism will define the messy, colorful, and vulnerable narrative that is a teaching career. By keeping your finger on the pulse of motivation, and by identifying where it may be breaking down, you will reach your students by speaking to what drives them internally, making them agents of their own experience and sharing the responsibility of personalizing their learning through their autonomy. There are ample opportunities to do this throughout a single school day. You just have to know how to look for them.

A FRAMEWORK FOR MEDIATED ACTION

The first time I witnessed intrinsic motivation in action wasn't even in a classroom. It was in San Francisco's Presidio on a beautiful Sunday afternoon. A cool breeze floated in from the bay, joy filled the air, children ran around freely, and I enjoyed snacks with new friends at one of San Francisco's Off the Grid food-truck events. In my periphery, I noticed a toddler stumbling around—a new walker, no doubt. Her eyes wandered with wonder, soaking in the beautiful day. She reveled in the radiance of the blue sky, the comfort of the wind on her face, and the feel of the prickly grass in between her tiny fingertips.

She noticed a dog across the way, and almost immediately, her eyes locked on it. She waddled perilously, step by step, over to the dog. Her parents eyed her every move, and so did I, curious as to her intentions with the furry animal. When she arrived, she laid her hands on its soft fur, smiling gleefully and tilting her face back into the warm sun. The dog sat patiently, comforted by the baby's tiny hands caressing its back. The child experienced pleasure: she was learning (or perhaps learning again) that it felt good to touch a dog.

But let's imagine a different scenario.

Let's imagine the child has walked over to the dog, her off-kilter stance somewhat unsettling to the skeptical animal. Upon her arrival, the animal becomes nervous as the little girl, now a perceived threat, continues to approach. The dog tightens its muscles, its ears sink, and it slowly moves its face toward the ground, grimacing. The girl is unable to pick up on the dog's subtle hints, for she has not yet experienced a dog in this way. So she approaches him anyway. When she reaches him, she lays her hands on his soft fur, just as she did in the actual scenario. The dog growls and barks ferociously, causing her to fall to her bottom and cry. Fear permeates every crevice of her body, and nerves shock her extremities. Her mother comes to her rescue, assuaging her trauma.

These are two incredibly different experiences—one of them merely hypothetical—and if we examine them in juxtaposition, both have the capacity to teach us a lesson about intrinsic motivation, engagement, and the learning process.

First and foremost, both scenarios are dictated by the media through which the child experiences them. In his book *Voices of the Mind* (1991), largely inspired by Vygotsky, James Wertsch argues a sociocultural approach to learning that emphasizes the importance of "cultural tools" that shape the way we think and act. Without a medium—in this instance, the dog—this little girl would not have been able to learn something new about animals or about independent exploration. Second, both scenarios depict the degree to which free will and independent decision-making affect intrinsic motivation. To delve into this further, let's break the situation down into even smaller steps, into what I call the *Framework for Mediated Action*, largely inspired by Wertsch's work (see Figure 4.2).

This framework consists of three phases, and similarly, our children go through these phases with innumerable "cultural tools" in our classrooms. While these steps generally occur sequentially, they also occur cyclically, returning to Phase 1 with each micro- and macro-learning experience. The three steps are as follows: stimulus and interpretation; decision and action; interaction and modification.

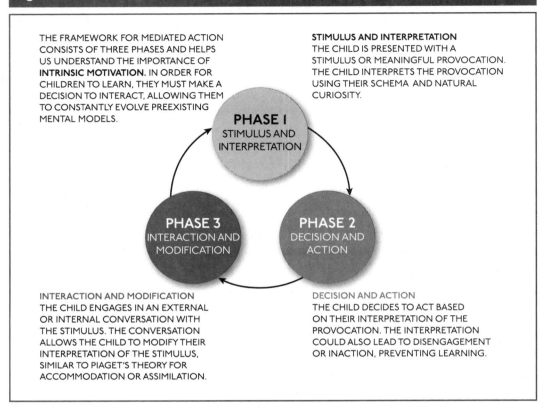

Figure 4.2: A Framework for Mediated Action

THE FRAMEWORK FOR MEDIATED ACTION CONSISTS OF THREE PHASES AND HELPS US UNDERSTAND THE IMPORTANCE OF **INTRINSIC MOTIVATION.** IN ORDER FOR CHILDREN TO LEARN, THEY MUST MAKE A DECISION TO INTERACT, ALLOWING THEM TO CONSTANTLY EVOLVE PREEXISTING MENTAL MODELS.

STIMULUS AND INTERPRETATION
THE CHILD IS PRESENTED WITH A STIMULUS OR MEANINGFUL PROVOCATION. THE CHILD INTERPRETS THE PROVOCATION USING THEIR SCHEMA AND NATURAL CURIOSITY.

PHASE 1
STIMULUS AND INTERPRETATION

PHASE 3
INTERACTION AND MODIFICATION

PHASE 2
DECISION AND ACTION

INTERACTION AND MODIFICATION
THE CHILD ENGAGES IN AN EXTERNAL OR INTERNAL CONVERSATION WITH THE STIMULUS. THE CONVERSATION ALLOWS THE CHILD TO MODIFY THEIR INTERPRETATION OF THE STIMULUS, SIMILAR TO PIAGET'S THEORY FOR ACCOMMODATION OR ASSIMILATION.

DECISION AND ACTION
THE CHILD DECIDES TO ACT BASED ON THEIR INTERPRETATION OF THE PROVOCATION. THE INTERPRETATION COULD ALSO LEAD TO DISENGAGEMENT OR INACTION, PREVENTING LEARNING.

PHASE 1: STIMULUS AND INTERPRETATION

Children must be trained to notice.

Children are born curious, with a sense of exploration and wonder. The child's experience in the park was no different. It started with a stimulus, with something she noticed: a dog. All learning experiences begin this way; children must *notice* in order to learn. Once the child noticed the dog from across the way, she *interpreted* it using her prior experiences and background knowledge.

In the real scenario, the little girl's eyes lit up. Perhaps she had seen such a furry creature before and had a positive experience with it; perhaps she had not and was curious about what it was. Regardless, she interpreted the creature as something worth approaching, something fun that would bring her joy. She was, in essence, *motivated* to go toward it.

PHASE 2: DECISION AND ACTION

In either scenario—real or hypothetical—the child *decided to act* on her positive interpretation of the furry creature across the way, making the possibility of learning from it much greater. Children are always interpreting, even when they are simply identifying something they've seen before. However, new learning may not occur if it's a familiar stimulus with which the child decides they'd rather not interact.

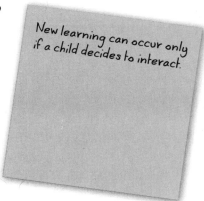

New learning can occur only if a child decides to interact.

The toddler *decided* to go play with the dog and *acted* on that by walking over. In her case, the decision was most likely impulsive, as she had not developed the metacognitive skills to go through a conscious decision-making process. As children age, they become more aware of decision-making processes; they become less impulsive. This is partially natural but can also be positively impacted by the explicit teaching of mindfulness, habits, and managing impulsivity, as we'll discuss in Section II.

This point in the Framework for Mediated Action is critical not just because the child has decided to act but also because now the child's behavior is observable to another. In an evidence-based learning environment, which all personalized learning environments must be, children's actions and the by-products of these actions are the only pieces of evidence we have to quantify learning.

In the first scenario, this resulted in a jubilant smile and overall joyful experience. In the second, hypothetical scenario, it resulted in shock and emotional pain. In turn, it is the interaction with the stimulus that modifies the existing mental model of said stimulus, and we can see this in the final phase of the Framework for Mediated Action: interaction and modification.

PHASE 3: INTERACTION AND MODIFICATION

Interaction is the most critical part of the framework. Interaction *is* the conversation I've referred to so many times already. It occurs when the stimulus reacts and communicates something back to us. Interaction is where *feedback* occurs, resulting in self-directed learning. It is also this phase of the framework that reveals the Piagetian nature of personalized learning, due to the fact it directly impacts the child's ability to assimilate or accommodate new experiences into an already existing schema.

In the first scenario—the one I actually witnessed on that sunny Sunday in San Francisco—the dog (the stimulus) gave the child positive feedback. By doing nothing and continuing to wag its tail, the dog sent the little girl a subtle signal that it enjoyed the sensation of little fingers running through its fur. However, in the hypothetical scenario, the dog gave quite different feedback. Instead, the dog shared its visceral disdain for the child's touch, giving her feedback to help change her decision-making process the next time.

This interaction step, along with the feedback associated, is applicable to innumerous contexts, such as teacher-child or peer-to-peer interactions where verbal feedback is exchanged through interpersonal conversation. But all the media in the world communicate with us—even inanimate media. Think of a cup of water overflowing after it's been filled too high, or two paint colors that are mixed together on a blank canvas. Even these inanimate media are engaging us in conversation and giving us feedback.

That is why this interaction phase is so critical. It shows us that all learning—even learning that happens independently—necessitates a conversation. Learning cannot be consumptive; it must be collaborative, for it is through interaction, feedback, and conversation that we push and pull on the media that occupy our world. It is through interaction that we modify our mental models of the world, resulting in learning.

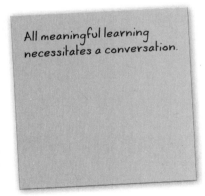

All meaningful learning necessitates a conversation.

In the final stage of the Framework for Mediated Action, the original stimulus is modified only after interaction occurs. I am going to invite you to broaden your definition of the term *modification*. While it can imply the creation or transformation of an object into a new entity, it can also imply either the assimilation or reorganization of new material, knowledge, or information into an already existing schema (Piaget & Cook, 1952).

In the first scenario of the child and the dog, she assimilated affirming experiences into her already existing mental model of the furry animal. Assuming she already associated the animal with joy, she then associated it even more with joy, making it more likely that she would approach the animal again in the same manner and maybe even develop a bountiful love of dogs. In the world of Piaget, this is known as *assimilation*, where new information fits into the already existing mental model.

In the second, hypothetical scenario, she would have modified the stimulus in a different way. Instead of adding more positive reinforcement to her preexisting mental model of the dog, she instead would take in information that contradicted the mental model, forcing her to reorganize it. When having to reorganize information, our brains *accommodate* new information that contradicts what we already know. This is why Piaget clearly differentiated between *assimilation*, the blending of new ideas into an already existing schema, and *accommodation*, the reorganization of the mental model to take new information into account.

Perhaps, after this second scenario, the child would pause before going to pet the next dog she saw in the park, or perhaps in the future she wouldn't pet dogs that looked similar to the one that growled. She would have reorganized her mental model of dogs, modifying the original stimulus and taking her back to the beginning of the Framework for Mediated Action. Most likely, resulting from the real scenario, the next time she sees another dog in the park and the framework repeats for the little girl, the same series of steps will begin again, giving her the potential to further modify her mental model of dogs.

NURTURING THE INNER DIALOGUE

The Framework for Mediated Action is applicable to all sorts of contexts, even in adulthood when we are our less malleable selves. Our internal and external environments are composed of varied stimuli: they are codified by the "cultural tools" through which we perceive and interact with the world. As a result, we are constantly interpreting, deciding to act on, interacting with, and modifying those stimuli to assimilate or accommodate new learning into preexisting mental models.

It is through the Framework for Mediated Action that all individuals learn, rung by rung, as the cycle infinitely repeats itself. And it is for this reason that intrinsic motivation is paramount when humanizing personalized learning, as it shines light onto moments when students decide whether they will—or whether they will *not*. Intrinsic motivation and the Framework for Mediated Action define the inner dialogues that occur for our students and, in turn, grant them the opportunity to be partners in personalizing learning.

But just because these define the inner dialogue doesn't mean that we, the educators, cannot impact intrinsic motivation through our pedagogy. In fact, this is the very reason why educators are invaluable in the process of humanizing personalization and why it is incumbent on school leaders and legislators to invest more in teachers around the country. Teachers are the ones who encourage students to access their agency, witness their autonomy, and find purpose in classrooms. They aid students' exploration of identity, unlock intrinsic motivation, and partner with them to nurture an ever-evolving inner dialogue that makes students independent.

Nurturing the inner dialogue is not easy work. It requires a presence of mind and a compassionate responsiveness to student behavior. It requires vulnerability and a relinquishing of the shame that comes from unmet expectations. It necessitates a complete immersion into the process of learning, because it is within this messy process that we connect with our humanity and connect with one another.

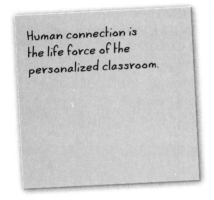

Human connection is the life force of the personalized classroom.

Connection is foundational to the human condition, and therefore it is foundational to the human experience of learning, as well. It is connection that allows us to continue learning conversations, to tolerate the discomfort that accompanies novel experiences, and to revel in the joy that comes with learning. Human connection is, by all means, the life force of the classroom and the life force of personalized learning. And it makes sense, because human connection unites all three dimensions of personalized learning.

To nurture the inner dialogues of a diverse group of learners, we must leverage human connection, because our students must trust one another and their teachers enough to consent to having their inner dialogues nurtured by the interpersonal conversations and feedback that permeate the classroom. As a result, we must create psychologically, emotionally, and physically safe spaces where students allow themselves and their identities to be shaped by the external forces of the classroom. Doing so allows educators an entry point into this inner dialogue by cultivating awareness, encouraging humility, and incentivizing vulnerability—all through a responsive and respectful pedagogy that has the potential to change the way students actualize their agency and autonomy within the personalized classroom.

CULTIVATE AWARENESS THROUGH EXECUTIVE FUNCTIONING

Awareness is foundational to building a culture of autonomy and agency, but fortunately, it can be developed in all three dimensions of personalization. In the first dimension, we can cultivate awareness through group mindfulness, explicit lessons intended to bolster social-emotional competencies, and modeling metacognition. But we can also cultivate awareness within our students by better understanding how executive functioning skills impact an individual's ability to think flexibly, regulate, and plan ahead.

Before we do so, it's important to define executive functioning by understanding its components. Executive functioning is composed of *cognitive flexibility*, *physical/emotional regulation*, and *planning/organizational skills*. Each year I teach, I notice executive functioning skills becoming more and more of a challenge, specifically with regard to planning, organization, and executing multistep directions. I surmise that this is a product of a world that increasingly incentivizes instant gratification within children, no doubt exacerbated by digital technology, overbooked schedules, and learned helplessness.

To start the school year, I recommend teaching children about working memory and how we can train it to help us easily recall multistep directions. This can be done through *rehearsal*. When I first introduce this concept to my kids, I model it by thinking aloud, meanwhile making a circular motion beside my head, like a gear is turning while I rehearse the directions.

"First, I'm going to get my writer's notebook out," I say.

"Then I will open up to the next clean page, the next clean page, the next clean page," I repeat rhythmically, knowing full well that many of my students forget this critical step.

"Last, I will title my page and write the date," I finish. "Okay, now it's your turn. Turn and tell your neighbor what the three steps are."

The children follow suit, going through the directions, some of them replicating the gear-like circular motion beside their heads. They walk to their seats, and even with classes where executive functioning is especially a challenge, I notice a great deal of success.

As the year goes on, I do this less and less. By early winter, I'm encouraging students to do this nonverbally in their minds, slowly scaffolding the process and intending to build automaticity and independence.

"Very soon," I say, "I'm going to expect you to rehearse the directions in your mind without a reminder from me."

Unsurprisingly, some students need more support than this. In the event that they do, I equip every student with a numbered sheet that lives inside an erasable plastic sleeve in their desks. If they have trouble remembering the directions, they can write them down for themselves. In some cases, challenges with multistep directions and executive functioning allow me to strike up a conversation when we set goals, which we aim to do once per season.

ENCOURAGE HUMILITY THROUGH A CULTURE OF GOAL SETTING

Goal setting is a skill, not an instinct. In fact, even high-achieving students need to learn how to set goals and pursue them to completion. Too many high achievers have succeeded through compliance and wit, unable to develop a vision for the not-so-distant future and identify action steps for it. To help with this, I scaffold the goal-setting process three times throughout the year: fall, winter, and spring. To do this, we go through a rather simple process consisting of four steps (see Figure 4.3a).

Figure 4.3a: Goal-Setting Process

Step 1: Identify strengths

Step 2: Identify obstacles

Step 3: Identify causes and consequences

Step 4: Identify action steps and consequences

To help my students organize their thinking, I leverage Thinking Maps (Hyerle, 1995). Thinking Maps are like mind maps. The key difference, however, is that there are only eight maps to choose from, and each of them is used for very specific purposes, which I will outline as we go. I recommend visiting www.thinkingmaps.com to learn more about them.

First, we identify strengths using a Circle Map, intended for brainstorming (see Figure 4.3b). This helps us see them as assets to the goal-setting process. Too often, goal setting is done only in the context of our deficits, and if we want to make it meaningful and growth-oriented, we must use our assets, too. Beginning with assets also paves a path to equity and inclusion within our classrooms. All children, regardless of identity, have assets to bring to the classroom; they all

Figure 4.3b: Strengths

Reflecting on Strengths
What has gone well for you so far this year? What progress have you made? What strengths do you have?

I noticed that when I make a plan with Mr. Fienre or take a break and take a deep breath it helps me calm down so I can finish my work.

have stories to share that enrich the collective conscious. Within these stories are strengths, and our job as educators is to allow those strengths to shine.

But we mustn't ignore challenges and obstacles. Doing so perpetuates a culture of perfectionism and invulnerability. We must, instead, embrace our challenges and identify them as obstacles that we *can* overcome by leveraging our assets and the encouragement of the learning community. Similarly, we use a Circle Map for this, as well, to aid students in brainstorming as many obstacles as possible (see Figure 4.3c).

Figure 4.3c: Obstacles

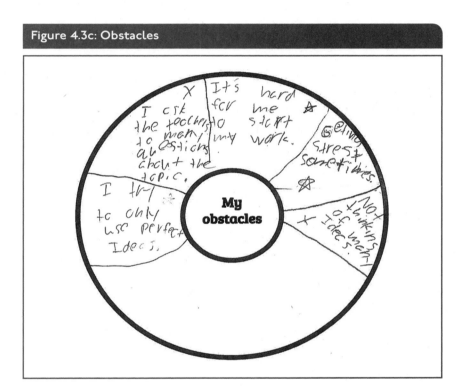

Part of cultivating awareness is helping students better understand what is within their locus of control. By identifying both the causes and the consequences of the goal, students may see that, if they are intentional about their actions, they can make the changes necessary to overcome an obstacle. To aid this, we use the Multi-Flow Map (see Figure 4.3d). On the left-hand side of the map are causes. The map itself allows for many causes for any one event or action. On the right-hand side, you'll see the effects of that same event or action. And then in the middle of the map you'll see the action or the event itself. In this instance, the middle action or event is the obstacle the child is experiencing. Using the Thinking Map helps children identify multiple causes and multiple effects, allowing them to concretely see how they might modify behaviors within their locus of control when setting their goal.

Figure 4.3d: Causes and Consequences of Obstacles

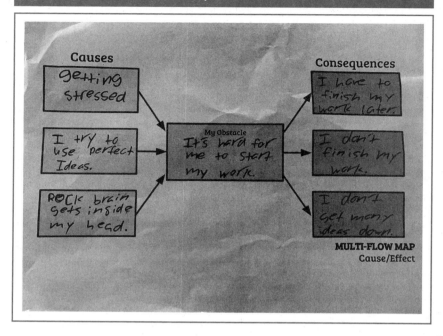

Causes

getting stressed

I try to use perfect Ideas.

ROCk brain gets inside my head.

My Obstacle
It's hard for me to start my work.

Consequences

I have to finish my work later.

I don't finish my work.

I don't get many ideas down.

MULTI-FLOW MAP
Cause/Effect

But it's also important to remember that *consequence* doesn't need to have such a negative connotation. There are consequences for everything—for our assets, our obstacles, and reaching our goals. That is why in the final part of this process we simply turn the paper over and likewise turn the obstacle into a goal (see Figure 4.3e). The causes on the left-hand side turn into concrete action steps for reaching the goal. On the right-hand side,

Figure 4.3e: Causes and Consequences of Goal

What I need to do:

use tools to understand the directions.

Take deep and mindful breaths.

Don't get distracted by the things around you.

Tell myself: "It doesn't have to be perfect!"

My Personal Goal
Try to start my work more efficiently.

How it helps me and others:

To stay on the group plan.

helps me finish my work faster

get to the choices.

MULTI-FLOW MAP
Cause/Effect

we identify the positive consequences of reaching our goals, allowing us to develop a vision for how good it will feel and the impact it will have on ourselves and our community. Even in personal goal setting, we must balance the collective and the individual, leveraging all three dimensions of personalization.

Does this always lead directly to success? Well, I suppose it depends on your definition of success. In my classroom, to succeed means to open yourself up to the possibility of growing. The first time we do this, many of my students don't meet their personal goals in their entirety, but what I hope for most of all is that we build a *culture* of goal setting. My intention is that this process becomes a part of the cultural fabric of our classroom, even if we don't meet all our goals.

"Mr. France?" one of my students said to me one day while reflecting on our goals and setting new ones. "I don't think I met my goal. I think I need some more time to work on it. I actually think it might be a goal for me all year since it's really hard for me to remember I don't have to have the perfect idea to get started. Is it okay if I keep the same goal?"

"Absolutely," I replied. "I love how *aware* you are of what you need."

An interaction like this shows me I've succeeded in creating a culture of goal setting. My students aren't concerned with superficially meeting a goal or faking their progress; they're intrinsically motivated to make progress and set goals for the purpose of personal growth. And this couldn't come without the trusting relationships we've built and the willingness to be vulnerable with one another. But this doesn't happen overnight. It happens with intention, and it happens by praising vulnerability and making it a part of the way you define success in your classroom.

INCENTIVIZE VULNERABILITY THROUGH BRAVE MISTAKES

Growth is a choice. It is something to which we must submit and consent. This goes for children, too, and it's why this notion of intrinsic motivation and training decision-making is so powerful when nurturing a child's inner dialogue. But the growth that comes from humility and enhanced awareness is precipitated by vulnerability—by the courage to admit to ourselves that even though we are *enough*, growth is still a part of the human condition.

We live in a society that too often incentivizes perfection and impenetrability, and this acts in opposition to growth, humility, and vulnerability. As educators, one of the many jobs we're faced with is counteracting this by modeling the courage necessary to be vulnerable and imperfect. We can model vulnerability and, in effect, take steps toward nurturing the inner dialogues of our students by sharing pieces of our identities and stories of our imperfection. In our final section, on equity, I'll share some of my own journey as an openly gay educator and how I've used my own identity to connect and be vulnerable with my students.

Learning to be vulnerable with students is a process. It took me more than five years to work up the courage to share my identity with my students. It's okay to be uncomfortable, and it's okay to give yourself space to build up some courage. There are other ways to be vulnerable. One of the best ways is to share our own mistakes and missteps with our students. Any teacher knows that mistakes and missteps are ubiquitous in our profession. It's hard for me to get through a half-hour without making one. To help my students, I let them into these moments in an effort to both normalize them and help them feel comfortable letting me into *their* missteps, mistakes, and vulnerabilities.

If you're like me and you need a process when trying new things, try the one in Figure 4.4.

Figure 4.4:
Process for Brave
Mistakes

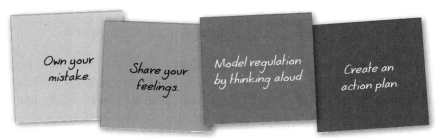

Own your mistake.

Share your feelings.

Model regulation by thinking aloud.

Create an action plan.

Step 1: Own the Mistake

"Oops, I think I made a mistake," I'll say to my class, owning my mistake. "I can't figure out where I put the math tasks."

It's true I could just give them something to do while I figured it out, but mistakes and missteps are there for a reason. They are there to help us learn something, and in the classroom, these moments are even more powerful: they grant us an opportunity to connect with our students through our imperfections. We must capitalize on those moments and be open about them.

Step 2: Share Your Feelings

I look at them, take a deep breath, and begin to share how my mistake is making me feel. "I'm feeling a little frustrated and nervous right now because I know I misplace things a lot. I'm also worried my mistake is going to make the whole class really unfocused," I continue, letting them into the natural and universal feelings that come up when any of us make mistakes.

Step 3: Model Regulation by Thinking Aloud

"But you know what? I know that mistakes help me learn, so I'm going to take a deep breath and remember that you are all here to support me when I make mistakes in our classroom," I say to them. "Will you help me while I work through my mistake?"

They generally nod or sit quietly, engaged by a vulnerability I imagine they are not accustomed to seeing in school.

Step 4: Create an Action Plan

"I'm going to look for the math tasks. In the meantime, can you all pull out your digit cards and play a couple rounds of Multiplication Top-It? While you are, I want you to think about what we learned yesterday about using more efficient strategies to multiply big numbers in your head. While you do that, I'm going to work to fix my mistake so we can do our math task."

Making an action plan with them wasn't a big deal or a laborious process. It kept them engaged, it bought me some time, and it bonded us over a common goal. It also allowed for an extra moment to teach about vulnerability and how in moments of vulnerability, we must lean on the collective to help us overcome our obstacles. It helps them see—albeit implicitly—that we're all connected through our vulnerabilities, our mistakes, and the growth that emerges as a result of them.

THE INTERSECTIONALITY OF PERSONALIZATION

Exploring the three dimensions of personalized learning has paradoxically brought us right back to the beginning—back to the collective. By now, I hope it's clear that these three dimensions are not orthogonal, that to embrace the paradox of personalization, we must allow both the interests of the individual and the needs of the collective to occupy the same space and to be of equal importance for learning to be personal and personalized.

Such is the nature of identity, as well—an oftentimes overlooked component of personalized learning, but a critical one when we're humanizing personalization. While identity is truly of the individual, it is simultaneously of the collective. It not only defines an individual as a unique entity; it describes entire groups of people, united by race, ethnicity, sexual orientation, gender identity, ability, religion, or socioeconomic status. It is the intersection of these group identities coupled with the compounded perspectives born from our individual experiences that build an identity. As a result, identity is contingent on both the individual and the collective.

When these group identities intersect, forming the individual, their orthogonality becomes palpable. It's hard to separate the *Black* from the *man* or the *White* from the *woman*. The intersection of these individual group identities takes on a life of its own. It's the age-old paradox that exists between the gestalt and the parts. The gestalt is greater than the sum of its parts. The parts don't necessarily function on their own; instead, each of the parts is dependent on the others to form an identity that's unique and intersectional.

Personalization is intersectional, just like identity. To serve each of our children within a classroom that values humanized personalization, we must allow each of the dimensions to exist in various proportions throughout the day, ebbing and flowing as new stories are told. Similarly, the identity of a humanized classroom becomes greater than the sum of its parts. It becomes a place where the collective community is honored and respected, and simultaneously where the individual is valued, seen, and heard.

In enabling this multidimensional, differentiated, and inclusive learning environment, we create an infinite number of pathways for student learning. The three dimensions of personalized learning are the same. They cannot exist without one another, and when they converge within our classrooms, we enable a multidimensional, differentiated, and inclusive learning environment; we create distinct classroom identities that are similarly intersectional due to the serendipitous collision of twenty or more human beings learning together. It is through these infinite pathways—and the cultivation of a classroom identity—that children may witness their autonomy and agency, become partners in the process of personalization, and integrate into the collective conscious of the classroom.

To reduce personalization down to the individualization of curriculum is to ignore the gestalt—to ignore the *identity* of the classroom and its inhabitants. When we strike a balance between shaping the collective conscious of the first dimension and nurturing the inner dialogues of our students in the third dimension, we actualize the agency of all learners, creating a learning environment where all are seen, heard, valued, and supported in their learning journeys.

While the intentions here were good—in individualizing curriculum to personalize learning—we now know better. We know this doesn't work. We focused our energy in the wrong place, falling victim to a culture that prizes fierce individualism and self-interest, taking the lead from the education technology industry and the wealthy tech elites that run it. And now it is our job as culturally responsive pedagogues to reclaim and repurpose personalization as a pedagogy that restores equity, humanity, and connection in our schools.

It is paramount that we do this *now*, and the greatest thing about it is that humanity and equity don't have to wait for a new update to software or a financial investment in new iPads or Chromebooks. Instead, it necessitates an emotional investment in ourselves and the people around us; it necessitates a presence of mind and willingness to enhance our awareness of what's right in front of us; it requires us to listen to and believe the many stories that come into our classroom so we may honor the identities of our learners and our learning environments.

And with that, let's get started.

SECTION I

FOUNDATIONS

Implications for Humanized Personalization

Personalized learning is the art of making learning personal. It is largely dependent on the classroom environment, which builds a strong foundation for learning that is inherently personal. Beware the common myths of personalized learning. Falling into them may make your practice of personalization unsustainable. If you find yourself falling into any of these myths, reconnect with what you've learned about personalized learning.

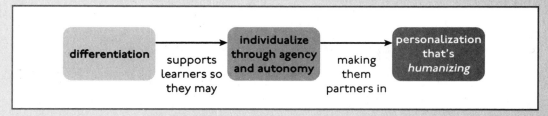

© Paul Emerich France, 2018 www.paulemerich.com, Twitter: @paul_emerich

Personalized learning necessitates an investment in people and pedagogy. To make learning personal, think of it in three dimensions:

- In the *first dimension*, we shape the collective conscious of the classroom. The learning environment must meet the basic, universal needs of a diverse group of students and foster human connection. In the first dimension, personalized learning necessitates points of *convergence* and *divergence*. Using a workshop model allows for this. Teachers can achieve this by starting with a minilesson and leveraging workshop times for small-group and individualized instruction. Coming together at the end of an instructional block allows for sharing and reflection on unique learning paths. While this exact structure is not always necessary, maintaining the *spirit* of the workshop model is critical so learners can benefit from points of convergence and divergence.

- In the *second dimension*, we focus on partnerships and small-group learning, leveraging dialogue, discourse, and formative assessment to strategically group students. In all cases, we must balance *heterogeneity* and *homogeneity* within the second dimension. Sometimes it makes sense to work with a group of learners who express any given similarity. This can be a path to a sustainable model for meeting individual needs. Other times, leveraging heterogeneity allows for peer modeling and for less obvious strengths to shine. But even heterogeneity has its limits. When leveraging heterogeneity, it's critical to take developmental differences into account so you may build points of convergence within individual lessons in the school day.

- In the *third dimension*, it's important to remember that individualized learning lies not in our curricular choices; instead, individualized learning lies in nurturing the child's inner dialogue, which builds agency and autonomy in the learning process. It is, in fact, possible to personalize with a curriculum that, at its outset, looks uniform to all. What's most important is that the curriculum you use is malleable, with varied entry points for a diverse group of learners. When you understand *motivation, engagement,* and learning as a *conversation,* the third dimension for personalized learning comes alive. Crucial to remember is that meaningful learning resides within the learner's decision to interact. As a result, our job as educators is to cultivate a learning environment where learners know that it's safe to take risks and make mistakes.

We must also remember that there are both humanizing and dehumanizing ways to personalize learning. We should always be striving to humanize personalization in our classrooms, which begins by putting human beings and human connection at the center of what we do. If any of our practices threaten human connection, we should immediately reconsider them. Please see the chart on the next page for a summary.

Humanized Personalization	Dehumanized Personalization
Powered by *humans*	Powered by *technology*
Connects learners through collaboration, vulnerability, and human connection	*Isolates* students through individualized tracks, competition, and cultures of shame
Uses assessment as a tool for *knowing learners*	Uses assessment to *compare* and *categorize*
Curates a high-interest curriculum that exposes learners to new and relevant topics to broaden experiences and schema	*Relies on interest-driven curriculum,* limiting learners to preferred learning topics and narrowing experiences and schema
Leverages *whole-group, small-group,* and *individualized* practices	Leverages technology tools that *individualize* curriculum
Understands individual learner's needs *in the context of* the collective learning community	Values individual needs *without considering* the collective learning community
Promotes *agency and autonomy* through social-emotional learning and structured choice	Limits *agency and autonomy* through automated, didactic curriculum delivered through digital technology
Uses technology to *preserve or enhance human connection*	Uses technology to *accelerate dissemination* of curriculum
Considers identity, *advocates* for representation, and *promotes equity*	*Ignores* identity, *limits* representation, and *proliferates inequity*

SECTION TWO

PEDAGOGY

CHAPTER FIVE

CULTIVATING AWARENESS

In biology, *ecosystems* are defined as *biological communities of interacting organisms and their physical environments*. Ecosystems are not necessarily defined by the organisms themselves but instead by the way they interact with one another and the environment. Theoretically, this process is pretty simple: primary producers (plants) are responsible for converting energy from the sun into usable energy that consumers (herbivores, omnivores, and carnivores) acquire by eating plants or other consumers who've already eaten the plants. In essence, energy transfer within an ecosystem is entirely dependent on the plants' ability to convert the sun's energy into usable energy. Without these primary producers, all life on Earth would cease to exist, as there would be no way to harness the sun's natural energy.

CLASSROOM ECOSYSTEM:

An interconnected and interdependent community of learners

The classroom is an ecosystem, too, much like the ecosystems that define natural life on Earth: those who occupy the classroom need an energy source to make yearlong learning sustainable. In too many classrooms, educators are expected to be the primary producers of education and learning—harnessing energy for learning from textbooks, industrialized curricula, or web-based adaptive technologies for direct transfer onto students. This, however, acts in opposition to learning that's personal and meaningful; it counteracts the notion of learning as a partnership between educator and learner.

When learning is industrialized, children become passive, mindless objects of the education system, as opposed to mindful and active subjects of an educational narrative. As a result, too many classrooms are unsustainable: teachers are carrying too much of the load, and students are leaving dependent, no more autonomous or empowered than before. In classrooms where technology-driven personalized learning is the norm, computer programs that disseminate content have become the primary producers of education, leaving both students and teachers to be passive consumers of learning. While technology offers an arguably more sustainable solution for individualizing learning, it's less human, more industrial, and utterly *impersonal*.

In a model that values *humanized personalization*—one where connection between human beings sustainably powers intrinsic motivation and meaningful interaction—students are partners in personalizing and humanizing the classroom. It is their curiosity, misconceptions, prior knowledge, and successes that propel learning forward. As Daniel Pink (2009) states, tapping into intrinsic motivation requires an understanding of autonomy. Far too many educators operate under a flawed definition of autonomy. Autonomy is not synonymous with unbridled independence; instead, it refers to an individual's ability to make decisions within social constraints and norms. This necessitates an understanding that one's autonomy exists in relationship with the collective. As a result, before fostering autonomy, we must cultivate self-awareness and an awareness of the collective.

A CLOSER LOOK

THE LIMITS OF VOICE AND CHOICE

There are good intentions behind "voice and choice." We want our students to be partners in the learning process, but too often, educators attempt to achieve voice and choice by having students design their own learning activities. In reality, there are more pragmatic, realistic, and sustainable ways to promote voice and choice without turning all the responsibility over to the children. We must remember that not just anyone can be a teacher. Being a teacher necessitates a nuanced understanding of the intersection of child development, curriculum design, and human-centered pedagogy. Children are not qualified to do this, nor should they be expected to. Providing them too much voice or choice can actually be paralyzing and dysregulating. We must, instead, scaffold voice and choice through the grades.

In primary grades, voice and choice include using centers for literacy and numeracy and may even mean providing play-based choice time in the school day. In the intermediate grades, this might look like allowing students to write about a topic of their choice, but still within the confines of the current genre of study

(Continued)

(i.e., expository, opinion, narrative). It may even look like initiating "quiet time" where students can read, write, draw, or make with found materials. In middle school and beyond, we can continue to expand voice and choice with elective classes and more autonomy with regard to topic and final demonstration of learning. We can do so increasingly in these older grades because they have begun to develop the executive functioning skills to handle their autonomy. If we don't build self-awareness and self-regulation prior to removing these scaffolds, voice and choice are actually counterproductive to learning.

In essence, when voice and choice are scaffolded properly, we are able to see all three dimensions for personalized learning: students may unite under the collective conscious of the class in which they are situated; engage in small-group dialogue or discourse around their learning; and finally, nurture a very personal, inner dialogue through exploration and discovery. But when voice and choice are not properly scaffolded, a culture of fierce individualism emerges, making for very few points of convergence in the classroom. It creates an entitlement that only exacerbates a desire for instant gratification. As educators, we have a responsibility to ensure that the collective interests of the classroom sit in balance with the interests of the individual. And we cannot do this without putting mindful boundaries around voice and choice in our classrooms.

Too often, educators jump right into designing learning experiences for students, when in reality, we first need to consider the greater ecosystem in which educators and learners are situated. In Figure 5.1, you'll see a preview of what's to come. Designing learning experiences entails three phases: (1) building a flexible frame with clear learning outcomes, (2) collecting or designing assessments that gauge learning, and (3) creating a plan for humanized instruction. All of these phases are grounded in the work of Grant Wiggins and Jay McTighe and inspired by the practices they suggest in their book *Understanding by Design* (1998). In the Thinking Map representing humanized pedagogy, I use a Flow Map, implying order or chronology and aligning with the process of backward design.

The first two chapters in this section address the context in which the design of learning experiences sits. The designers of Thinking Maps use what they call a "frame of reference" to illustrate this. In our case, awareness, agency, and autonomy encompass the frame of reference, build classroom culture, and contextualize the process of designing learning experiences. Think of it like a lens or a prism: it is through this lens of learner awareness, agency, and autonomy that humanized personalization can shine in colorful abundance. Outside of the frame of reference—without this lens of awareness, agency, and autonomy—exist practices or tools of *dehumanized personalization*,

Figure 5.1: Humanized Pedagogy

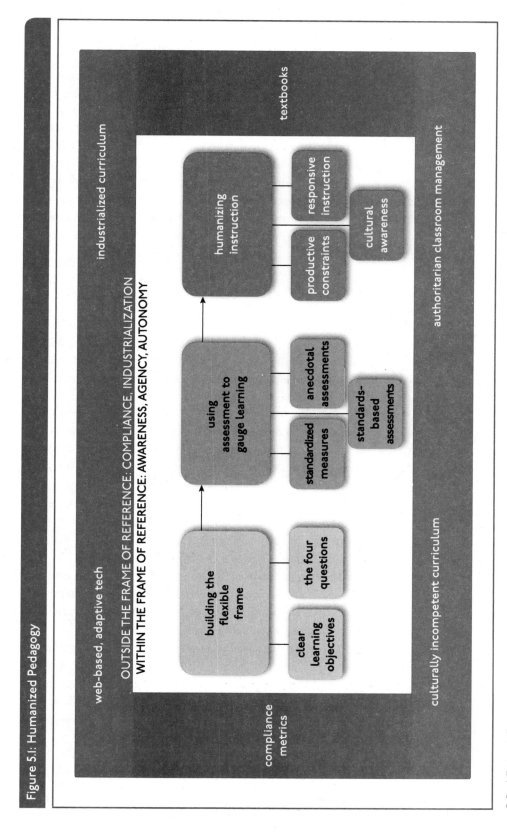

which oftentimes neglect to cultivate awareness, agency, and autonomy in students. These practices tend to dehumanize learning in classrooms.

DEFINING AWARENESS

Awareness is an oftentimes overlooked enigma. But it's incredibly important to discuss when humanizing personalization, as our awareness is what makes us undeniably human. While most animals learn out of a mere reptilian need to survive, humans fulfill a need quite unlike most other species. In addition to our instinctual need to survive, humans are hardwired to be curious, resulting in complex emotional experiences, ranging from boundless joy to overwhelming shame; inexhaustible passion to tiresome disengagement; visceral connection to ignorant disconnection.

When we examine learning in this context, it comes as no surprise that human awareness is difficult to quantify, understand, and embrace, for it is formed in a manner similar to the environment of a natural ecosystem. The everyday forces that act upon us—forces of success, failure, joy, anger, shame, vulnerability, and connection—form the peaks, valleys, cracks, crevices, flowing rivers, barren deserts, and bountiful plains of our intersectional identities.

In the Framework for Mediated Action, we can sense the importance of awareness even though it's not thoroughly described. In the first phase, stimulus and interpretation, we rely on children to *notice* the initial stimulus; we rely on them to be *aware* of it. For our children to autonomously connect to learning experiences in the classroom, they must develop self-awareness before they can autonomously persist through obstacles and fruitfully revel in the overwhelming joy of their successes.

Awareness is such an enigma because it brings with it the infamous chicken-or-egg conundrum. We ask ourselves, what comes first: self-awareness or an awareness of one's surroundings? Perhaps it depends on the individual or the situation. Regardless, both self-awareness and an awareness of the surrounding world must be cultivated in tandem, for it's nearly impossible to divorce the two. They are irrevocably connected, as they mediate each other. A child's surroundings impact what happens internally, while a child's internal dialogue affects their interaction with the world around them. It is not the origin that matters; it is instead how we cultivate an awareness of both the internal and external that matters the most.

In this chapter, my thoughts are structured from internal to external. In Section I: Foundations, we began with the collective, gradually zooming in to the individual learner and their inner dialogue. Now we start with the inner dialogue and zoom back out to the collective, not only to offer some parallelism in our approach to defining humanized personalization but also to help mimic the process by which we must reach our children: we must constantly toggle between environmental and personal factors that affect a child's ability to learn. Both the internal dialogue and the learning environment impact the degree to which learning is personal and inherently meaningful.

SELF-AWARENESS

Children are constantly developing and refining self-awareness from the minute they first witness themselves in a mirror, the mirror serving as a simple and poignant example of the external environment mediating internal self-awareness. Self-awareness is enhanced by the infant's ability to see themselves in the mirror—a tool from the external environment. There are infinite "mirrors" in the real world, if you will, mirrors that have the capacity to reflect information about ourselves back to us—from books and movies to art, music, and mathematics—allowing them to continuously interact with and refine our self-concept over time. This constant redefinition of a child's identity and self-awareness never ceases. It is not something to ever be mastered but, instead, something to continuously tend to and hone into adulthood.

Cultivating self-awareness is a more and more emerging need in schools. Nowadays, adults do far too much on behalf of children, limiting opportunities to build self-awareness. Not only has technology changed the way they access games and entertainment; it's also changed the way families access goods and services. Children are now accustomed to an Uber picking them up whenever they need a car; they're used to groceries being delivered to their doorstep. They're enrolled in myriad after-school classes and activities intended to provide a well-rounded education.

While our intentions are good, the reality is that many kids are micromanaged, tending to a desire for instant gratification. If they're bored, they can access nearly any form of entertainment on a computer or tablet, and if they're not bored, they're exhausted from the constant shuffling between activities and classes. As a result, they're wholly unaware of the significant role they play in their own lives. They're unaware of the fact that they belong to *themselves*.

I see this firsthand in my classrooms. The children who are accustomed to being micromanaged look up at me doe-eyed the first time I ask them to solve a multistep problem or answer an open-ended question. They shy away from the challenge of uncertainty, for fear of coloring outside the lines. They don't know that the fear, discomfort, and pain that come with uncertainty can actually be constructive and beneficial—that is, if you allow yourself to actually feel them. They don't see these experiences as opportunities for learning; instead, adults have conditioned them to see these as experiences to avoid. This, in turn, squashes agency, autonomy, and resilience, as they are constantly looking for guaranteed success.

This increased mindlessness knows no bounds. While it does not discriminate, it has the potential to have an even greater impact on our most vulnerable populations. In *Culturally Responsive Teaching and the Brain*, Zaretta Hammond (2014) implores readers to "support dependent learners to become independent thinkers." She states that "underserved English learners, poor students, and students of color routinely receive less instruction in higher order skills development than other students." This compounds over time, their dependency making them less apt to conquer rigorous academic tasks that require flexible thinking, problem-solving skills, or metacognition—all of which necessitate enhanced self-awareness, as well as the ability to exude resilience in the face of risk-taking and mistake-making. This worsens when populations of vulnerable students are subjected to the dehumanizing effects of personalized learning technologies, fostering even more dependence by limiting critical thinking, problem-solving, and metacognition.

Students will never learn to experience failure in a constructive way if they are not aware how fleeting the fear, discomfort, and pain of failure can be, especially if we are reinforcing dependent learning and a lack of self-awareness. We must cultivate self-awareness first by partnering with our students to help them personalize their own experience through their agency and autonomy. Self-awareness precedes autonomy, mastery, and a sense of purpose, and serves as a platform for risk-taking, mistake-making, regulation, and resilience (see Figure 5.2).

Figure 5.2: Awareness Precedes Intrinsic Motivation

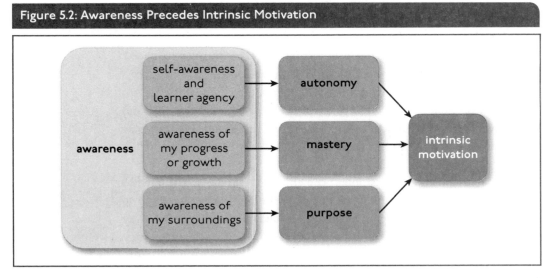

© Paul Emerich France, 2018 www.paulemerich.com, Twitter: @paul_emerich

I find it helpful to examine self-awareness from four different vantage points: emotional awareness, physical awareness, cognitive awareness (metacognition), and social awareness. It's important to remember that these are neither orthogonal nor sequential; they hang in a harmonious tension, impacting one another.

EMOTIONAL AWARENESS

I'm reminded of a conversation I had with Evelyn, an energetic, loving, and artistic six-year-old. She was navigating a number of obstacles to her learning, including some prohibitive sensory needs and difficulties with attention. She was also grappling with a new family structure. She was between two homes frequently, and it was starting to weigh on her. It impacted her academics and, at times, her ability to interact with peers. One day, I sat next to her while she was writing. She looked wiggly, distracted, and a bit forlorn.

"I'm feeling in the blue zone today," she said, referring to the Zones of Regulation.

The Zones of Regulation is a framework developed by Leah Kuypers (2011). Originally developed for students with autism, it concretizes emotions into four colors: red, yellow, green, and blue, accounting for state of arousal and energy level, as well. In the green zone, students feel regulated and "ready to learn." In the yellow and red zones, they feel less regulated, perhaps needing to slow down or take a break. In the blue zone, students generally are at a low state of arousal, usually sad, bored, or tired.

"How come?" I replied to Evelyn.

"I'm feeling sad about my family," she confided in me. "It's really hard to have two homes sometimes."

"I understand," I replied. "I think that would put me in the blue zone, too. And it's okay to feel sad about it. But you know what I learned recently?"

She looked at me inquisitively, curious about what I was going to say next.

"I learned that we can't always control the feelings we have, but we can control how we respond to them. I like to think of them like waves at the ocean. Do you know what happens to waves at the ocean?"

She thought for a second, and then replied, "They move in and out, right?"

"They do," I continued. "And I like to think of our feelings like waves. They wash over us and eventually wash away. You feel sad right now, and that's okay. But you won't always feel sad about it. Eventually, you'll feel okay again. Then you'll probably feel sad again at some point, too. But it won't last forever."

"I think I need a hug," she said to me shortly after. We hugged for quite a while. I was sure not to let go until she did. I was so proud of her for having the courage to sit in this palpable sadness. It's not easy to sit in sadness— even for adults.

Evelyn was not always this reflective, though. When we started the year, she frequently snapped at other children and, more or less, seemed wholly unaware of her emotions, her friendships, her body, and how to manage the intersection of all of them. And now, about two thirds of the way through the school year, I was able to see the fruits of our labor: I had before me a child comfortable with the discomfort of her own tough emotions, courageous enough to be vulnerable, and humble enough to recognize that she needed someone to sit in an uncomfortable space with her and tell her it was okay to be sad.

But she never would have gotten there without emotional awareness—had it not been for the fact that she communicated to me that she was in the blue zone.

I now introduce the Zones of Regulation every year. I find them incredibly helpful in concretizing emotions, serving as a scaffold for children who do not yet have the vocabulary to communicate the nuances of emotion.

PHYSICAL AWARENESS

I cannot claim the waves analogy as my own. It came from a therapist I worked with while living in San Francisco. His name was Kip, and he helped me connect my own emotional awareness with the physiological manifestations of my anxiety. He did this masterfully through clearly defined boundaries and a mindfulness practice that helped me learn to manage the uncomfortable feelings and sensations that come as a result of my anxiety.

My anxiety manifests not only through cyclical thought patterns but also through a racing heartbeat, sweaty palms, and a prickly uncomfortable rush of heat over my entire body. When I'm especially anxious, I want to crawl out of my skin. It wasn't until one of my sessions when Kip engaged me in a mindfulness practice that I realized how powerful this waves analogy was.

We sat in silence, our eyes closed, feet on the floor, and hands resting on our knees. He asked me to focus on my breathing. He helped me sit with the physiological symptoms of my anxiety, my racing heartbeat and tight chest;

he helped me become more physically aware of the inner workings of my body and their connection to my emotions. He coached me through allowing these waves of emotion to wash over me in a way I had never allowed them to before. I had, instead, tried to push them away—to build levees to keep them from coming in.

Engaging in this mindful process made me aware of a toxic pattern. I had repressed so many emotions that were now impacting my ability to function in my everyday life. Over time, Kip helped me get in touch with some of these underlying emotions, stemming from my own obstacles with coming out as gay and overcoming the trauma of physical and emotional abuse in childhood. Through this process, I learned that I was still angry. I was still sad. My body and mind hadn't yet processed those two things together.

I share this personal story for a few reasons. First, it's important for teachers to normalize our challenges with mental health. Mental illness is a pervasive but silent epidemic in our country. We cannot change this for our children if we don't change it for ourselves first. I also share this because it is this enhanced awareness, understanding, and compassion for myself that has allowed me to reach my students in a more powerful way than I ever had before. Had I not reached this understanding for myself, I doubt I would have been able to extend it to Evelyn.

Emotional awareness and physical awareness are inextricably connected. While our emotions may lie outside our control, they lie underneath the surface to tell us something, to encourage us to act. But we also have to be smarter than them and interact with them in a manner that's productive. Knowing that emotions come in waves, I now am able to ride out my panic, sit with my feelings, and let them run their course—because I know that they will eventually wash away.

We cannot normalize emotional health for our children until we normalize it for ourselves.

Our kids need to know this, too. They need to know that, when uncomfortable emotions wash over them, they have a choice about what to do with their bodies. That said, they will not have access to these choices if we don't help cultivate emotional and physical awareness first.

Kuypers's framework also provides examples of tools for regulation. This could entail taking a body break, using cyclical breathing, or reaching out to a trusted friend or adult to talk about how they're feeling. There are limitless possibilities for what children might do to regulate their bodies and their emotions. It all begins with cultivating emotional and physical awareness, and helping them understand what they need.

METACOGNITION

I'm a firm believer that there is no such thing as a stupid question, but I do believe there are lots of questions that don't need to be asked. Many kids are conditioned to ask questions not for the purpose of genuine curiosity but instead out of a need for reassurance, a by-product of a culture that makes them afraid to fail. By constantly preventing them from failing, hovering over them, and micromanaging them, we've engendered a mindless anxiety in them. Many are rigid and concerned only with perfectionism, for they have so infrequently experienced the emotions associated with failure and uncertainty. This impacts so much more than their ability to regulate their bodies and their emotions: it impacts their cognition, as well. Our job, then, is to cultivate an awareness of their own cognition, to discern between the times they *need* to ask us questions and the times they're simply looking for validation.

> Many children are rigid and concerned only with perfectionism, for they have so infrequently experienced the emotions associated with failure and uncertainty.

Metacognition is defined as the ability to think about one's thinking. Developing metacognition is critical to humanized personalization; it is an important component of the inner dialogue we nurture in the third dimension of personalized learning. Ellin Keene and Susan Zimmermann, authors of *Mosaic of Thought* (2007), first introduced me to the idea of *think-alouds*. Think-alouds are a popular practice for building reading comprehension, beckoning students to call on a variety of strategies such as visualizing, synthesizing, and making inferences to problem-solve while reading. Thinking aloud in front of children serves as a model for proficient thinking while reading. Through the process of thinking aloud, teachers may gradually release the responsibilities of metacognition and problem-solving to children while they're reading independently. Eventually, these think-alouds are internalized, fundamentally changing the inner dialogues of students. But this isn't only limited to reading. Think-alouds are useful at any moment in the school day.

Part of my work with Japanese Lesson Study was to be observed by a team of teachers while engaging my students in an open-ended math task. Dr. Takahashi, aforementioned expert in Japanese Lesson Study, accompanied my team of teachers on the day I was observed. Shortly after my lesson concluded, I sat down with the teachers, Dr. Takahashi included, and received some feedback on the lesson, its design, and my instruction. Dr. Takahashi's feedback was focused solely on my students' *logical thinking*, sharing that many of my students didn't seem to know how to think logically. They didn't make plausible assumptions, organize their work in a way that made logical sense, or exhaust all possibilities before moving on from the problem.

As you can imagine, *logical thinking* was not an explicitly stated part of our curriculum. This sort of thinking requires a carefully trained awareness of problem-solving, one I had not yet cultivated within my students (see Figure 5.3).

The very next day, I started using the term *logical thinking* in my classroom. While we tried to define it together, I knew that it would take quite a while for this to stick. I'd have to repeat the term frequently, modeling it with my own behavior but also through think-alouds (see Figure 5.4).

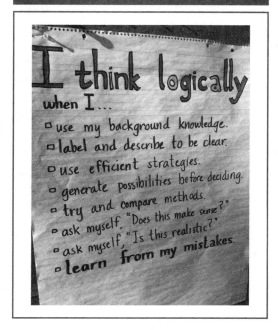

Figure 5.3: Logical Thinking Anchor Chart

I think logically
when I...
- use my background knowledge.
- label and describe to be clear.
- use efficient strategies.
- generate possibilities before deciding.
- try and compare methods.
- ask myself, "Does this make sense?"
- ask myself, "Is this realistic?"
- learn from my mistakes.

"I know that part of being a mathematician is thinking logically. I want to make sure that my work is organized in a way that makes sense to a reader, so I'm going to use the boxes and try to show my steps in the order that I did them."

"I can tell Jacob is trying to show that he's thinking logically right now," when referring to work he shared with the class. "He probably thought I am going to think logically by trying some more possibilities to make sure that I didn't miss anything."

"I know it's logical for lots of math problems to have patterns in them. I'm not seeing a pattern here, so it's making me think my solution is not logical."

Figure 5.4:
Think-Alouds for
Logical Thinking

Of course, it's not as simple as saying these things in isolation. Modeling cognitive awareness and nudging children to be metacognitive is a sensitive process. As a result, these practices must be a part of an embodied and humanized pedagogy for personalization, woven in to every part of the day.

About a month later, my class had begun a project that infused both social studies and math skills—an urban planning project where they built structures for a community based on needs identified in scenarios like the ones in Figure 5.5.

Figure 5.5: Urban Planning Scenarios

Neighborhood 1

General Information

This neighborhood is growing rapidly! There are many single-family townhomes, but it is running out of space for all the new people moving there. People who want to live by the water flock to this neighborhood. An issue this neighborhood faces is that many people work downtown, which is not a walkable distance. Most people do not have cars. With all the new people, some neighbors are concerned about it remaining a safe place, and having enough access to their needs. Residents wonder if the many parks should remain parks, or if they should convert some of these to accommodate the growing population.

Neighborhood 2

General Information

People in this neighborhood are worried the population might begin to decline. As families grow and change, many people are realizing that all their needs cannot be met. Specifically, an airport was recently built that provided many jobs, but they had to close a big school to make room. Now the one school in the neighborhood is overcrowded. In addition, children don't have anywhere to play. The airport is very loud, so residents do not want to live close by. The neighborhood planners realize that many people travel to and from the airport, and want to figure out how to use the land surrounding the noisy airport.

Neighborhood 3

General Information

This neighborhood has financial difficulties. The residents don't have access to health care or a library. They have to travel far for both of those. The alderman wants to make money by putting in high-rise apartments along the lake. Unfortunately, much of the land in front of the lake is swampy and won't support buildings. The community members want the limited lake space to be a place to gather and come together, as the residents complain there are no spaces for them to interact and meet other members in the neighborhood. Many residents of this neighborhood are concerned about the environment, so they ride bikes, recycle, and love green space!

Part of the project required them to work individually, and some parts of the project allowed them to work in partnerships. Two students, AJ and Gavin, were working on a mall for their neighborhood, in response to the fact that their neighborhood had a growing population. I noticed them building the walls out to the very edge of the lot (given to them on a piece of grid paper).

"How are people going to get in?" I asked the boys.

"They can just go right from the street," AJ said.

"No, wait, that's not *logical*," Gavin replied. "Buildings don't usually go up to the road like that. People need a place to walk next to the building."

After weeks of using that term with my students, it was clear that it had begun to stick. It had become so meaningful that it transferred to this project. I was beyond thrilled.

I also talk about *cognitive flexibility* with my students a great deal, so much that it, too, is interwoven into every instructional block. For this, I prefer to use Stephanie Madrigal and Michele Garcia Winner's (2008) Superflex stories and characters. The Superflex curriculum personifies a variety of emotions and behaviors through characters like Rock Brain and Glassman. These characters invade children's brains, trying to make them inflexible. Using these characters depersonalizes these experiences, sending the implicit message that impulsive behaviors and uncomfortable emotions are experiences that happen *to* them; they are not linked with their identity or sense of self-worth. With the right metacognitive skills and proper scaffolding, children can learn to conquer these tough feelings and behaviors on their own. I'll explain these more thoroughly toward the end of the chapter.

With time, children's emotional, physical, and cognitive awareness interweave and manifest externally so they may draw on them in social situations. The supports I've mentioned thus far—the Zones of Regulation and Superflex—are intended to be scaffolds for younger students and/or older students who struggle with emotional awareness and regulation. As children age, they are capable of taking on these metacognitive skills through verbal modeling, role-playing, and coaching with students, always leveraging our relationships with them to do so. We cannot expect them to do this on their own, though. We must explicitly teach children *how* to be physically, emotionally, metacognitively, and socially aware.

SOCIAL AWARENESS

I'm reminded of Ellie, an innately curious girl with a whimsical yet mature imagination. She struggled with regulating her emotions and resolving conflicts when the school year began. I'd see her shut down during math when a problem became frustrating, and I'd witness her snapping at friends when she felt something was unfair. It wasn't until about halfway through the year that, again, I saw the fruits of this laborious awareness training.

We were in closing circle, and it was time for "shout-outs." Shout-outs happen at the end of the day so we can praise individuals and express gratitude for their positive contributions to our classroom. They can be about anything really, from showing persistence to practicing our weekly intention to being extra kind to a friend.

That day, Avery raised her hand to give a shout-out.

"I want to give a shout-out to Ellie," she said. "Today, we were working on our informational text about Jane Addams, and Ellie didn't feel like she got to do enough work on it. She said she hadn't done much work on the writing and that she wanted to be more included. I didn't notice that Ellie hadn't written that much, and I'm glad she told me."

I sat in the circle, stunned. I realized then and there that our lessons on conflict resolution had worked exceedingly well. Avery was using many of the steps for conflict resolution that we had learned just weeks before (see Figure 5.6).

Figure 5.6:
Steps for Conflict
Resolution

Thinking and sentence stems accompanied these four steps (see Figure 5.7), and in this scenario, I could see that this flexible framework had helped them mitigate a conflict that could have occurred rather easily, especially knowing Ellie's history with expressing her feelings and frustrations. I could tell, from the simple recounting of the interaction during our end-of-day shout-outs, that both Ellie and Avery had assumed positive intent, that Ellie had very kindly and eloquently advocated for herself, and that each person had been able to live their own truth and constructively work together to complete the assignment. I reveled in my pride for them, affirmed by the practices that we'd put in place in the classroom.

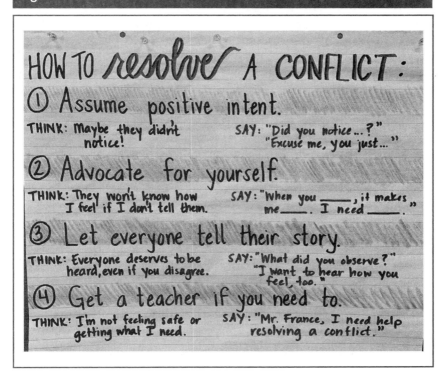

HOW TO *resolve* A CONFLICT:

① Assume positive intent.

THINK: Maybe they didn't notice!

SAY: "Did you notice...?"
"Excuse me, you just..."

② Advocate for yourself.

THINK: They won't know how I feel if I don't tell them.

SAY: "When you _____, it makes me_____. I need _____."

③ Let everyone tell their story.

THINK: Everyone deserves to be heard, even if you disagree.

SAY: "What did you observe?"
"I want to hear how you feel, too."

④ Get a teacher if you need to.

THINK: I'm not feeling safe or getting what I need.

SAY: "Mr. France, I need help resolving a conflict."

It is in moments like these we can see that these different types of awareness cannot operate in isolation. Ellie's increased emotional awareness, supported by former struggles with emotional regulation, helped her more productively resolve conflicts. We cannot possibly make the choice to be vulnerable, regulate our emotions, and interact with others in a wholehearted way without the development of self-awareness first.

This may look different for different groups of children, largely dependent on age or developmental level. In some classes, it begins with making eye contact and being aware of body language. In others, it could be more sophisticated, focusing on tone of voice and word choice. Regardless, cultivating social awareness in a developmentally appropriate manner is critical to humanized personalization.

SIX GUIDEPOSTS FOR CULTIVATING AWARENESS IN CHILDREN

If we are going to expect children to be partners in decision-making in our classroom and rely heavily on their agency, autonomy, and intrinsic motivation, then we *must* invest time cultivating awareness within them. We must be intentional, yet emergent; we must provide structure, yet be flexible and responsive. But most of all, we must allow ourselves to be vulnerable with our practice. We, too, must be willing to take risks and make mistakes. We must model the wholeheartedness, vulnerability, and humility we try to instill in our children, not only to make them compassionate and kind human beings but also to make the process of learning feel all the more *personal* and *human*. Use these six guideposts to get you started.

GUIDEPOST 1: SET UP A MINDFULNESS PRACTICE

Mindfulness has been shown to enhance awareness in both adults and children (Langer, 1989, 1997) because it trains them to quiet their bodies and minds and notice the little details in the world around them. It also trains them to willfully interpret the world around them differently. I introduce mindfulness to my children by channeling their awareness to how they are sitting and breathing, and I focus on this for the first six to eight weeks of school because it is so challenging for them. I teach them to notice their posture, the location of their legs, and how to breathe through their diaphragms.

We practice sitting for about a minute each day, focusing on our breathing. At the end of the minute, I ring our singing bowl three times. When the singing bowl has been rung, the sound very gradually dissipates until it is inaudible. When they no longer hear the sound—when it has "walked away"—they raise their hands to signal they can no longer hear the sound. This practice enhances noticing because they are forced to listen to something that could be imperceptible.

As we become more sophisticated with our mindfulness practice, I invite them to practice gratitude, do body scans, notice the temperature of the room, or keep tabs on their hearts beating in their chests. I may even ask them to think about our class's intention for the week.

I also use mindfulness as a management strategy during transitions or moments of dysregulation. I assume a mindful position, closing my eyes, resting my feet on the floor, and touching the fingertips of my opposing hands together to signal to the children that it's time for a reboot. Because of the culture we built around mindfulness in the beginning of the year, it generally works to get their attention.

But it's important to remember that mindfulness and meditation are not synonymous. Mindfulness is the art of being intentional, of being fully present in the here and now. It entails being aware of one's surroundings and thinking carefully before responding. While meditation can support mindfulness,

mindfulness must become a way of being within your classroom to truly cultivate a mindful inner dialogue within students. This is yet another practice that knows no bounds and does not discriminate. It doesn't require new textbooks or expensive technology; it requires sentient, empathetic teachers who want to help students become the best versions of themselves.

In 2016, the *Washington Post* featured Robert W. Coleman Elementary, an urban school in Baltimore where mindfulness practice helped reduce suspensions dramatically, the result of more reflective and aware students who "are more willing to take responsibility for their behaviors," Principal Carlillian Thompson mentioned, gradually helping students become more independent learners with time (George, 2016).

While mindfulness is not a panacea for overcoming systemic oppression or barriers related to discrimination, it is helping many students—including low-income students and students of color—gradually grow from dependent learners into independent thinkers.

GUIDEPOST 2: SET WEEKLY INTENTIONS WITH YOUR STUDENTS

This came to me once after a yoga class. For those of you who don't go to yoga, it's not uncommon for yoga instructors to read a quote or set an intention. After witnessing how one of the yoga instructor's intentions helped me, I thought it might benefit my students, as well, to draw their awareness to a specific virtue or quality each week, cultivating collective awareness and building community through a common goal (see Figure 5.8).

Each week, we set an intention that coincides with our mindfulness practice. To start the year, I choose intentions such as exploration, authenticity, connection, and compassion to lay the foundation for agency, autonomy, and community building, and as the year progresses, I choose intentions that correspond with our needs. For instance, if I notice a need for increased attention to regulation, I choose an intention of *awareness* to help us focus on finding ways to stay aware and regulated throughout the week. Drawing

Figure 5.8: Intentions

authenticity	gratitude
connection	compassion
courage	resilience
calm	adventure
play	rest
creativity	trust
joy	awareness
hope	love
celebration	freedom
stillness	reflection
forgiveness	letting go
exploration	imagination
focus	change

their attention to this each day, both in the morning and at various points throughout the day, makes a surprising difference: it engenders a mindful culture in the classroom and unites the classroom in a shared goal.

As the year persists, I invite the children to set their own intentions. We discuss these in morning meeting and closing circle, where students "turn and talk" about ways they have realized their intention.

GUIDEPOST 3: EXPLICITLY TEACH EMOTIONAL AWARENESS AND EMOTIONAL REGULATION

Due to a variety of factors, it's becoming increasingly important to explicitly teach these skills. They are neither instinctual nor naturally acquired with time. I rely on the Zones of Regulation and Superflex to explicitly teach emotional awareness and regulation.

I sprinkle lessons about the Zones and the Unthinkables into my morning meetings throughout the year, generally starting the school year with the Zones of Regulation and, by winter break, explicitly teaching cognitive flexibility through the Superflex stories. With time, it becomes easier to use these resources in response to student behaviors, but at first, it's best to take a more didactic approach and introduce both the Zones of Regulation and Superflex through read-alouds and direct instruction. With time, you'll see the natural entry points for these socioemotional resources throughout the school day. For instance, one of my classes struggled a great deal with humor. While I believe humor is critical to a positive learning environment, I know that it can also be a road to dysregulation. WasFunnyOnce, one of the Unthinkables, is great to talk about when this happens.

"I think we have an Unthinkable close by," I will say. "Do you know who?"

The students will identify one or two Unthinkables that could be floating around, and shortly thereafter, we talk about how to get rid of them. Generally, students suggest a moment of mindfulness, a few deep breaths, or maybe even a change in seat.

GUIDEPOST 4: MODEL THE THINKING AND SPEAKING YOU EXPECT TO HEAR FROM YOUR CHILDREN

"I'm feeling really frustrated right now," I said to Jemma. Jemma struggled with focus, attention, and processing speed. I was mindful of this when giving her assignments. I frequently gave her extended time, large pieces of paper on which she could organize her thinking, and extra supports for organizing ideas.

But one day, I began to notice an emerging pattern. She was consistently late to circle, usually talking to friends instead of doing her routines. I finally saw she wasn't making much progress on her writing, and I found out why when going through the revision history on her iPad. She had lost an entire paragraph of her work, and when I pressed the undo button, I saw that she had been playing with the keyboard, typing emojis and other nonsense words instead of editing her spelling. I knew it was time for an intervention.

"Jemma," I said with a kind sternness in my voice, "I know that you sometimes need extra time for things, and I am very happy to give you that time. But when you use your time to play and not to work, it makes me feel frustrated. I'm trying to help you, but you're not helping yourself. I need you to notice when you're getting off task or distracted, and I need you to ask for help if you are."

I was using the very same guidelines that Avery and Ellie used to proactively mitigate their conflict. I assumed positive intent from Jemma; I advocated for myself; I told my story. I was compassionate through my kindness, understanding, and explanation but also through my willingness to draw boundaries with her. Brené Brown tells us that compassionate people draw boundaries with others, and as compassionate teachers, we must do the same.

I could see tears welling up in her eyes. My instinct was to hug her and tell her she didn't need to feel sad—that I understood it was challenging for her. But I thought back to experiences such as the one I had with Evelyn. *Emotions wash over us in waves*, I thought. *Jemma is strong enough to feel this and move on from it.* I remembered that Jemma was hardwired for struggle, and this pain she felt was going to help her in the long run.

"It's okay to feel sad," I said. "And I'm glad you feel sad, because it shows me that you care. Remember that making mistakes is a part of learning, and what's more important is what we do after we make the mistake. What are you going to do next time?"

"Not get distracted," she said.

"Well," I replied, "I don't know if that's something you can do. I can't even do that. We all get distracted. What could we do if you *notice* you get distracted?"

"Find a more successful spot?" she queried.

"Exactly," I replied, my expression softening into a smile, remembering just how critical awareness is.

Later that day, Jemma came up to me during reading workshop.

"I need to sit up at the white table," she said, referring to my kidney table for guided reading.

"Oh, okay," I replied. "How come?"

"I noticed I was playing with my keyboard again," she confessed with a half smile.

> Personalizing learning means empowering students to make changes on their own.

I was so proud of her for noticing and doing something about it. It appeared that by modeling my feelings in a compassionate way and drawing boundaries with her, I helped her gain a sense of agency at times when she felt distracted, empowering her to make a change on her own. *That* is personalized learning. *That* is what we want for our kids: to make choices for themselves so they may continue learning independently.

GUIDEPOST 5: REMEMBER THAT SOCIAL AND EMOTIONAL LEARNING ARE NOT BENIGN SUBJECTS

I'm not a proponent of boxed curricula. In my experience, they engender mindlessness when planning instruction. Teachers become convinced that to be successful and to teach with consistency, they must follow every word of the curriculum. This, however, acts in opposition to learning that's personal and instruction that's responsive.

> Rigidly implemented boxed curricula act in opposition to learning that's personal.

Likewise, I struggle to understand how one can use boxed curricula designed to teach social and emotional competencies. While it's incredibly important to explicitly teach lessons related to social and emotional competencies, it shouldn't be done in lockstep with a scripted curriculum. It's most meaningful when it comes from real issues that children are facing in the classroom—and there are ample opportunities for that. Moreover, teaching social and emotional lessons shouldn't be confined to a certain time of day; it should, instead, be embedded into everything we do. More often than not, boxed curricula do not allow for seamless integration into other subject areas.

Social and emotional learning need authentic contexts in which they can root themselves. Otherwise, children are learning socioemotional competencies in a decontextualized manner, unable to see how they can use them in their everyday lives. For this reason, it's critical to remember that social and emotional competencies are not benign skills that exist on their own; they are, instead, skills that must dig their roots deep into the fabric of the classroom culture, ultimately present in all academic subjects and every interaction in the classroom.

In fact, the most *personal* way one can learn core academic subjects is to connect with them viscerally—to understand them in a social and emotional manner. This requires an awareness of the obstacles associated with each core subject and how to overcome the obstacles one might face.

> Social and emotional learning need authentic contexts in which they can root themselves.

Take Owen, for instance. When Owen began the school year, he looked at our math tasks with terror. He sat in front of the open-ended task, unsure of how to proceed, as he had been trained for years to fill in blank spaces on a worksheet. Without the rigid structure and safety of a worksheet, Owen was unsure what to do. His fear and anxiety were palpable even from across the room. He looked around at his classmates until, finally, he raised his hand and told me that he "didn't get it."

I replied with my usual response, asking Owen to tell me precisely what he got and precisely what he didn't get from the question in front of him. It was a classic case of black-and-white, rigid thinking. He didn't understand the problem in its entirety, and as a result, he collapsed under the uncertainty.

I anticipated this would be the case for many of my students, but I knew that this problem would not solve itself overnight. I addressed it by regularly doing think-alouds when approaching the math tasks, and by explicitly talking about the habits of mathematicians (see Figure 5.9).

Figure 5.9:
Things to Say in Response to "I Don't Know"

"Sometimes when I see a problem I don't understand, I get in the yellow zone. I start to feel nervous that I won't do the problem right or that I'll make a mistake.

Then I remember that it's okay to make mistakes and that mistakes actually help me learn."

"I'm going to just jump in and try something that will tell my teacher what I know and what I don't know, so he can help me learn what I need to know."

"I may not know everything in this problem, but there is something I can figure out even if it's just drawing a picture of what the problem is saying."

"I'm not sure what to do here, so I'm going to write Mr. France a note about what I understand from the problem and what I don't understand from the problem.

Even though I'm in the yellow zone, I know that I'm in school because there are certain things I'm not supposed to know yet. I'm here to learn, after all!"

Think-alouds like this help model the type of thinking that we want our children to do when faced with complex academic tasks. With time, the children begin to use internal self-talk like this, enhancing their awareness of their own emotions and academic obstacles and eventually helping them learn how to problem-solve and regulate their emotions independently.

Months later, Owen's disposition toward these complex tasks had changed remarkably.

"Mr. France!" he said to me one day. "I wasn't sure what to do, so I decided to draw a picture, and once I did that, I was able to figure out what the question was asking!"

He smiled, empowered by his own agency, excited to continue to the next problem and explain his strategy. He even began to check and double-check his work, signaling to me that he had, in fact, enhanced his awareness a great deal over the first half of the school year.

Teaching thinking is hard to do, though. It's helpful to remember that with every word we say, we are rewiring our kids' brains. That's why it's important to model thinking with think-alouds, and to do so with fidelity and consistent language. Modeling and remodeling create the scaffolds on which our children can climb and eventually internalize their own version of resilient thinking. This can't be disingenuous, though. Children know when our actions are not authentic, and as a result there is one last tip I have for cultivating awareness and building social and emotional competencies in the classroom.

GUIDEPOST 6: REMEMBER THAT IT STARTS WITH US, THE ADULTS

It's really easy for adults, me included, to forget this one. Energy is contagious, and when adults are unable to regulate their emotions, respond to conflicts constructively, or practice strong habits for resilient thinking and a growth mindset, it trickles down to our children.

I see this most demonstrably when setting personal goals with students. Generally speaking, when children set goals, they set superficial ones that don't actually stretch them. And this makes a lot of sense; kids are naturally looking for the path of least resistance, as many of us do. As the adults in the room, we must help them find the path of just-right resistance.

In response, I generally model goal setting for them with my own personal goals. One time, in particular, I noticed that my reading and writing mini-lessons were going far too long. This was prohibiting me from meeting with small groups and individual students, exacerbated by an already shortened literacy block. To model the goal-setting process authentically, I shared this obstacle with them. I confided in them that I wanted desperately to be able to meet with more of them individually and in small groups but that I was constantly falling short because my lessons were too long.

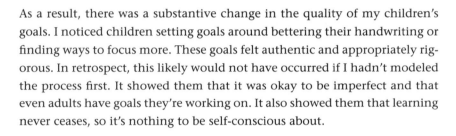

Help students find the path of just-right resistance.

As a result, I was able to be vulnerable with my own obstacles and model how to use them to make a meaningful change. I even went so far as to tell them about vulnerability and the importance of sharing our goals with the collective classroom community, for if our friends know our goals, they can help us reach them.

As a result, there was a substantive change in the quality of my children's goals. I noticed children setting goals around bettering their handwriting or finding ways to focus more. These goals felt authentic and appropriately rigorous. In retrospect, this likely would not have occurred if I hadn't modeled the process first. It showed them that it was okay to be imperfect and that even adults have goals they're working on. It also showed them that learning never ceases, so it's nothing to be self-conscious about.

EXPANDING AWARENESS

When we cultivate emotional, physical, cognitive, and social awareness in our students, we are also able to cultivate a sense of *agency* in the classroom. While *agency* and *autonomy* are oftentimes used interchangeably, they are quite different. Agency is a sense from within, while autonomy is externally manifested. Cultivating a sense of agency means helping students understand that they play the most significant role in their learning experience, that through their choices, dispositions, and habits, they can chart their own learning paths.

Of course, there are limits to this. When I say "chart their own learning paths," I am not suggesting they design all their own learning experiences. Instead, I mean that they are able to make choices within constraints, all carefully designed by a mindful educator.

The process of autonomous decision-making must be scaffolded for young children, as they are not developmentally ready to make educative choices. They're not aware of the skills necessary to be functioning adults, and they're not aware of how skills progress. That's the job of the teacher. In the next chapter, we'll discuss how children can use this newly cultivated self-awareness to help them access their agency and make decisions autonomously. And we'll discuss how you, the teacher, can structure and support that.

DEVELOPING AGENCY AND AUTONOMY

John Dewey, the father of progressive education, had a vision for agency and autonomy: in his vision, students were active constructors of their own knowledge and experiences. He also understood the importance of knowledgeable, sentient teachers—of structure and boundaries. His vision for real-world, experiential learning rested on the idea that the adults knew which experiences were worthy of the children's valuable learning time. He recognized that agency and autonomy didn't entail a radical sense of individualism or an unbounded independence; instead, he knew that true autonomy allowed children to flourish within the mindful constraints of a well-structured learning environment.

BALANCING AUTONOMY AND AUTHORITY

"All experiences are not genuinely educative," Dewey (1938) suggested in *Experience and Education*. "An experience may be immediately enjoyable and yet promote the formation of a slack and careless attitude."

This text was published almost a century ago, yet it's interesting to see educators still misinterpreting what we mean when we promote student agency and autonomy. When I was working in Silicon Valley, this misinterpretation of agency and autonomy was the ideal, especially in the company's early stages—that children would be able to choose the topics about which they wanted to learn. It presupposed that motivation and engagement lay primarily within teaching to a child's interests. It assumed that the best authority figure in the child's education was the child, not the teacher.

This sounds rosy at first, but it's neither practical nor desirable. Education needs to serve multiple purposes: we want children to find *new* topics of interest; we hope they'll see the value in lifelong learning; we hope to expose them to new experiences they otherwise would not encounter; we also hope it serves the purpose of socializing and intellectualizing our children so they may contribute to society.

Dewey (1938) states this a bit more succinctly. He says, "Education is a process of overcoming natural inclination and substituting in its place habits acquired under external pressure."

"Education is a process of overcoming natural inclination and substituting in its place habits acquired under external pressure."

In essence, Dewey argued that while school exists to build agency and autonomy, it is also there to build long-term habits that will help children become productive members of a democratic society—a democratic society bounded by rules and social norms.

Dewey is not alone. Even less-common ideologies such as Montessori or Reggio Emilia advocate for a great deal of student choice—within constraints. Montessori advocates for children to choose from a relatively limited number of intentionally designed learning tools; Reggio Emilia advocates for mindfully designed provocations, intended to promote the playful construction of knowledge. In both of these student-driven ideologies, learning outcomes and learning tools are intentionally chosen by teachers. The educator's mindful selection of a provocation coupled with the illusion of choice makes space for children to construct knowledge in partnership with the educator.

Here, partnership doesn't mean that the child is owning all decision-making. Instead, the child is exercising autonomous decision-making within the boundaries of the provocations specifically chosen by the educator. By design, these provocations have a limited number of outcomes, already anticipated and planned for accordingly.

It's important to note that partnership doesn't necessarily mean that the child is owning all decision-making.

Even with these strong examples of student-driven pedagogy that embrace boundaries, student-driven learning is too often conflated with a resistance to authority. The most radical forms of this turn teachers into mere babysitters that are not required to do what they've been trained to do: curate stimulating learning environments where children are pushed outside their comfort zones. True student-driven education values authority in the classroom, but not as an authoritarian entity that knows and controls all. Instead, authority in the personalized classroom is an *authoritative* entity that is trusted with evaluating learning experiences and determining which ones will be the most educative for the children (see Figure 6.1; Baumrind, 1967).

Figure 6.1: Teaching Styles

	SUPPORTIVE	UNSUPPORTIVE
DEMANDING	**AUTHORITATIVE** TEACHERS CREATE POSITIVE AND TRUSTING RELATIONSHIPS GROUNDED IN PARTNERSHIP, HOLDING STUDENTS ACCOUNTABLE FOR CLASSROOM BEHAVIOR AND ACADEMIC EXPECTATIONS, MEANWHILE ALLOWING MINDFUL ENTRY POINTS FOR INTERESTS AND IDENTITIES.	**AUTHORITARIAN** TEACHERS RELY ONLY ON OBEDIENCE TO ELICIT DESIRABLE BEHAVIORS AND RESULTS. AUTHORITARIAN TEACHERS LIMIT STUDENT VOICE IN ESTABLISHING BEHAVIORAL EXPECTATIONS AND DENY OPPORTUNITIES FOR INDIVIDUAL INTERESTS AND IDENTITIES TO CONTRIBUTE TO THE CLASSROOM.
UNDEMANDING	**PERMISSIVE** TEACHERS HONOR STUDENT INTERESTS AND NATURAL CURIOSITY BUT PROVIDE LITTLE ACCOUNTABILITY FOR BEHAVIOR EXPECTATIONS OR STRUCTURE FOR RIGOROUS ACADEMIC LEARNING.	**NEGLECTFUL** TEACHERS PROVIDE LITTLE GUIDANCE OR PERSONALIZED ATTENTION. NEGLECTFUL TEACHING IS USUALLY INFLEXIBLE, MINDLESS, AND UNRESPONSIVE TO STUDENT NEEDS.

Authoritarian practices are pervasive in education. School is not often a place that promotes humanized, student-centered, and student-driven pedagogy. School, more often than not, promotes shame, fear, and compliance with standardized practices, which in turn strip children and adults of their autonomy, crushing the intrinsic motivation of those who should be the primary producers of education—the educators and the students. It comes as no surprise that the response to this has been to remove most, if not all, authority in progressive spaces that value personalized and student-driven learning. Self-proclaimed progressives do not dare mold their classrooms in this authoritarian image but, instead, have engineered classrooms that are overly permissive and sometimes even neglectful of what's best for children. Their response to authoritarian schooling has gone too far. In many progressive classrooms, it is anarchy, which can be far more damaging to agency and autonomy.

I experienced this firsthand in Silicon Valley. I fielded criticism from even the director of education at my school for my emphasis on standards-based assessment and a well-rounded curriculum that held students accountable for language, mathematics, and the sciences, regardless of whether students wanted to learn about them. But her prevailing theory was that students would learn better if they learned about things they said they were interested in. She once even told me that young children could learn how to read by playing *Minecraft*, simply through reading about it online. This sort of misguided thinking acts in opposition to the best interests of our children—children who are too young to make informed decisions about what they need to learn.

As we've learned, the answer generally lies somewhere in the middle. Authoritarianism and anarchy both act in opposition to personalizing learning. These two schools of thought dehumanize individuals, and as a result, dehumanize the learning process, chipping away at a learning environment that values student agency, diversity, and equity. We can strike a balance between these two by managing our classrooms using authoritative practices, which preserve adults' roles as authority figures, meanwhile partnering with students to build agency and autonomous decision-making.

TEN TIPS FOR TEACHING AGENCY AND AUTONOMY

While it may sound counterintuitive, agency and autonomy can be taught only within mindful boundaries. Such is the nature of *authoritative* classroom management. There is a palpable tension between autonomy and authority, but it is one that also offers beautiful harmony if we can find a healthy balance between the two. But striking this balance is not easy. I don't think it's something that any teacher masters, myself included.

The question then becomes, How can we build autonomy and agency within children, all the while using our authority in the classroom to ensure that we're building experiences alongside them that are educative and worth their time and investment? The following ten tips for this encompass the remainder of the chapter, but I encourage you to mold them to meet your needs so you may constantly explore new ways to partner with children to build agency and autonomy.

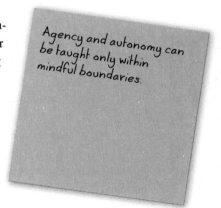

Agency and autonomy can be taught only within mindful boundaries.

TIP #1: FIRST IMPRESSIONS ARE EVERYTHING

Respect is earned. Plain and simple. And I'm not talking about the kind of respect that comes with fear; I'm talking about the kind of respect where children intuitively trust and understand that you have their best interests at heart. Children quickly pick up on a lack of structure, and within the first few weeks of the school year, they will know which boundaries to test. For this reason, it's important that the first impression your children have of you is one of clear routines and boundaries. While it seems counterintuitive, this will support a classroom of autonomy and agency later on.

Sure, the first days and weeks of school are also going to be times when you show your children extra compassion. You'll let them make social mistakes as they learn the ropes. I'm not suggesting you go into your classroom with a stern face and demand that your children listen to your every word; I'm suggesting you begin the school year by setting clear boundaries that the children are, by no means, able to cross. Starting your year like this will help your children see that boundaries are there to make the classroom run smoothly. Here's an example.

It was the first day of school, and the hallway outside my classroom was chaotic. I was greeting parents, meeting children, and otherwise embracing the chaos of the first day of school. As the clock approached 8:15, I said goodbye to families and pulled out my chime. I rang it, and mostly due to novelty, most of my children stopped talking. Most of the parents did, too.

"Excellent," I said. "I see you all already know what to do. But just for practice, let's try it again. This is the chime, and it will be the way I get your attention in the classroom. When I ring the chime, I need you to stop talking and put your eyes on me."

I asked them to turn and pretend to talk to one another. Within seconds, I rang the chime again. The children stopped talking immediately and looked at me. Then we entered the classroom to start our day. One of the moms looked at me and winked, confident that I had the class under control already.

This set the tone not only for the first day but for the entire year. You might be wondering why I've chosen to first discuss a rigid routine when this is supposed to be a chapter about autonomy. This is so we can explore the paradox that emerges when we consider autonomy and authority as partners in humanizing personalization. Once your children see that you are an authoritative figure in the classroom, you are able to build a foundation on which your children can work autonomously. The structures and routines put into the classroom become authoritative in and of themselves, creating a space that feels safe for them to explore their own autonomy.

More often than not, when a classroom lacks structure, children abuse their autonomy. The chaos that accompanies a lack of structure turns on an instinctual fight-or-flight response, causing children to become impulsive and unaware of what's going on around them. Furthermore, this chaos acts as a threat to an equitable and inclusive classroom. Without clear boundaries or supportive structures, children may be limited in getting what they need—and they may inadvertently limit others in reaching their full potential, as well. On the contrary, with clear structures and expectations, children may exercise their autonomy in a way that feels safe and aligns with your expectations. It also ensures that every child in a diverse classroom full of learners can reach their full potential.

TIP #2: BUILD EXPECTATIONS AND ROUTINES AS A CLASS

Responsive Classroom (2015) provides an evidence-based approach for building social-emotional competencies that ultimately support academic learning in the classroom, helping students step into their agency and autonomy so they become independent learners. They advocate for clear boundaries, empathetically responding to misbehavior, and setting clear boundaries with students so they may thrive within structure. If you're unfamiliar with them, I recommend going to their website (www.ResponsiveClassroom.org) to learn about their work. I love their ideas for generating rules, interactive modeling, and helping the children explore their autonomy within boundaries. I use their methods for generating classroom rules and consequences, only with a slight technological twist.

iCardSort is a digital card-sorting application for the iPad, allowing students to sort words, pictures, or anything that you can put on a digital card. Once you've created the sort in iCardSort, you can send it to them wirelessly via Bluetooth. It allows them to manipulate information concretely without all the waste.

We used iCardSort to generate rules as a class. With my iPad projected on the front screen, I asked them to turn and talk to propose expectations for our classrooms. They mentioned a lot of the usual rules, such as "Use walking feet" or "Don't talk while the teacher is talking." After they shared ideas with partners, some students shared with the whole class, and while they did, I added the rules to iCardSort. It wasn't long before we had a ton of rules on the screen (see Figure 6.2). I followed the Responsive Classroom approach and suggested that we pare these down a bit.

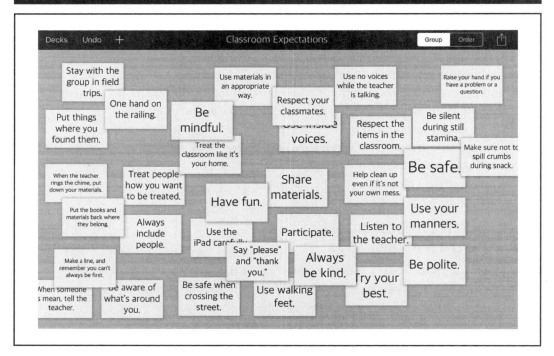

Source: iCardSort App, https://icardsort.com/. Cards created by Paul Emerich France.

"I don't think I can remember all of these," I said. "Can you?"

They agreed, so I asked them to go back to their seats to synthesize the agreements into just a few all-encompassing rules that accounted for more specific rules, such as walking in the classroom.

"Synthesizing is when we take lots of little things and turn them into a big idea," I told the class, also drawing their awareness to metacognition. "I want you to come up with a big rule for the groups that you made so they're easier for us to remember."

They followed suit, sorting the rules into groups and creating three or four "big" rules that we'd potentially be able to use as our classroom agreements. When they finished, we listed all the rules on the board, checking for duplicates. We then pared these down into four general classroom expectations by which we all could abide (see Figure 6.3).

Room 402
classroom agreements:
- Treat the classroom like it's your home.
- Treat everyone like family.
- Try new things.
- Be your **BEST** self.

This simple step in building classroom culture is often overlooked, despite the fact that it pays off in large dividends. By taking this very active approach to creating classroom agreements—and by allowing them to have very active conversations around the expectations—children are more likely to internalize these expectations and apply them so they may function autonomously in the classroom later.

TIP #3: REVIEW AND MODEL ROUTINES

Naturally, kids become comfortable and complacent at various points throughout the year, and this requires reviewing expectations and routines. When this happens, we review our routines and practice them again while I wait patiently until the entire classroom demonstrates their understanding. While inconvenient, reestablishing and reviewing routines is critical: it's important for the children to see that there are no exceptions when it comes to classroom agreements. Learners need structure; they need to know someone is holding them accountable—all the way through the end of the school year.

Reviewing routines and agreements also serves as a great lesson on mindfulness. Generally, when kids forget routines or expectations, it's because they are operating without intention. This is a great time to think aloud and model what it's like to reconnect with an old goal or former obstacle.

"This happens to me, too," I'll say. "I get really good at something, and then I start to think that I don't have to worry about that goal anymore. But then I make a mistake and realize I need to practice again. I realize I need to be a bit more mindful."

This type of think-aloud models cognition but also takes the shame out of making mistakes. It allows us to move away from "You should have known better" to "I know what I'm supposed to do, but next time I need to be more aware and make the *choice* to do that."

TIP #4: HELP KIDS SEE NATURAL CONSEQUENCES

Cultivating awareness around routines also entails partnering with students to identify logical consequences. Usually, we default to a negative connotation for the word *consequence*. It generally implies an undesired by-product of a behavior, and children bring this connotation into the classroom. But consequences can be by-products of *any* behavior—positive, negative, or neutral. So before we begin generating consequences for unexpected behaviors, I reframe the conversation, defining *consequence* neutrally. We define *consequence* as "the result of a behavior." We then discuss the causes and effects of all types of behaviors in the classroom, both expected and unexpected.

I use the terms *expected* and *unexpected* from *Thinking About You Thinking About Me* by Michelle Garcia Winner (2002), founder of Social Thinking. *Good* and *bad* are loaded words; they often carry a shaming and dehumanizing tone, causing students to label themselves as "good" or "bad." This is not only detrimental to their senses of self but also detrimental to the classroom culture. By labeling *behaviors* as "expected" and "unexpected," we help children separate themselves from their behaviors, seeing them as social mistakes that make an impact on others. In some ways, this makes social learning a bit less personal but only in the sense that it divorces behaviors from their identities, helping children remember that all people make social mistakes. What becomes most important, I tell them, is what you learn from your mistakes and how you make amends.

To show these causes and effects, I use the Multi-Flow Thinking Map in Figure 6.4 (Hyerle, 1995). This map is especially helpful because it shows that causes and effects aren't necessarily dichotomous. An unexpected behavior is, after all, both a cause and an effect. It can be the effect of a lack of awareness, a desire to rebel, dysregulated emotions, or even just part of the human condition. Likewise, unexpected behaviors cause others to feel uncomfortable, the class to function ineffectively, a lack of productivity, or a number of other effects that limit the individual from contributing to the classroom or learning on their own.

Figure 6.4: Multi-Flow Maps for Logical Consequences

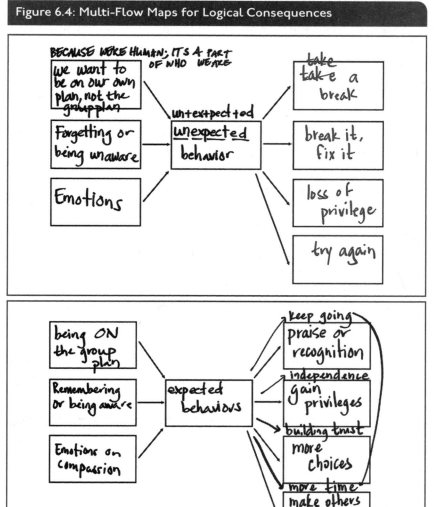

Figure A: Here, we explore the causes and effects of unexpected behaviors, which we used to generate our natural consequences. The term *group plan* comes from Michele Garcia Winner's *Think social! A social thinking curriculum for school-age students.*

Figure B: Here, we explore the causes and effects of expected behaviors, appealing to the universal human desire for connection with others.

Expected behaviors also have causes and effects. They can be the result of compassion, awareness, or motivation to be part of a group; expected behaviors can bring us praise and recognition, as well as more privileges, choices, and independence. They can also build relationships with the people around us by earning trust, making others feel good, and otherwise helping us be seen as good role models and citizens.

In these situations, I am consciously trying to appeal to our students' innate desire for human connection. As Brené Brown would say, we are "hardwired" for connection. Human connection is one of the most naturally motivating factors in a classroom that values humanized personalization. By helping children understand the impact of their behaviors, they see that their behaviors can either bring them closer to their peers or isolate them. By reframing the conversation around consequences and linking it directly to human connection, we create an authentic context for cultivating awareness around the logical social consequences for exhibiting unexpected behaviors.

TIP #5: BUILD TRUST

Autonomy cannot happen without trust, and it's important that our students know this. They must know that autonomy is not a right in the classroom; it is, instead, a skill that can be learned through risk-taking, mistake-making, and proper scaffolding. Hammond (2014) tells us that we must build trust, grounded in affirmation and a strong rapport, to build quality partnerships with students.

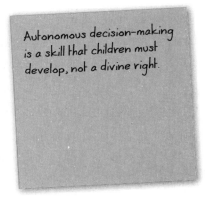

Autonomous decision-making is a skill that children must develop, not a divine right.

A tower is an excellent analogy for building trust, especially for our youngest ones. I learned this analogy of the Trust Tower from a colleague in San Francisco. She was explaining to one of our five-year-old students that trust is built slowly over time, much like a tower is built one block at a time. I took the analogy with me, and I've found that children of all ages connect with it.

"Trust is like building a tower," I'll say to my students. "We build trust block by block over time, and the more we build the trust tower, the more choices you will be able to make on your own."

I've even gone so far as to build a trust tower in my classroom as a way to call out specific behaviors that build the trust tower, behaviors like "doing what you're supposed to even when the teacher is not looking" or "cleaning up materials I didn't use" (see Figure 6.5). This tool serves as a concrete reminder that trust is built through observable behaviors and that autonomy is learned by demonstrating awareness of what's happening around you.

What's more, it sends a very clear message that the individuals in the classroom do not exist in isolation. Even in an era when we strive for learning to be as personalized as possible—when we are aiming to actualize a vision for agency and autonomy in the classroom—students must still be held accountable to the collective classroom community.

TIP #6: PRAISE THE JOURNEY, NOT THE ACHIEVEMENT

Winnie came to me for a reason one year. When I first met her, we struggled to understand each other. I saw her as a child who needed incredibly clear boundaries and even clearer consequences. But each time she received a consequence, it seemed painful and counterproductive for her. Ironically, she was taking it *too* personally. She saw my feedback and her consequences as an indicator of her self-worth.

I learned throughout the year that there were many factors at play. Not only had her mother passed away just a few years prior; she was struggling with depression. Her self-confidence was low, and as a result, critical feedback about her performance only made her feel more unlovable. It wasn't until I spoke with her therapist that I really understood what was going on for Winnie. As her therapist mentioned, Winnie was concerned with the "performance" and how she was being perceived. As a result, she put a great deal, if not all, of her self-worth into these "performances," whether it was writing a narrative, solving a math problem, or even sharing a video of herself performing in a singing competition. While it seemed beneficial to praise these exemplary performances, it wasn't nurturing Winnie's inner dialogue or building her self-worth.

Winnie's therapist encouraged me to start celebrating Winnie's internal journey through praise and thinking aloud. But instead of praising the neatness of her handwriting directly, I started to say things like, "I can tell you put a lot of effort into this. Because you did, I can read your handwriting really well and learn about the great thoughts you have in your mind." Or I would say something like, "Winnie, when you show me how you've double-checked your answer on your math task, it really shows me that you care about math and that you're trying to share all of your thoughts with me. I really appreciate that because it helps me get to know you better."

The change was subtle—but powerful. And it didn't require me individualizing Winnie's curriculum. It didn't entail Winnie designing her own learning activities in a flippant effort to help her "own" her learning; instead, personalizing for Winnie meant getting to know her as a human being and slightly altering the way I gave her feedback.

I believe the universe sent me Winnie that year because I needed to learn that lesson for myself, too. I have always tended to focus on my performances over my journey. As I've grown through my own struggles with anxiety, children such as Winnie have helped me see that the journey itself—not the product of the journey—provides a greater indication of how we're thriving. What's more, praising the journey builds intrinsic motivation and agency within all of us, making the learning process all the more personal because it serves as an avenue for human connection. It is only with a humanized and deindustrialized view of the classroom that we can truly see this.

> Praising the journey serves as an avenue for human connection.

TIP #7: PRAISE RISK-TAKING AND MISTAKE-MAKING

This journey we speak of is riddled with risks, mistakes, joy, and pain. It requires learners to be vulnerable, to acknowledge and love self-identified imperfections, and to embrace pain and discomfort. Perhaps it's our paternal instincts that motivate us to protect our children from risks, mistakes, and pain. Or perhaps it's our preoccupation with perfection. The industrialized classroom prizes perfection; it puts the mass production of an idealized product at the center, sending both implicit and explicit messages to our students (see Figure 6.6).

Figure 6.6

Brené Brown agrees. In her now famous TEDxHouston talk from 2010, she reflects on perfectionism and the effect it has on our kids.

"[Children are] hardwired for struggle when they get here. And when you hold those perfect little babies in your hand, our job is not to say, 'Look at her, she's perfect. My job is just to keep her perfect—make sure she makes the tennis team by fifth grade and Yale by seventh.'

That's not our job. Our job is to look and say, 'You know what? You're imperfect, and you're wired for struggle, but you are worthy of love and belonging.' That's our job. Show me a generation of kids raised like that, and we'll end the problems, I think, that we see today."

I made a conscious choice early in my career to express gratitude for mistakes—and to model this for children. Don't get me wrong: I don't mean to praise a lack of effort or intentional mediocrity, but I do believe that we can always find something to praise, even if it's our students' willingness to be vulnerable. There are lessons to be learned in everything we do, and it takes a great deal of courage and vulnerability to make a conscious decision to interact with uncertainty, even if it means simply having the courage to show up. This is something we are asking children to do every day in school, and they deserve more credit than we give them for constantly putting themselves out there.

It might feel unnatural when you explicitly start praising the journey. The words may not feel quite right on your tongue. If you're unsure of what to say, you're welcome to borrow some of my words and use them to come up with more of your own (see Figure 6.7). I think you'll be surprised at how your children respond to them.

Figure 6.7

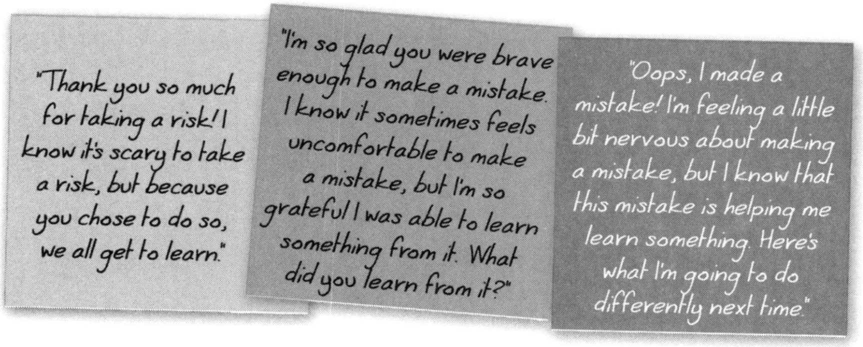

"Thank you so much for taking a risk! I know it's scary to take a risk, but because you chose to do so, we all get to learn."

"I'm so glad you were brave enough to make a mistake. I know it sometimes feels uncomfortable to make a mistake, but I'm so grateful I was able to learn something from it. What did you learn from it?"

"Oops, I made a mistake! I'm feeling a little bit nervous about making a mistake, but I know that this mistake is helping me learn something. Here's what I'm going to do differently next time."

By giving them credit for making these "brave mistakes," we humanize and normalize imperfection. We make it desirable because it gives so much more than it takes. What's more, by making our own thinking visible through these types of think-alouds, we allow them into our own thinking processes as adults, helping nurture their inner dialogues toward vulnerability and resilience.

TIP #8: LET GO AND LET KIDS STRUGGLE

We learn the most through our struggles and our pain. The darkness that can come with failure counterintuitively illuminates the joy we feel when we've succeeded. By not allowing our children to fail, we are, effectively, taking away future opportunities for them to feel the boundless joy that comes as a result of their successes. They will never know this joy unless we allow them to feel the stinging pain that often accompanies failure.

Our job, as Dr. Brown says, is not to protect them from this pain. It is to remind them that they are imperfect, that they can handle struggle, and that every bit of them belongs here with us—regardless of how they perform (see Figure 6.8). This includes their joy and success, but more

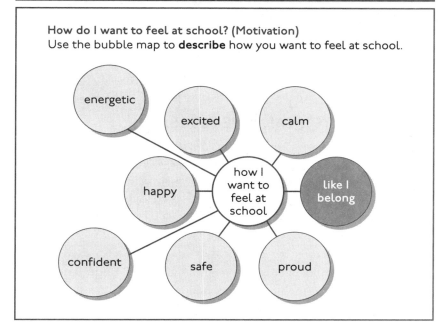

How do I want to feel at school? (Motivation)
Use the bubble map to **describe** how you want to feel at school.

energetic

excited

calm

happy

how I want to feel at school

like I belong

confident

safe

proud

Before identifying hopes and dreams for the year, I found it necessary to talk about our motivation, specifically our hopes and dreams for how we want to feel at school. Leah quietly raised her hand, and when I called on her, she poignantly said, "Like I belong." It served as a nice reminder that we all want to feel as though every bit of us belongs in our classroom, regardless of how we perform.

important, it includes their failures, pain, and the mishaps that bring about discomfort.

It's so hard, though. I know firsthand how this feels as a teacher. While I don't yet know what it feels like as a parent—to watch your child struggle and fail—I'd imagine it's even harder. But in those moments when we tell ourselves we are trying to take away our children's failure and their associated pain, we must ask whose pain we are really trying to assuage. I'd imagine that, more often than not, we are doing more to avoid our own discomfort, when instead we should be sitting in that space with our children, letting them know we've been there, and reassuring them that it will pass when it's ready to—like the tides of the ocean. It is here that we adults have a unique power to offer our children. It's not the ability to stop pain but instead to serve as a model for how to hold, feel, and process pain so we may use it for learning.

We must ask ourselves, who are we serving when we try to prevent our children from experiencing failure, struggle, or pain?

This attitude toward failure and the method for helping our kids learn how to process disappointment, struggle, and pain can truly rehumanize our classrooms, personalize learning, and change the world. After all, there is nothing more personal than pain and struggle. The beauty of it is this: we need nothing more than our own open hearts to achieve it. This willingness to connect and open our hearts to each other—in times of success, joy, pain, and struggle—is far more important than ensuring our children experience success every moment of the day.

TIP #9: ASK IF YOU CAN GIVE FEEDBACK

Everyone should teach kindergarten at some point in their career. Kindergarten is a place to observe and interact with children in the modern wild. It is a wonderful place to learn about agency, autonomy, and intrinsic motivation. Those of you who have taught kindergarten or worked with small children already know that kindergarteners do whatever they want, whenever they want, however they want to do it.

Nolan became a symbol of agency and autonomy in my kindergarten classroom, but he wasn't at the start of the school year. When I met him, he was afraid to write on his own, always worried he would misspell words; he was afraid to read on his own if he didn't know how to read *all* the words aloud. However, with time—by praising the journey, supporting risk-taking and mistake-making, and processing these small moments that defined Nolan's learning journey—he truly became the writer, narrator, and protagonist of his story.

But my favorite memory of Nolan is not his writing growth, his unquenchable thirst for challenging math, or even his project on the planets that he completed toward the end of his kindergarten year. It was his love of feedback.

It was the end of writing workshop one morning, and we were sitting in a circle with the author's chair in front of us. Oftentimes, especially in kindergarten, I found the author's chair to be a great way to reflect on a writing workshop session. It allowed the kids to build confidence by sharing their work, but it also allowed me to praise the journey, as I could see the fruits of the laborious mistakes and tenuous risks the children took over the course of the hour. It also allowed the kids to practice giving feedback.

"Now," I said to my kindergarteners and first-graders, "we have to make sure someone is ready to receive feedback. If someone doesn't want feedback, they probably won't be able to use our feedback to learn."

I modeled how to do this.

"Can I give you some feedback?" I said to one of my students in the author's chair.

The child nodded in reply, and I followed, modeling how to give clear feedback about writing. I told them how it was important to say not only *what* you liked but also *why* you liked it. Feedback, I conveyed to them, was a way to help people know what they should keep doing, as well as what they could change to make something better.

As a result, we also addressed how to give constructive and corrective feedback. I suggested they use phrases such as "I wonder" or "Maybe next time" to keep it positive but also to help everyone see that each of us can always find something new to try or something to improve on.

A CLOSER LOOK

TIPS FOR GIVING FEEDBACK

Giving feedback is an art. It is a strong indicator of flexible and responsive teaching, and as a result, it's a cornerstone of humanized pedagogy. It is the conversation that keeps learning going in our classrooms. In fact, Hattie's research in *Visible Learning* (2008) shows that it has an effect size of .70, which is far within the range of desired effects. Here are some tips for giving feedback in the classroom.

Tip	Example 1 (Writing)	Example 2 (Math)
Ask if you can give feedback.	"Can I give you some feedback?"	"Are you ready for some feedback?"
Start with praise and provide a rationale.	"I really liked your lead because it helped me make a movie in my mind."	"That method seems really logical to me because it goes in order."
Balance praise with constructive, honest, and specific feedback providing a rationale.	"Have you considered starting with dialogue? It might make the story come to life even more."	"I can see that you've put the steps in order, but it's unclear to me how you got from step three to step four."

(Continued)

(Continued)

Tip	Example 1 (Writing)	Example 2 (Math)
Make it actionable by making a recommendation or providing some advice.	"What sorts of things did the characters say or do? Make a list of those things, and choose one that might work for this lead."	"Prove to me that crossing out the 4 and making it a 3 works. Try it with another method. You can draw a picture or use base-ten blocks."
Ask the child to summarize the feedback and/or the recommendation.	"Can you summarize the feedback I gave you?"	"Let's review. What are you going to do before I check in with you again?"
Follow up in a timely manner.	"I'm excited to see what dialogue you've chosen! Can you show me?"	"How did that other method go? Were you able to prove it in a different way?"

This method for giving feedback worked very well. In fact, with enough practice, I overheard the children asking if they could give each other feedback when they needed it during workshops.

Nolan *loved* to give feedback. And when I say loved, I mean it was probably one of his favorite things to do. He would wander around the classroom asking if he could give feedback. His mother told me that he even went so far as to give her some "feedback" about dinner, which she was *very excited* to tell me about the following day.

Alas, Nolan did not enjoy receiving feedback as much as he enjoyed handing it out. In fact, one day, it was Nolan's turn to be in the author's chair. He read his writing and smiled up at me afterward.

Another student, Lex, raised his hand.

"Nolan, can I give you some feedback?" Lex said.

"No, thanks," Nolan replied matter-of-factly.

I nearly died laughing. Even so, it was important to me to honor Nolan's choice. It's true, after all, that some days we don't want feedback. Sometimes we're just not in the mood, and other times, we just want to feel seen and heard. Feedback is not, by any means, always necessary, and in that moment,

Nolan was communicating something about himself to all of us—not to mention providing me some great data on his cognitive flexibility.

"Okay, Nolan, well if you don't want feedback right now, I think we should let someone else sit in the author's chair. Thanks for sharing."

He went back to his seat on the carpet, participating in the remainder of sharing, offering feedback to many of his friends. It wasn't long before he wanted to sit in the author's chair another day. As you might guess, the same thing happened again. He turned down the opportunity to get feedback, but this time I was prepared.

"Nolan, it makes me feel yellow when you go in the author's chair but won't accept feedback," I said to him in front of the class, referring to the Zones of Regulation.

"If we are going to learn, it's important that we open ourselves up to feedback from others, just like your friends do for you."

Nolan looked down at the ground, his large chestnut eyes softening.

"Okay, Paul," he said to me with a knowing tone. "Bailey, you can give me some feedback."

From that point on, he was much more open to feedback, and as a result, he learned a lesson that many adults struggle to understand: feedback is beneficial, even when it makes us uncomfortable.

Nolan is a poignant and comedic outlier. I've never encountered another child who has turned down feedback, but I'm grateful for Nolan's authenticity, as I'm grateful for all the moments when my children make the brave choice to be their authentic selves. It's these authentic moments that humanize our classrooms and allow for teachable moments that truly make learning feel personal.

In this authentic, humanizing, and utterly personal moment, Nolan's learning was not about writing or even about feedback itself; it was about vulnerability and an acknowledgment of imperfection. What's more, my response to him was not one of compliance but instead one of a social agreement—that he would be held accountable to the collective norms of our classroom culture.

It is here that we see authoritative classroom management shine and support agency and autonomy. To be a part of the experience, he had to sign the social contract and act in an equitable manner. But the beauty of it is that this lesson came as a result of offering him the choice. It all came as a result of giving Nolan the agency to choose the feedback, which he so autonomously decided not to do. If I had not allowed him to make this choice, explore his own autonomy, and better understand the effects of the choices he was making, he may not have learned this valuable lesson about vulnerability and feedback. It was one he learned quickly, and he soon felt comfortable receiving feedback from the group regularly.

TIP #10: REFLECT, REFLECT, REFLECT

Risk-taking, mistake-making, and failure are, in so many ways, the only pathways to agency and autonomy, which is why it's so critical to make space for them in our classrooms. They provide concrete reference points for the many invisible boundaries that exist in the world. However, they exist purposelessly if we neglect to reflect on the lessons we can learn from them. Reflecting on learning allows children a chance to continue an internal dialogue—an internal learning conversation that allows them to interact with their thoughts and feelings and continue to modify an existing mental model of themselves that's increasingly more resilient and self-appreciative.

Oftentimes, reflection is overlooked in the classroom. The industrialized philosophy tells us that all children need to know is the grade they received, and that this alone will help them see what they need to do differently. This may seem like it's working just fine for the children who fit the industrialized mold—the ones who have the skills to strategically comply with the demands of traditional education. In actuality, it doesn't support any children in the classroom—especially our learners who struggle the most.

The children who struggle the most are oftentimes the ones who need the most structured reflection. Students who struggle academically are more often lacking executive functioning skills rather than academic content. This is especially true for students in urban settings, most often serving communities of color and/or low-income students. A variety of systemic and societal factors exacerbate this—ranging from basic needs that sometimes go unmet to excessive strain on parents who are forced to work multiple jobs to make ends meet. This is only worsened by the fact that struggling schools are held to rigid structures for implementing boxed curricula and collecting assessment data, making them unable to promote executive functioning skills and structured reflection. Most boxed curricula overlook the importance of structured reflection and instead prioritize the consumption of content.

Technology-powered personalized learning programs are no different. While they may provide "feedback" in the form of a correct answer, these tools do not provide support in helping children process and learn from their mistakes in the way a sentient educator can. We know that students from historically underserved communities are best supported when we support them in transition from dependent to independent learners (Hammond, 2014). To transition them to independence, we must make more time for children to reflect on their learning so reflections can become valuable assets that support independence.

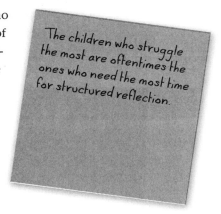

All children need honest, actionable, and timely feedback. They need the chance to connect their efforts to improvements in their work. Such is the nature of Pink's (2009) definition of *mastery*. It is this process that helps them see that they have control over their learning journeys.

Reflecting can do more than create a positive and autonomous attitude toward learning. It can also help empower children in their academics. Before starting any of my units, I do my best to give a pre-assessment, aligned to the standards I've chosen for the unit. This provides a concrete artifact for reflection later in the unit, helping my students see their growth by comparing work samples.

In most cases, their performance will not change *what* I teach, but it may change *how* I teach it. While pre-assessments may show areas of need, areas of strength, or even gaps in conceptual knowledge, they also give me insight into my students' processes and serve as a means for previewing content. Early in the year, this scares my children. When I give the first assessment, they look at me fearfully, unsure of what to do and scared to fail.

"I don't know how to do this," someone will say to me.

"Excellent!" I say back to them. "That means we get to learn it together."

This doesn't necessarily assuage their fears immediately, but with time, they begin to understand why I give them assessments before any teaching or learning has occurred.

"Remember, everyone," I repeatedly say to the kids, in so many words, "an assessment is not to tell me if you did a good or bad job. An assessment tells me what we need to learn next. So, if you don't know how to do something, please feel free to write me a note, ask me a question, or ex it out."

It takes a while for them to become comfortable with this, but it certainly comes with time. I'm reminded, specifically, of Sydney when I think of this. She came to me with anxiety, oftentimes paralyzed by a fear of what might happen when she failed. This manifested most acutely in writing, where she found it difficult to even generate an idea.

In our first pre-assessment, an on-demand writing task from Lucy Calkins's Units of Study, Sydney sat and looked at her paper listlessly. I walked over and checked in on her to see if she was okay.

"I don't know what to write," she said to me, the corners of her eyes drooping, her body melting into her chair.

"I know, it's really hard to come up with an idea sometimes," I said back to her. "Just do your best. You'll get another opportunity to try it again."

Now, this is critical: I could have stepped in. I could have helped her generate an idea. I could have asked her a ton of questions, modeled again how I come up with ideas, or given her something to write about. But I specifically chose not to. Sydney was dependent, attempting to take the path of least resistance with a subconscious intention of self-preservation. It was a less vulnerable, safer choice to have me generate an idea. By putting her idea out there, she'd be putting a piece of herself out there for all to see. It was too high-stakes for her in the first weeks of school. I completely understood and identified with the feeling.

Self-preservation: The act of protecting oneself from perceived harm

Despite the fact that she completed nothing, this pre-assessment gave me precisely the data I needed. Sydney's needs in writing were not mechanical, grammatical, or even about idea development—yet. Sydney's writing needs were socioemotional.

We approached the end of the assessment window. I walked back over to her to find that she'd still written nothing.

"I know this was tough, Sydney," I said to her. "But I'm really proud of you for sticking with it even though it was hard."

She looked up at me, exhausted.

"Hey, I've got an idea," I continued. "How about we set a goal? The next time we do this, I want you to do your best to just write one sentence—just one. What do you think of that?"

She looked at me, unsure.

"We'll work on building some strategies for generating ideas. We won't worry about the idea itself, and we won't worry about spelling or grammar. We'll just set a goal to get something on the paper. How do you feel about that?"

She shrugged, unconvinced.

Over the next few weeks, we settled into a writing routine that embraced the three dimensions of personalization, allowing me to build a collective classroom culture where we take risks, make mistakes, and embrace vulnerability. I formed heterogeneous and homogenous small groups to foster collaboration and feedback, and I conferred with students, coaching them on writing skills, praising the inner journey, and offering constructive feedback to nurture an evolving inner dialogue around writing. While this supported all students, it especially supported students such as Sydney, creating a safe space where she could open herself up to the writing process. With these supports in place, it wasn't long before Sydney started to take risks, and when she did, my feedback was all about the journey. I would say things like the examples in Figure 6.9.

"Wow, Sydney, I am so glad to see that you've written three sentences today. It's really helping me get to know you and learn about the stories you like to tell."

"My goodness, you wrote so much in such a short period of time! I'm so happy to see that you're taking some risks. I hope you're feeling proud of yourself."

"Wow, Sydney! I'm thinking back to that writing assessment we did the first week of school and how hard it was for you to come up with an idea. It looks like you are settling into your ideas and taking some more risks. How do you feel?"

Figure 6.9: More Things to Say

This story ends well. Almost two months later, when we completed another on-demand writing task to end the unit, Sydney shined. She took a minute or two to come up with an idea, but when she did, she wrote ferociously. Where did her confidence come from? It came from investing in the process. By seeing where she started and embracing the writing journey, she was able to find safety in taking risks and making mistakes. What's more, letting her struggle and fail during the pre-assessment established a boundary in our relationship—a healthy, compassionate boundary that helped her witness her own agency and autonomy specifically in writing. She learned that *she* had to tell her own stories and that there was no way I'd be able to do it for her.

UNDERSTANDING THE INNER WORLD OF A CHILD

Agency and autonomy are ultimately about empowerment and equity. It's not necessarily the choice itself that instills a sense of agency or helps children see the autonomy that comes from their own decision-making power; instead, it's the notion of *having* a choice that makes it possible for students to witness their own agency. It is this process of evaluating and choosing that helps them see that they are the protagonists of their own stories and they must be willing to advocate for themselves and what they need.

This requires a significant cultural and cognitive shift in the way you manage your classroom and engineer the learning environment. This isn't something you can teach only in morning meeting or talk about occasionally; it's something you must embody every moment of every class you teach. What's more, it takes an emergent understanding of the inner world of a child, coupled with the humble realization that you'll never fully understand what it's like to think, feel, and experience the world in the same way they do.

This makes the process of developing agency and autonomy in a complex classroom ecosystem scary. It doesn't only mean that you need to allow your children to make mistakes and fail; it also means you must be kind to yourself and allow yourself to fail, as well, as you embrace the tender, personal, and human experience of learning alongside your children. As we unpack curriculum design over the next three chapters, you'll see that you, too, will need to open yourself up to risk-taking, mistake-making, and failure when building your own agency and autonomy with curriculum design, humanized assessment, and responsive pedagogy.

CHAPTER SEVEN

DESIGNING CURRICULUM WITH A FLEXIBLE FRAME

For many reasons, self-proclaimed "progressive" educators advocate against using standards in the classroom. Instead of seeing them as supportive structures that provide a common language for learning, they argue that standards act in opposition to child-centered education. When they hear the words *standard* or *standardize*, they immediately imagine an industrialized model for education, even though standards are critical to humanizing personalization and rehumanizing our classrooms.

"Compassionate people draw boundaries," says Brené Brown, and they do so because it provides a healing structure to the classroom. Standards do the same for curriculum design and student learning. They are merely mindful boundaries that form a common language for what students should know and be able to do.

If used correctly, standards can scale effective teaching and learning practices to the masses, promoting access and protecting equity through a common language and clear expectations. They provide a flexible yet structured foundation for building a curriculum that supports the unique needs of a diverse group of learners, scaffolding their autonomy over time.

"Compassionate people draw boundaries." —Brené Brown

Standards are critical in a personalized environment.

But this was not a popular idea when I began teaching in Silicon Valley. While most technologists understood the benefit of standards and their role in helping us measure our effectiveness, many progressive educators struggled to understand their benefit. In retrospect, they seemed so adamant in their reaction to mainstream public education and the shortcomings of the standardization era that they neglected to see the inherent value of structure in curriculum design. It seemed as though their negative preconceptions and experiences with standards-based education made it nearly impossible for them to even consider using a framework for standards, standardized assessments, and standards-based measures to add structure to learner-driven experiences.

When we strip away the bias and emotional baggage that comes with the words *standard* and *standardize*, it's clear that the intention behind standardization is to create consistency with regard to what students should know and be able to do. In fact, standardization helps ensure that all learners—regardless of race, home language, or zip code—are afforded access to an appropriately rigorous curriculum. The intent of standardization is to ensure that certain groups are not afforded access to a more rigorous curriculum while others are oppressed or suppressed by a less rigorous or less stimulating curriculum.

Many fail to realize that standards' bad reputation is born of misuse. Standards should not be used as a bar we hold over students' and teachers' heads, as some school systems do. They should not be created as an unreasonable performance indicator, used to punish learners for opportunity gaps and obstacles outside of their control. Instead, they should be created in a manner that allows all children to be represented, regardless of race, ethnicity, class, or any other identity marker. If they are, they can serve as a meaningful reference point for the efficacy of our pedagogy or the obstacles of our students.

If not for standards, I would not have been able to communicate to Viola's parents that she had unique struggles with counting, cardinality, and numeracy as a first-grader. Without standards, I would not have been able to create an intervention plan for Ari when I noticed he was two grade levels behind in decoding and reading comprehension—an intervention plan that helped him build his confidence and make a year and a half's worth of progress in reading in a year. Without standards, my team and I would not have been able to build meaningful project-based learning experiences, such as the urban planning project I'll share with you shortly, which required my students to draw on literacy, numeracy, and humanities skills to plan a town based on the needs of fictional residents (see Figure 7.1).

Figure 7.1: Urban Planning Project

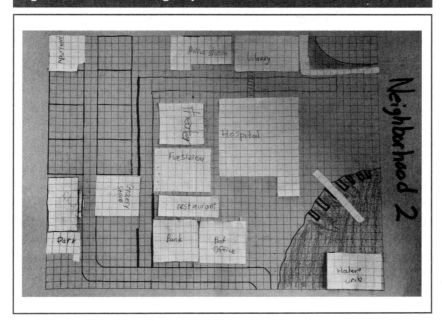

Photo Credit: Ryan MacLeod

In effect, by adopting an appropriately rigorous set of standards, we forge a path to equity. But we must also make sure that schools and the systems that run them are well-equipped to help diverse groups of students reach them through varied paces and modalities. The call for this isn't new. In a 1999 report released by Brown University, titled "Standards, Equity, and Cultural Diversity," Mary Ann Lachat calls for standards as a path to equity, stating that all children—including children from historically low-achieving communities—can indeed excel in an appropriately rigorous curriculum. She, too, agrees that the standards themselves are not enough: "The success of standards-based reform depends on a comprehensive set of changes involving access to resources, access to highly-skilled teachers, access to high-quality instruction, and a safe and supportive school environment (Neill, 1995; Stevens, 1996)."

Nearly a decade later, a report released by the Organisation for Economic Co-operation and Development (OECD) echoed similar sentiments. In the report, OECD defines *equity* in terms of both fairness and inclusion. To be fair and inclusive, it's necessary to remove barriers that limit access to a rigorous education, ensuring that "personal circumstances" do not limit one's ability to reach one's full potential. To be inclusive, the report conveys, schools must ensure a "basic minimum standard of education for all" (OECD, 2008).

Even recent reports on personalized learning convey the need for standards as a path to equity, reiterating the same message that the structure of a common, agreed-on set of educational standards increases our chances of ensuring educational equity through appropriately rigorous content. In the RAND Corporation's 2017 report on personalized learning, the authors identify competency-based progressions as a key feature of personalized learning models, meanwhile citing the challenges of competency-based models that allow for flexibility with regard to the pace at which children master content (Pane et al., 2017). In a competency-based progression, children do not advance to the next skill until they've mastered the current one. The benefits here are clear: by not rushing children through curriculum, we ensure that children master what they need to learn; on the other hand, extending the amount of time a child needs to master a specific skill might put them at risk of falling behind peers, threatening equity and inclusion.

This doesn't necessarily mean we simply let children master skills at their own pace. Doing so is likely to create more points of divergence and incentivize an over-individualization of the curriculum that works in opposition to equity, inclusion, and a sense of belonging in classrooms. In instances where we notice gaps in skill development, it is important to leverage the human resources in the school—including interventionists and intervention programs—to collect more data on what is causing any children to need more time to master a given skill. Neglecting to do so is a threat to equity, as well.

In essence, if used correctly, standards can *humanize* our curriculum and help us offer an equitable education to all who enter our classrooms. They create *points of convergence* within our classrooms around which students can collaborate on similar skills and learn in concert with one another. These points of convergence build structure, routine, and predictability, not only providing clarity on what students should know and be able to do but also creating sustainability with data collection. They also allow for *points of divergence* where we can enrich or remediate learning experiences by unpacking standards to account for various levels of proficiency and other individual differences. Without the structure that standards provide, we create an unsustainable and unscalable chaos that dehumanizes learning.

THE DANGER OF TEACHING WITHOUT STANDARDS

Teaching without standards is like being dropped into an open field on a cloudy night, with no compass, stars, or landmarks to guide your path. This is neither liberating nor motivating; instead, it's chaotic and traumatic. It creates unproductive anxiety and directionless discomfort. While some euphemize this lack of structure as "freedom" or "autonomy," this amount of freedom can actually be paralyzing, triggering the parts of our brains that are hardwired to respond to fear and chaos. Conversely, teaching with standards can be empowering and liberating if done correctly. It's like being dropped into that same field but instead with the tools necessary to succeed, like the compass that helps us determine which way is north and which way is south, or the map that helps us develop an action plan. Standards are the trees on the horizon that provide a reference point for the direction we might start heading; they're the stars in the night sky that orient and guide us when things become messy and uncertain.

Standards are productive constraints that guide us when things get tough.

Initially, in our personalized learning schools in Silicon Valley, we were in this open field, wandering around, unsure of what to teach and how best to support children. Growth and achievement were too often defined in terms of a child's happiness and comfort level, without incorporating valid and reliable metrics for academic growth. While it's important that our children feel happy to be at school, we mustn't ignore the idea that growth is sometimes uncomfortable. In trying to constantly ensure our children are entertained—and attempting to elicit only positive feelings from them—we may actually be doing them a disservice. We teachers are neither entertainers nor performers; we are coaches who help young human beings cultivate an ever-evolving sense of self. This work is sometimes uncomfortable—and quite frankly, sometimes it hurts.

Furthermore, we have a responsibility to ensure that our children are getting what they need academically, which is impossible to do without a common language with which we can gauge academic progress. Children *must* learn how to read, write, and compute in our modern world, even if it's challenging or uncomfortable. They must be able to do these things to engage in the collective conscious of the modern world.

When we do not identify standards and build an assessment framework through which we can measure the efficacy of our pedagogy, it becomes challenging to give every child what they need in the classroom—operating in direct opposition to personalization and equity—and struggling students fall through the cracks.

"We were told, 'No big deal—kids learn differently,'" one parent reflected in a *Business Insider* article (Robinson, 2017). "'We were always told our child was doing fine and not to be concerned.'

"She later found out that this was *not* the case—when the school asked her to provide a full-time aide for her child."

I, too, felt concerned about the approach to assessment and documentation at my school in Silicon Valley. It seemed to lack this critical step of identifying a rigorous set of standards that would allow us to gauge the efficacy of our practice. As a result, I began my first year there by identifying standards and mapping out the curriculum for the year, ensuring that I was providing my students with a well-rounded set of educative experiences.

While the school eventually initiated changes to these flawed practices, I can't help wondering if clear standards for teaching and learning, coupled with a watertight assessment framework, could have caught this child's learning disability sooner. Never mind the fact that the company's primary interests lay in scaling its technology to the masses; they had attempted to scale this approach without an evidence-based, small-scale model that was truly meeting the needs of every child.

It's true that simply identifying a standard set would not have solved all these problems. Schools require thoroughly designed and well-functioning systems to catch children who are struggling and then provide them the support they need. Not having these systems in place is also a threat to equity in schools. But identifying a standard set is a necessary first step. Doing so creates a common language for what's expected and, as a result, helps educators identify students who struggle. While the company eventually attempted to do this with more fidelity, it was far too late by the time they had. Too many children had already slipped through the cracks, creating a large mess that was tough to clean up.

The company even went so far as to streamline instructional resources and pedagogy, requiring that all teachers pull from a common set of teacher manuals to course-correct and streamline effectiveness—a far cry from the initial vision of the school, a vision that beckoned us to capitalize on the interests of children to build a dynamic curriculum that was personalized. This seemingly progressive education technology company that the education world idolized for such a short period of time had become a microcosm for the downfalls of public education—attempting to boost results on assessments through standardizing practice and resources, and to clean up a PR nightmare and prove that their technology-driven approach to personalization was, in fact, effective—even though there was ample evidence to suggest it was not.

Too many schools struggle to see personalization and standardization as a relationship—that standards and standardization support meaningful learning that's inherently personal. But that doesn't mean schools should be standardizing pedagogy and forcing teachers to instruct from manuals. When used well, standards and standardization build a foundation and *flexible frame* for learning—one that allows teachers to be emboldened by their autonomy so they may be creative practitioners who reach students on a personal level.

Standardization and personalization exist in a supportive and harmonious relationship.

THE FLEXIBLE FRAME

My kindergarten and first-grade multiage class had just finished our field trip to the San Francisco Botanic Gardens. We were in Golden Gate Park, San Francisco's version of Central Park, featuring museums, green spaces, and community areas. Golden Gate Park always felt like a respite in the middle of an urban jungle. When enveloped in the park's warm embrace, it was easy to get lost in it.

My class and I walked down the sidewalks, past the tennis courts, and up to an enormous play space adorned with stone slides that were at least five times my height, a large fortlike structure begging for a game of tag, and an enormous climbing structure augmented with a mountain of ropes and metal piping. You know the ones I'm talking about. They look like oversize spider webs. Or death traps. Or something else thrilling but terrifying at the same time. The thought of my kids going up there scared me, but alas, my inner child came out and I hopped right up there with them, abandoning my fear, my trepidation, and my adult self on the ground below.

It was liberating to climb higher and higher with my students, hearing the laughter and excitement that came from this thrilling play structure. It fascinated me to think that this one structure could be so liberating, not only to me but also to children more than twenty years my juniors. It seemed that, even though the structure was fixed and static and—dare

I say—*standard* to all of us, we managed to stay engaged, regardless of age and ability. We were all capable of playing on the structure independently but also with one another.

I later realized that while the play structure was fixed and static, our experiences were flexible and malleable due to our agency and autonomy. The structure allowed for points of both convergence *and* divergence. It neither limited us in our creativity nor restricted our ability to connect with one another. It instead provoked us to try new things, create new games, connect with one another, and travel on our own paths when it seemed appropriate and fulfilling.

After I'd climbed to the very top, I looked down to see Parker starting her ascent. She seemed invigorated and intimidated but determined to get up as high as she could. I noticed Keely, in contrast, sitting on the bottom rung just a few feet above the sandpit, content with her progress for the day.

Without that play structure, sure, the children would still have been able to interact and play with one another, even in a boundless open field. On the other hand, with a rather fixed and static play structure— one that was flexible enough to open us up to new possibilities but also sturdy enough to help us find safety and comfort—we were able to posit new possibilities, take risks, fall on our faces, and most important, learn something new.

This is, after all, what structure does in any environment. Through productive boundaries and mindful limits on choice, structure provides just enough flexibility to be motivating and supportive, offering multiple pathways for exploration. It's why the play structure is the perfect metaphor for humanized personalization. It illustrates an intimate and healthy relationship between standardization and personalization, and it helps us see how we can capitalize on it to sustainably humanize personalization.

SUPPORTING HUMANIZED PERSONALIZATION WITH STANDARDS

The final three chapters of Section II illustrate how to plan for personalized instruction, assess its efficacy, and enable humanized instruction. While these three components of pedagogy are not orthogonal—and while I think the inability to entirely divorce them from one another will be evident in the story I'll tell about our urban planning project—the remainder of this chapter will be about how to use standards to promote humanized personalization. It is my hope that you'll see how the flexible frame my team and I built not only created consistency and a common language but also allowed learners to personalize their own experiences by accessing their agency and exercising autonomy. It is also my hope that you'll see that humanized personalization incorporates project-based learning that is bounded by a very narrow range of choices.

This style of planning and preparation is neither new nor revolutionary. To attempt to illustrate the planning process for the urban planning project, I'll use the four professional learning community questions (DuFour, DuFour, Eaker, & Many, 2010) as a guide, but you'll also sense that it aligns nicely with *Understanding by Design* (Wiggins & McTighe, 1998), which entails identifying desired results (standards), designing assessments to gather evidence for student learning, and finally, creating a learning plan that meets the needs of all learners. The four questions are shown in Figure 7.2.

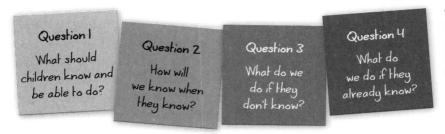

Figure 7.2:
Four Professional
Learning Community
Questions

Authors Fisher, Frey, Almarode, Flories, and Nagel (2019) have also advocated for adding a fifth, equity-focused question to the original list: *Who benefited and who did not?* Before we dive in to how we answered each of the questions and how we used those answers to structure the project, I feel it necessary to provide a bit of context around the project, specifically about why we chose to have the children build a community.

After I left Silicon Valley, I was teaching third grade in Chicago. Historically, the third grade's social studies curriculum was focused on the city of Chicago—primarily its history. This aligned not only with typical third-grade curriculum but also with what's developmentally appropriate for young children. It's important they learn about their surroundings, since they're not yet capable of deeply understanding world affairs. But my team wanted to go beyond Chicago history. We wanted to teach them more than just facts and figures about Chicago: we wanted them to know that understanding Chicago's history could also help them understand Chicago's present and future. We wanted them to understand that the problems of history are not unique to the past and that human beings are constantly solving new problems in their own communities and the world at-large. In essence, we wanted to make history and social studies personally meaningful to them.

The first half of the year was dedicated to understanding Chicago's history, from the intersection of various ethnic groups in early Chicago to the Great Migration and beyond. With that underlying historical context, we launched into a neighborhood study, where we examined our neighborhood, Gold Coast, and visited another Chicago neighborhood, a socioeconomically and racially diverse borough on the north side of Chicago called Uptown. We learned about issues the neighborhood was facing, from rising home prices to the displacement of low-income residents due to gentrification. The neighborhood study, which took place in the third quarter, culminated with students writing letters to city council members, proposing solutions to some of these issues, and creating public service announcement posters for other neighborhoods they'd studied.

Because we'd studied the past and the present, it only made sense to look to the future. To achieve this, we gave the students blank slates—open maps of cities to help them build a neighborhood given the needs of a group of people. To start the project, we provided one of three scenarios around which to build their neighborhood. Over the course of the eight-week unit, they would construct a variety of buildings to meet the needs of the residents. While complex, nuanced, and messy, it was always supported by a flexible frame of clear learning outcomes, leading us through the uncertainty and discomfort that oftentimes accompany project-based learning.

WHAT SHOULD CHILDREN KNOW AND BE ABLE TO DO?

This was a pretty simple process for our team, seeing as we'd spent time early in the year building a curriculum map as a foundation for the rest of the year. This curriculum map was a "living and breathing document," as we like to call it, subject to change when evidentiary need presents itself. Because we had chosen the Common Core State Standards as a guide for identifying math standards, we paced these out over the course of the school year, ensuring that we'd be able to give all four domains of Common Core Mathematics some airtime, as well as gauge understanding of the standards within the framework. We began the year with the "Number and Operations in Base Ten" and "Operations in Algebraic Thinking" strands, taking the first four months of the school year to build number sense and computation skills, and using the latter half of the year for measurement, data, fractions, and geometry concepts. For this reason, we already knew that the end of the school year would entail teaching geometry and geometric measurement, aligning nicely with a project on urban planning. By the end of the unit, we expected students to be able to do certain tasks in mathematics (see Figure 7.3).

Figure 7.3: Selected Math Standards

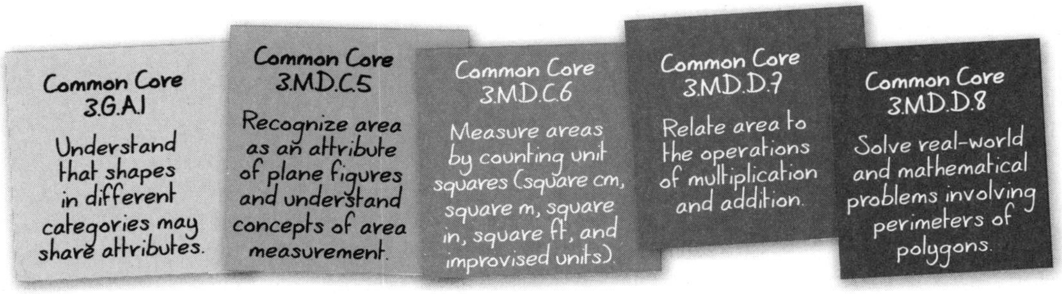

Common Core 3.G.A.1

Understand that shapes in different categories may share attributes.

Common Core 3.MD.C.5

Recognize area as an attribute of plane figures and understand concepts of area measurement.

Common Core 3.MD.C.6

Measure areas by counting unit squares (square cm, square m, square in, square ft, and improvised units).

Common Core 3.MD.D.7

Relate area to the operations of multiplication and addition.

Common Core 3.MD.D.8

Solve real-world and mathematical problems involving perimeters of polygons.

Due to the project's interdisciplinary nature, we didn't limit our standard selection to mathematics. We also pulled from the Illinois State Standards for Social Studies (see Figure 7.4).

Figure 7.4: Selected Social Studies Standards

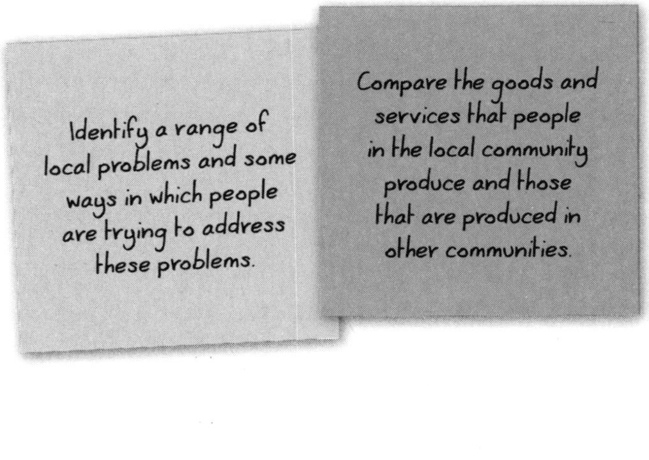

Identify a range of local problems and some ways in which people are trying to address these problems.

Compare the goods and services that people in the local community produce and those that are produced in other communities.

As we've illustrated thus far in this chapter, these standards served as guides throughout the unit. They served as a North Star—a reference point for when things became messy over the course of the project.

HOW WILL WE KNOW WHEN THEY KNOW?

In the following chapter, we'll discuss assessment practices and how to reliably assess against standards in a humanizing way. I like to think of assessment in terms of three major categories: standardized assessments, standards-based assessments (both formative and summative), and anecdotal assessments of the inner dialogue. For this project, our standards-based summative assessments occurred during math workshop, where we routinely engaged in open-ended mathematics tasks that allowed children to grapple with shapes—their attributes, area, and perimeter—decontextualized from the urban planning project. In Figure 7.5 you can see samples of assessment items from our post-assessment. We gave an assessment at the beginning of the unit and at the end of the unit.

A CLOSER LOOK

STANDARDS-BASED ASSESSMENT

When choosing standards, it is imperative that we also consider the ways we will gauge mastery of the standards. Standards and assessment exist in a relationship. The standards define what children should know and be able to do, while the assessments offer concrete experiences and a context for determining if children know and are able to perform these identified skills.

In Figures 7.5a through 7.5d, you'll see how the assessment is clearly designed to elicit valuable information about students' mastery of the standards we identified for the unit. The pre-assessment, post-assessment, and intermittent formal formative assessments were structured similarly, in an effort to gauge short-term progress in a valid and reliable way, meanwhile informing instruction throughout the unit.

Figure 7.5a

Name _____ Date _____

Unit 5 Post-Assessment

Section 1: Shapes and Attributes

Use the shapes below to sort into the three categories.

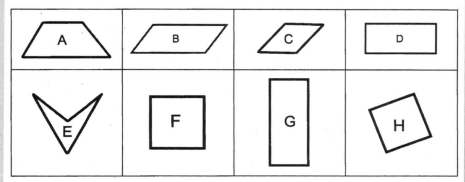

Squares	Rectangles	Rhombuses
Which of the shapes above are **squares**? You may write the letters of the shapes.	Which of the shapes above are **rectangles**? You may write the letters of the shapes.	Which of the shapes above are **rhombuses**? You may write the letters of the shapes.
How do you know?	How do you know?	How do you know?

(Continued)

(Continued)

Figure 7.5b

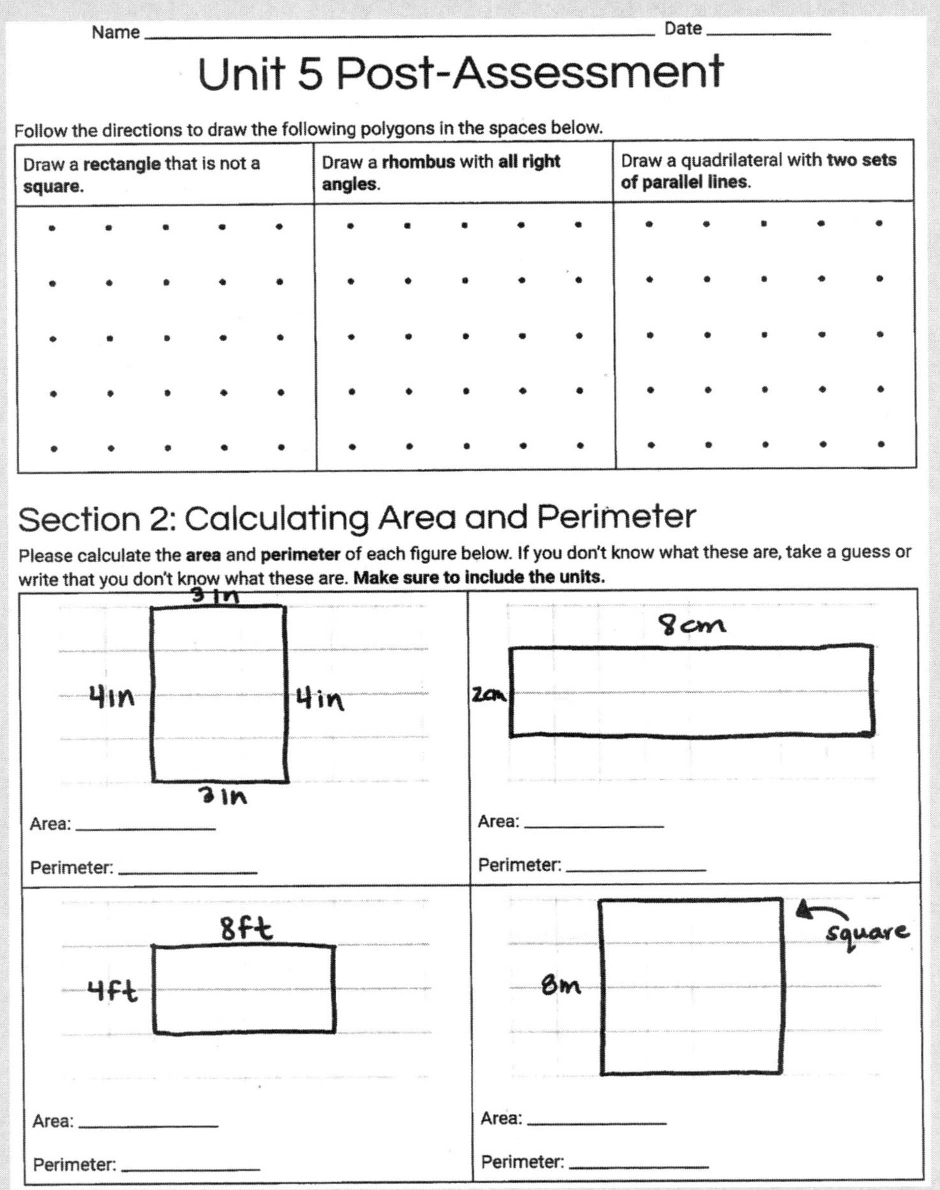

Name _____ Date _____

Unit 5 Post-Assessment

Follow the directions to draw the following polygons in the spaces below.

Draw a **rectangle** that is not a **square**.	Draw a **rhombus** with **all right angles**.	Draw a quadrilateral with **two sets of parallel lines**.

Section 2: Calculating Area and Perimeter

Please calculate the **area** and **perimeter** of each figure below. If you don't know what these are, take a guess or write that you don't know what these are. **Make sure to include the units.**

3 in

4in   4in

3 in

Area: _____

Perimeter: _____

8 cm

2cm

Area: _____

Perimeter: _____

8ft

4ft

Area: _____

Perimeter: _____

8m   square

Area: _____

Perimeter: _____

Figure 7.5c

Name _____ Date _____

Unit 5 Post-Assessment

Mrs. Northover is redoing a closet in her house. The floorplan is pictured below. Each square represents 1 square foot.

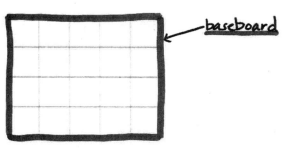

baseboard

She is going to buy square tiles to cover the floor. Each square tile is 1 square foot. How many square tiles should she buy to cover the floor?

She is also going to put baseboards down. Baseboards are pieces of wood that go around the edge of the room. How many feet of baseboard does Mrs. Northover need?

(Continued)

Figure 7.5d

Unit 5 Post-Assessment

Section 3: Three Hidden Rectangles

There are several ways to find the area of this figure:

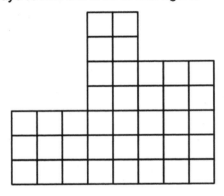

a) Find a way to split this figure into **three separate rectangles**. Use three different colors to show your different rectangles.

b) For every rectangle you find, write an equation to show the area. **Write each equation near each rectangle.**

c) Use the space below to find the total area.

During math workshop and our social studies blocks, we engaged in both formal and informal formative assessment practices at various points throughout the unit. In some cases, we administered formal formative assessments, and in other cases, we used the project as a means for observing students' ability to calculate area and perimeter in a novel context, given the constraints of the project.

To create constraints around the buildings they would construct, we came up with a series of "zoning laws" that gave children lot sizes and maximum sizes for floor plans. This served as a forcing function for applying area and perimeter skills and an authentic way to observe our students' transfer of the skills. Children were required to recall the definition of area and determine how to work within the zoning laws (see Figure 7.6).

Phase 3: Reviewing the Zoning Laws

Use the chart below to figure out the guidelines for your building. Highlight the zoning law that applies to your building.

Building	Maximum Area	Maximum # of Floors
Apartments	24 square units (2,400 square feet)	8
Police and fire stations	64 square units (6,400 square feet)	3
Hospitals	150 square units (15,000 square feet)	5
Schools	64 square units (6,400 square feet)	3
Museums and libraries	64 square units (6,400 square feet)	2
Parks	16 square units (1,600 square feet)	0
Community recreation	64 square units (6,400 square feet)	3
Restaurants	24 square units (2,400 square feet)	2
Entertainment	36 square units (3,600 square feet)	2
Stores and shops	36 square units (3,600 square feet)	2

In reviewing the children's designs, we could gauge their understanding of area and perimeter. They were required to record the area of their building, ensuring it was built within the constraints of the zoning laws. Then they were required to calculate the perimeter to figure out the amount of cardboard they'd need to go around the edge of the building. By the end of the project, all students had had ample opportunities to go through this process several times over, allowing for varied but repeated practice with the skills, supported by focused feedback. The end result was an assessment in and of itself—a stunning one at that (see Figure 7.7).

Figure 7.7: Final Product

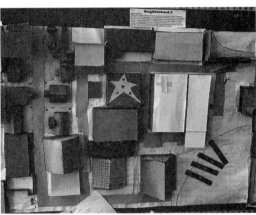

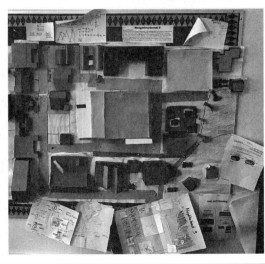

Photo Credit: Ryan MacLeod

But it's also important to note that we had to gradually build them up to this. We weren't able to simply open up the project and ask them to jump into it. We had to slowly scaffold the experience of applying area and perimeter. To do this, we began by giving each child a character profile. This character lived in the community they were building. To help them learn how to design within constraints, their first task was to build a house that was no more than ten square units on a twenty-five-square-unit lot, designing a floor plan based on the character's profile (see Figure 7.8).

Figure 7.8: Zahara

Name: Zahara Malik

Age: 24

Profession: Zahara is a student at DePaul University. She works as a babysitter and tutor in her spare time, since she has a degree in education from her home country in Syria.

Family: Zahara's grandmother, mother, father, and sister live in her home with her. Like Zahara, they are refugees from Syria. Her sister, mother, and father work as well.

Hobbies: Zahara doesn't have much time for hobbies since she is working and going to school. She loves kickboxing and playing her guitar.

Values: Zahara is so thrilled to have her family with her, and she spends a great deal of time enjoying meals and playing games with them. Zahara also volunteers at the local animal shelter when she can.

Source: Vitaliy Vladimirov

Through mindfully designed constraints and intentionally designed points of convergence (i.e., common standards, zoning laws), children were able to personalize their own experience within the boundaries of the collective. Despite the fact that the constraints and the learning outcomes were standardized, the designs and final products were incredibly diverse (see Figure 7.9).

Some explored only rectangular figures, while others explored complex rectilinear figures. Not only did this allow the children to access their agency and exercise their autonomy, it served as a meaningful assessment. Some children needed to build the perimeter of the buildings one unit by one

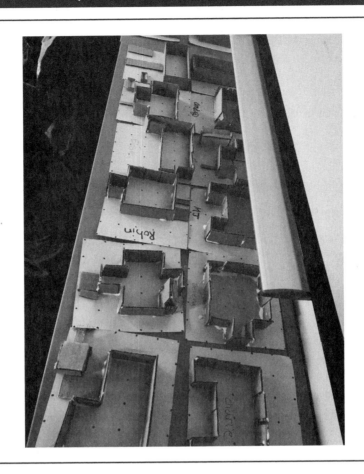

unit, while others were able to cut the lengths of the sides of their build-ings, directly translating from their design books to the real model. There were also a few students who needed extra support in completing this first task, providing an opportunity to review and reinforce area and perimeter through both small-group and one-on-one intervention.

WHAT DO WE DO IF THEY DON'T KNOW?

Project-based learning isn't valuable if there are not mindfully designed paths for all students to experience at least some level of success at one point or another. This is why equity and access are critical to humanizing personalization: all children need to be able to engage successfully in the points of both convergence and divergence over the course of any given learning experience or project. To anticipate and plan for this, my team and I deconstructed the standards to figure out what they looked like at various levels of proficiency. We then used these to make a rubric (see Figure 7.10).

Figure 7.10: Rubric

	Emerging	Developing	Approaching	Meeting
Attributes of shapes	With help, I can sort shapes.	I can sort shapes, but my sorting isn't based on attributes.	I can sort shapes based on their attributes without explaining my reasoning.	I can sort and describe shapes based on their attributes.
Calculate area	With help, I can define area and calculate the area of a rectangle.	I can calculate the area of a rectangle, but I make errors when counting squares or using the area formula.	I can calculate the area of a rectangle by counting unit squares.	I can calculate the area of a rectangle using the formula for area.
Calculate perimeter	With help, I can calculate the perimeter of a figure.	I can calculate the perimeter of a figure, but I make some errors.	I can calculate the perimeter of a figure when I'm given all the side lengths.	I can calculate the perimeter of a figure, including figures with unknown side lengths.

There are some very clear limitations to this rubric, many of which we experienced over the course of the unit. Student proficiency was not always clear when using the rubric. The following year, we switched to checklists that provided more detail for how the standards were deconstructed. This took away the hierarchical nature of the rubric and instead helped us more objectively check off what children knew and were able to do (see Figure 7.11).

Figure 7.11: Checklist

Skill	Checklist	Feedback
Attributes of shapes	❑ I can sort shapes. ❑ I can sort shapes based on specific attributes. ❑ I can explain my reasoning when I sort shapes.	
Calculating area	❑ I can define area. ❑ I can calculate the area of a rectangle by counting squares. ❑ I can calculate the area of a rectangle by using the area formula.	

(Continued)

Figure 7.II (Continued)

Skill	Checklist	Feedback
Calculating perimeter	❑ I can calculate the perimeter of a rectangle by counting. ❑ I can calculate the perimeter of a rectangle when I'm given all the side lengths. ❑ I can calculate the perimeter of a rectangle using addition and/or multiplication.	
Journaling	❑ I showed my thinking using pictures or numbers. ❑ I explained my thinking in words. ❑ My work is legible and organized. ❑ My final answer is circled and stated in a complete sentence with units.	

Annie, one of my third-graders, frequently needed extra support to access the curriculum. Due to a combination of factors, including a slow processing speed and some challenges with fine motor control, Annie struggled to access the curriculum, math especially, in previous grades. She struggled in third grade, too, and it turned out that deconstructing the standards helped me not only support Annie but also examine her skill set in terms of what she *could* do, as opposed to what she *couldn't* do.

Based on her pre-assessment for the unit, I knew that the concept of area was new to her. Likewise, from previous math assessments, I knew that she still struggled to calculate the products of single-digit numbers. Armed with this information, I was able to help her access the curriculum—in this case, calculating area and perimeter—by counting unit squares. In doing so, Annie was able to access the project and engage in valuable points of convergence where social learning occurred during the project, but also diverge and interact with the curriculum in her own way that worked within her current skill set. That's not to say that I completely ignored the fact that she was still working on multiplication. In fact, I frequently illustrated the relationship between counting the squares in groups (i.e., two groups of five) and multiplication to continue to push her toward third-grade mastery of calculating area using multiplication, both supporting her unique needs and trying to close the gap between her and her peers in an empathetic and compassionate way.

WHAT DO WE DO IF THEY ALREADY KNOW?

Conversely, there were a number of children who showed they needed something more. Take Amber, for example. In our minilessons around making some of the larger buildings, we pointed out that a great deal of buildings are not actually rectangles but are instead rectilinear (having only right angles) or even nonrectilinear (having varied angles). We encouraged students to challenge themselves by thinking differently about their buildings and trying to build some more "interesting" shapes. Amber did just that. She created a rectilinear shape still amounting to an area that met the constraints of the zoning laws (see Figure 7.12).

It's important to note, however, that this was not achieved by an individualized or even an accelerated curriculum. The curriculum was, instead, personalized through Amber's agency and enriched by her innate curiosity. It was as simple as giving her the option to explore other rectilinear shapes, making this choice available to her and others like her. Some weren't as successful as Amber. Some failed in their quest to make rectilinear shapes, but this allowed them to feel challenged in a different way, not only through an enriched curriculum but also with the emotional hurdles of trying something new and overcoming the feelings that accompany risk-taking and mistake-making—something many high achievers do not often feel.

Figure 7.12: Amber's Post Office

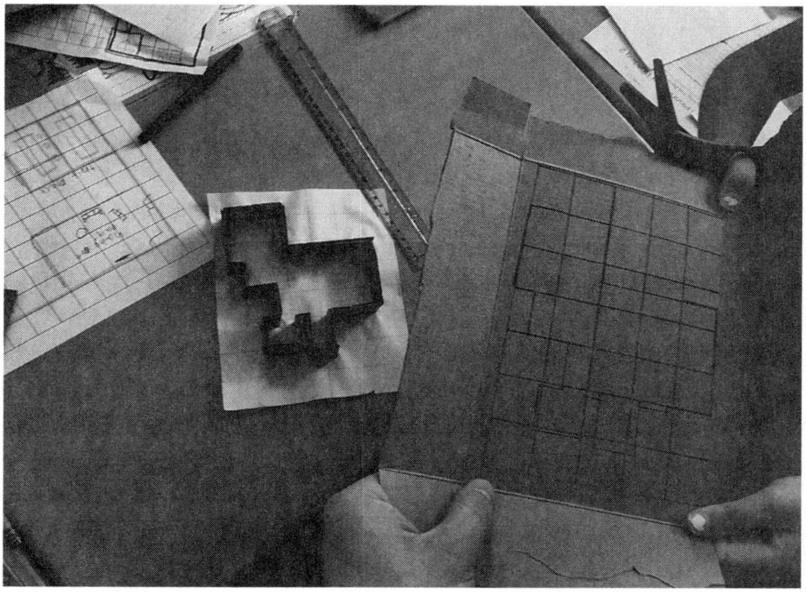

USING THE FLEXIBLE FRAME TO PERSONALIZE IN THREE DIMENSIONS

Without standards and the flexible frame, it would be impossible to support three-dimensional, humanized personalization. In the first dimension for personalized learning, we build the collective conscious of the classroom. It is here that we leverage the workshop model and use minilessons to have students converge around common provocations or projects, as we did with the urban planning project. The flexible frame supports the collective conscious because common experiences and a common language are necessary for building a collective conscious. In this case, the geometry and social studies standards—universal to the entire class—help them make meaning around common content and in a common enough way that's simultaneously universal but also able to be molded to meet their needs.

We find that the flexible frame also supports the second dimension, where we leverage the power of small-group experiences. This project-based experience was collaborative in nature, with groups of students working together to design a neighborhood. Again, if not for the common language and boundaries of the project—built on a limited number of standards—students would not have been able to collaborate so intimately. Without this structure, they would not have been able to engage in discourse about where to put certain buildings; productive conflicts and disagreements that sparked serendipitous social and emotional learning would not have emerged.

Most important, the flexible frame supported the third dimension of personalized learning, where we nurture the inner dialogues of our learners. Without a flexible frame fortified with productive constraints, we could not have engendered a learning environment where productive struggle and cognitive dissonance occurred frequently. Likewise, we could not have scaffolded autonomous decision-making and self-reflection. To nurture an inner dialogue sustainably in a diverse classroom of more than twenty learners, we needed a common medium, and in this case, the medium was the urban planning project and its clearly defined standards.

It's nearly impossible to divorce assessment from standards, which is why the next chapter on assessment is an extension of this flexible frame. When we use assessment not only to gauge learning but also to jump-start future learning, it supports the three dimensions of personalized learning, helping teachers continue to shape the collective conscious and nurture the inner dialogues of students—all based on the invaluable information they've collected about students and their learning.

CHAPTER EIGHT

HUMANIZING ASSESSMENT

I spent the first four years of my teaching career in the north suburbs of Chicago, tucked away on Chicago's North Shore. It was the ideal job for a brand-new teacher. During that time, I built the foundation of a career of professional learning. The school district supported me in earning my master's degree in language and literacy and achieving National Board Certification. Moreover, the board was committed to in-house professional development in curriculum design, technology integration, and assessment. It was within those first four years of teaching that I learned how to use backward design to create interdisciplinary units of instruction, leveraging both my team's knowledge and the work of Jay McTighe and Grant Wiggins to do so. Under the guidance of our grant writer and trailblazer, Katy Fatalleh, my team and I also explored technology integration, using emerging models like the SAMR Model to develop scalable and sustainable practices for using one-to-one iPads in the classroom. But perhaps some of the most important work we did was around assessment. Over the course of my four years there, I explored Chappuis's (2009) *Seven Strategies of Assessment for Learning*, as well as Robert Marzano's work with proficiency scales.

In a relatively short period of time, my assessment practices grew from tallying decontextualized point totals in an electronic gradebook to developing the foundations for a competency-based system that allowed my students and me to use assessment not only for learning but *as* learning. It laid the foundation for assessment practices that continue to develop to this day, almost ten years after I set foot in that classroom in the north suburbs of Chicago.

In my latter two years there, my teammates and I began to explore portfolio-based assessment. It began with paper portfolios, with collections of pre-assessments, post-assessments, and formative assessments, intended to tell the story of each child's unique learning journey. It eventually evolved into electronic portfolios, using apps like Evernote or Google Drive to increase efficiency through digitized organization. Much to our chagrin, it was hard to categorize their work and make it easily accessible. We even flirted with the idea of creating blog portfolios, where children would post work to a blog and tag it with a standard or learning objective to keep things organized.

That could be our million-dollar idea, I thought. *We could develop a portfolio where we tag standards, like you would with a hashtag on Twitter.*

Little did I know that wasn't *my* million-dollar idea; it was an idea that was already being developed some two thousand miles away in Silicon Valley. It wasn't long before I found myself there—in Silicon Valley—working for a personalized learning start-up company and network of microschools that was doing the very thing I'd imagined in my mind's eye. Their goal was to create individualized playlists of activities, intended to personalize learning for every child in the classroom. Each activity on the playlist, called a card, contained not only instructional materials but tags, as well. These tags related directly to learning objectives, developed in-house by the company. While admirable, their objectives related mostly to what they called "ways of being, thinking, and interacting," which we later found out were too nonspecific and amorphous to actually be used as assessment criteria.

That first year in Silicon Valley, my classroom was the second- through fifth-grade multiage classroom I mentioned in Chapter 3. To manage the complexity that accompanied that kind of developmental breadth, I used the Common Core (www.corestandards.org) to structure curriculum creation, building multiyear rubrics to aid in identifying student needs, despite the fact that few other educators were doing so (see Figure 8.1). Given age-level and anecdotal assessments, I used these rubrics to create and/or assign through the playlist activities that were directly correlated to their age and ability levels. At any given time, I could have as many activities going on in the classroom as I had students. In other classrooms within the network, teachers relied on Khan Academy to provide this kind of individualization. In this way, the playlist was already obsolete, because more sophisticated web-based technologies such as Khan Academy could provide this level of individualization by adapting to correct and incorrect answers, providing instructional videos along the way.

Figure 8.1: Multiyear Rubrics

Anchor	Skill	K	1	2	3	4	5
Understand place value	Base-ten system	Compose and decompose numbers 11 to 19 into tens and ones (K.NBT.1).	The two digits of a two-digit number represent the amount of tens and ones (1.NBT.2).	The four digits of a four-digit number represent the amount of thousands, hundreds, tens, and ones.	The digits of a number represent the amount of that place value (up through the billions).	Recognize in multi-digit whole numbers that one place represents ten times what it represents in the place to its right (4.NBT.1).	Recognize in multi-digit numbers that a digit in one place represents ten times as much as what it represents in the place to its right and one tenth of what it represents in the place to its left (5.NBT.1).
	Extended math facts			Use extended math facts to add and subtract numbers ending in repeated zeros within 1,000.	Use extended math facts to multiply numbers ending in zero.	Use extended math facts to calculate products ending in repeated zeros within 1,000,000.	Use whole number exponents to denote powers of ten and explain the patterns in the number of zeros or decimal places when multiplying or dividing (5.NBT.2).
	Read and write numbers	When counting objects and writing objects, say the number names in the standard order, pairing each object with one and only one number name and each number name with one and only one object through 100.	Count to 120, starting at any number less than 120. In this range, read and write numerals and represent a number of objects with a written numeral.	Read and write numbers to 1,000 using base-ten numerals, number names, and expanded form (2.NBT.3).	Read and write numbers to 1,000,000 using base-ten numerals, number names, and expanded form, including those with placeholders.	Read and write multi-digit whole numbers using base-ten numerals, number names, and expanded form (4.NBT.2a).	Read and write decimals to the thousandth place using base-ten numerals, number names, exponential notation, and expanded form (5.NBT.3a).
	Compare and order numbers in base ten	Identify and compare whether the number of objects in one group is greater than, less than, or equal to the number of objects in another group (e.g., by using matching and counting strategies).	Compare two two-digit numbers based on meanings of the tens and ones, recording the results of comparisons with the symbols >, =, and <.	Compare two three-digit whole numbers based on place value using >, <, or = (2.NBT.4).	Compare six-digit whole numbers based on place value using >, <, or =.	Compare two multi-digit whole numbers based on meaning of the digits using >, <, or = (4.NBT.2b).	Compare decimals to the thousandth place based on meanings of symbols using >, <, or = (5.NBT.3b).
	Rounding				Use place value and "1/2 concept" to round whole numbers to nearest 10 or 100 (3.NBT.1).	Use place value to round multi-digit whole numbers to any place (4.NBT.3).	Use place value to round decimals to any place (5.NBT.4).

Source: Figure 8.1 is adapted from the Common Core State Standards: www.corestandards.org

I, too, eventually succumbed to this method of individualizing. Using my rubrics and creating activities on my own became unsustainable. My choice to pivot to Khan Academy was a last-ditch effort to make sure each of my students was getting what they needed in the classroom. But I saw what it did to them. They became addicted to the point totals and digital badges that come with technologies such as those. They measured their growth and worth in terms of levels and content consumption. It didn't prompt them to look internally, to see math as a language, or to work through obstacles with persistence. If anything, it only contributed to a fixed mathematical mindset, grounded solely in a pervasive and toxic achievement culture that is more damaging to competency in mathematics than it is supportive.

The following year, I was determined to do it differently. This time, it would be with a transitional kindergarten through first grade multiage class in Palo Alto. It was that year that I took a more embodied approach to personalization, learning from the prior year's mistakes. I leveraged the workshop model, allowing children to converge around common topics and provocations, using small-group and individual conferencing to make learning more intimate and personal.

But I was still intent on capturing as much learning as I could. I leveraged the playlist tool that year not to individualize content but, instead, to curate a learning narrative, mostly through photos of student work. The hardest part about working with primary-age children (preschool through second grade) is navigating their emerging communication abilities. Without fully developed reading, writing, and speaking skills, collecting assessment data and providing feedback is tricky. So much of it needs to be delivered verbally, since few of them can read well enough to receive feedback in that manner. But that didn't stop me from doing a lot of assessment work behind the scenes.

I'd spend hours before school, after school, and in my prep periods making sure I logged pictures of their work in each playlist card. This allowed me to assess learning against the aforementioned tags that were also in each card. For some assignments, I'd tag upward of ten to fifteen learning objectives because I thought I could meaningfully assess their work if I did so. This was especially true of writing, where one written piece lent itself to assessing coherence of ideas, letter formation, and myriad language conventions that I thought needed to be mastered over the course of kindergarten and first grade.

In short, this type of documentation was arduous and unsustainable. Just imagine documenting the work they produce in writing workshop alone over the course of a given week. Not only is it time-consuming to view each sample and consider next instructional steps; it's even more time-consuming to then formally document and assess against ten to fifteen learning objectives for each child. About halfway through the school year, I became curious about just how many assessments I'd entered.

I reached out to one of the technologists who had access to all the data we'd entered. She shared a spreadsheet with me that documented each learning objective I'd assessed so far that year. It turned out that more than seven thousand rows in that spreadsheet had assessment data, meaning I'd assessed seven thousand learning objectives over the course of about four months.

Seven thousand.

I probably don't have to tell you that this wasn't worth the labor. I didn't feel as though I was entering data to better my practice or improve learning experiences for my students. Quite the opposite actually: I felt that I was entering the data to pander to parents and my superiors. I was desperate for their approval—desperate to prove to them that I was doing a good job, desperate to prove that I was a *good enough* teacher and employee. In reality, entering data to this degree wasn't helping my children reflect on their work or step into their agency; it was instead pulling me away from what was truly important in the classroom. The time I was using before school, after school, and during my prep periods to enter data could have been used far more effectively. I could have been researching and booking more fun field trips for my kids. I could have interacted more with my colleagues or spent time planning engaging projects. I could have allowed myself to take a break, to leave my work at school, and to take care of myself instead of bringing so much work with me everywhere.

While I refused to admit it at the time, the workload was burning me out and dehumanizing my practice. I was so exhausted and distracted by excess work that was only adding counterproductive complexity. It caused me to turn toward a machine far more than I was turning toward human beings and human experiences.

Clearly, at that point I wasn't familiar with the inverted U. I wasn't aware that it was, in fact, possible to collect too much data on our children and overdocument, even if it was happening behind the scenes. Little did I know I was falling victim to the seductive desire to control and predict all student learning in my classroom through overdocumentation (see Figure 8.2).

Figure 8.2: Inverted U for Data Collection

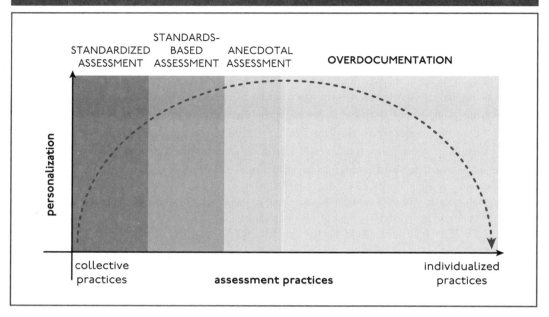

© Paul Emerich France, 2018 www.paulemerich.com, Twitter: @paul_emerich

It took me almost two years at the personalized learning school in Silicon Valley to realize that we had reduced personalization to overdocumentation, overlooking relationships, school culture, and the need for human connection, none of which could be captured in the space behind our screens. We forgot that our school system was a human system, not a technological one. We forgot that learning was the never-ending evolution of a story, with each chapter building on the preceding ones to create a lifelong narrative for learning.

Our hypothesis, instead, was that the more data we had in our system, the more developed the portrait of the learner would be, allowing technology to do the work of personalizing on our behalf. This charge for gathering as much data as possible had us using technology in largely unproductive ways. In addition to assessment practices that had us turning toward computers and away from our students, we had video cameras taping every corner of the classroom and every moment of the school day; later, there were even talks of facial recognition and reading emotions through cameras, and discussions of using artificial intelligence (AI) to help us assess our students.

The mere thought that AI should replace some of the jobs teachers do—even if it was *possible*—was utterly offensive. After all, teaching is so much more than simply looking at assessment data, coming up with a diagnosis, and suggesting a new activity. It's a matter of engaging in the *process* of assessing. It's a matter of considering context, empathizing with a child, and sensing their misconceptions. It's a matter of knowing and appreciating students unconditionally for their idiosyncrasies, strengths, and obstacles. This is something I'd never want a robot to do, even if it could.

I ended that year exhausted again but grateful for having learned a valuable lesson: it's not the product of assessment that is inherently meaningful for educators, students, and parents alike. It is instead the *process* of assessing that is inherently meaningful and personal. By engaging in the process, we allow time for reflection—to consider where we were, to express pride and gratitude for how far we've come, and to develop a vision for the future. This is the true purpose and value of assessment in the classroom. It's equally as emotional as it is concrete and physical. And our assessment practices need to mirror this.

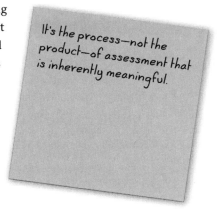

It's the process—not the product—of assessment that is inherently meaningful.

I started to wonder about the origin of these flawed hypotheses on which our company was built. I was perplexed at how we'd lost sight of the importance of human connection, a sense of belonging, and the *people* who made up this intricate system. Most of all, I was puzzled by how *I'd* lost this and become a part of a vision for teaching and learning that was so dehumanizing. How could we have gotten to a place where evidence-based assessment and data-driven instruction had turned into documenting every move our children made?

Shortly thereafter, it dawned on me that I'd been blind to education's pervasive culture of shame and fear. There were so many educators like me, on a quest to overdocument learning experiences in the classroom in an effort to prove something—to prove to superiors, parents, or maybe even themselves that they were *enough*.

CULTURES OF SHAME AND FEAR

It was still my second year in Silicon Valley, a few months before I reached out to the engineer and asked to see my seven thousand assessments. Jax's mom sat across from me in a conference room, her face sprinkled with the redness that comes only with anger and anxiety.

"Well," she said to me sharply, "if he were in public school, this would be a *really* big problem. According to Reading Recovery, he should be getting *at least* three half hours of one-to-one reading intervention from a reading specialist each week in order to catch up."

She wasn't *wrong*, per se, but she also wasn't seeing the whole picture. It's true that Jax was reading slightly behind grade level, and as a result, I was doing my best to work with him on building his phonological awareness and decoding skills, since that seemed to be his primary need.

However, by that point in the school year, Jax had missed almost 25 percent of class time for various reasons. Jax also struggled to develop strong reading routines—both in school and at home. Surely his truancy was not helping him overcome this obstacle. He was not a persistent reader and frequently struggled with book selection, likely a product of an inconsistent school routine and a permissive style of parenting that allowed him to rule the roost.

I attempted to convey some of this to his mother, specifically with regard to his reading habits, his attendance, and how strong reading routines would help him step into his agency and autonomy as a reader. Shortly thereafter, the conversation pivoted; her tone became harsher with every word she spoke.

"Well," she scoffed, "these author lists you sent me weren't any help at all."

She threw them in front of me, the papers rotating forcefully on the table. I had sent these lists to her a few weeks prior to help her find some more books for her home library. Stunned, I sat and continued to absorb her disrespectful and combative words. The more she spoke, the clearer it became to me that I was simply a container for her anger and frustration—as so many educators are. She assumed she was in a position of power—that her tuition dollars would motivate me to cave to her requests and tell her that she was correct. She was a clear and concrete manifestation of the degree to which schools and schooling had become so dehumanized. There she was, sitting in front of me, feeling as though she could make demands, speak disrespectfully, and otherwise dehumanize another human being, all because she believed she was financially entitled to it. I knew I had to change the course of the conversation and take a different approach. I had to appeal to and advocate for the humanity that existed within both of us.

> When in a disagreement, sometimes the only common ground two people can find is their humanity.

"Listen," I said to her, realizing that in just minutes I would need to go and start morning meeting, "I want you to know that we really care about your son. We really care about his learning, and we really, truly are doing everything we can to help him to the best of our ability. I think your feedback about documenting our reading conferences better and trying to include parent volunteers is great. I also appreciated your suggestion on starting the take-home book program. So many families have benefited from that."

I paused, took a deep breath, and then continued with the hard part.

"I have to tell you, though, that sometimes when you speak to me, or when you send me e-mails, I feel like you aren't assuming positive intent. From where I sit, it feels like you don't think we are trying our best to help Jax become a better reader. But I want you to know, we really care, and we really are trying our best. I think, in order for us to move forward and to help him, we must assume positive intent; we need to work together and be partners in this. I'm not sure we can move forward until we can do that."

She looked at me, speechless. I could tell that my words, honest, respectful, and powerful, had stopped her in her tracks. They reflected back to her the way I was perceiving her. Her eyes welled up with tears, and she blinked quickly to combat the war they were waging on her eyelids.

"I'm so sorry, Paul," she said to me. "I never ever wanted to make you feel that way."

I couldn't believe it, but it turned out that by leading with vulnerability, I was able to diffuse our conflict and start us down a road to understanding. We both stood up from the table, still a bit shaken. We looked at each other, and we even hugged. Even though I was still upset, I knew that it wasn't entirely her fault. She was a victim of the environment in which she'd grown up and lived: one that perpetuates a culture of fear and shame in schools, one that assumes we must micromanage every step of the way, one that assumes cold, hard academic data tell the whole story of personalization.

Jax's mom is not alone. All teachers have stories of parent interactions like this: stories where parents come in, guns blazing, ready to blame, shame, and demonize teachers for not doing enough—for not *being* enough—when in reality, we teachers are not powerful enough to singlehandedly make or break a child's education. It takes a village.

The reality is this: the village is dysfunctional. This village in which all of us play a role is in desperate need of systemic and cultural reform. It's in need of mindful individuals, ready to confront their own bias, privilege, and upbringing, ready to question why the education system is the way it is and how we got to this place where we blame, shame, and demonize teachers and the teaching profession. It will require individuals to overcome their shame and fear—to lead with vulnerability and a whole heart, as Brené Brown would tell us. But to do so, it's incredibly important we go back in time and understand where this fear, shame, and blame originated. Once we deconstruct this and name our fear and shame, we can take steps toward overcoming it.

THE ORIGIN OF FEAR AND SHAME

"Comparison kills joy," says Brené Brown (2010a). Comparison is, in fact, a clear symptom of shame—of not feeling like we're enough. We compare to prove that we're better than one another, and too often, we use assessment for this: to compare students with one another, proliferating a silent culture of fear and shame. The American way of thinking about education is responsible for this. We live in a society grounded in rugged individualism, self-interest, and competition. It is the capitalist way, and our assessment practices reflect this.

In 1983, the Reagan administration published *A Nation at Risk*, an incendiary initiative intended to reform the educational system in our country due to deficits in test scores and in response to nearly forty years of international competition fueled by World War II, the Space Race, and the Cold War. In retrospect, it's clear that fear and shame were palpable at this time:

> The risk is not only that the Japanese make automobiles more efficiently than Americans and have government subsidies for development and export. It is not just that the South Koreans recently built the world's most efficient steel mill, or that American machine tools, once the pride of the world, are being displaced by German products. It is also that these developments signify a redistribution of trained capability throughout the globe. . . . If only to keep and improve on the slim competitive edge we still retain in world markets, we must dedicate ourselves to the reform of our educational system for the benefit of all—old and young alike, affluent and poor, majority and minority. Learning is the indispensable investment required for success in the "information age" we are entering. (National Commission on Excellence in Education, 1983)

Not only does *A Nation at Risk* mention the achievements of other countries specifically, it also uses the words "competitive edge" to persuade Americans into supporting this new era of education focused on assessment and accountability. While the document later goes on to address domestic concerns, as well, such as "the chance [for all] to participate fully in national life," the motivation for the creation of this initiative seems overwhelmingly influenced by an obsession with exceptionalism.

Constant comparison and an obsession with exceptionalism are symptomatic of something that lies deep beneath test scores, technological innovation, and economics. They're symptomatic of unworthiness, a fear of failure, and a lack of self-compassion and vulnerability within American culture. Education's culture of fear has bred this into all of us. It tempts us to seek as much control as possible, all for the sake of making the uncertain certain. By overdocumenting and capturing as much data as possible, we can guard ourselves from imperfection and ensure that we'll no longer have to grapple with the uncertainty and vulnerability that come with educating the future of our society. It makes us think that we—and our kids—will be safe.

"I hate vulnerability," Brown (2010b) says in her now famous TED Talk on shame and vulnerability. "And so I thought, this is my chance to beat it back with my measuring stick. I'm going in, I'm going to figure this stuff out, I'm going to spend a year, I'm going to totally deconstruct shame, I'm going to understand how vulnerability works, and I'm going to outsmart it."

As she goes on to say in her TED Talk, it didn't work out as she had originally hoped. Through an immense amount of qualitative research around shame and vulnerability, Brown discovered that the secret to conquering shame was to live with vulnerability. It was, in fact, to live and lead with a "whole heart," to stop trying to control and predict, and to find solace in a strengthened sense of belonging and worthiness. She called people who were able to do this the "wholehearted":

> They fully embraced vulnerability. They believed that what made them vulnerable made them beautiful. They didn't talk about vulnerability being comfortable, nor did they really talk about it being excruciating—as I had heard it earlier in the shame interviewing. They just talked about it being necessary. They talked about the willingness to say I love you first, the willingness to do something where there are no guarantees, the willingness to breathe through waiting for the doctor to call after your mammogram, the willingness to invest in a relationship that may or may not work out. They thought this was fundamental.

> I personally thought it was betrayal. I could not believe I had pledged allegiance to research, where our job—you know, the definition of research is to control and predict, to study phenomena for the explicit reason to control and predict. And now my mission to control and predict had turned up the answer that the way to live is with vulnerability and to stop controlling and predicting.

The education system, as it currently stands, is not a place where we can embrace our vulnerabilities; it is not a place where we can help all individuals find a sense of worthiness; it is not a place where we can prioritize a sense of belonging. It is instead a place where we attempt to control and predict outcomes, where we try to promote perfectionism. This has resulted in school cultures that crush pedagogical innovation and instructional creativity. It's caused teachers to turn to curriculum manuals and step-by-step guides for teaching. While it's true that many of the metrics we've put in place have exacerbated these cultures of fear and shame, we must open our eyes to the fact that an American culture that values competition, self-interest, and exceptionalism is the place where this all originates.

> We must expand our perception of the meaning behind assessment.

The first step in fixing this problem is enhancing our awareness and expanding our perception of what *assessment* truly means. Once we are more aware of the factors at play, we can slowly shift our conscious. We can cultivate awareness around the very metrics and policies we currently have in place and see how they are, in fact, destroying the education system from the inside out.

The reality is this: initiatives like *A Nation at Risk*—as well as the Goals 2000 campaign that trailed behind, or even the No Child Left Behind era of the early twenty-first century—have created such a significant change in the culture of education that these measures have actually distorted the original processes that standardized assessment is intended to monitor. It's not supposed to monitor our competition with other countries; it's supposed to monitor the health of an institution critical in supporting a democracy that is under attack. And it's not currently doing that.

CAMPBELL'S LAW

> Campbell's Law states that "the more any quantitative social indicator (or even some qualitative indicator) is used for social decision-making, the more subject it will be to corruption pressures and the more apt it will be to distort and corrupt the social processes it is intended to monitor."

Donald T. Campbell was a psychologist and social scientist known for his contributions to research methodology. Campbell's Law, developed in 1976, is well-known in the research and education communities. It states that "the more any quantitative social indicator (or even some qualitative indicator) is used for social decision-making, the more subject it will be to corruption pressures and the more apt it will be to distort and corrupt the social processes it is intended to monitor" (Campbell, 1979).

I liken Campbell's Law to treating a fever. One of the ways to get rid of a fever is to take a fever reducer like acetaminophen or ibuprofen. While it may lower one's body temperature, many doctors advise against this because it's not curing the underlying ailment. It's curing only a symptom—an indicator of the ailment.

The rise in an individual's body temperature is usually caused by an infection or virus. Until the infection or virus is eradicated, the fever will continue to spike. What's truly necessary in this situation is to treat the infection itself. By treating only the fever, we run the risk of worsening the ailment or even spreading it to others.

This is analogous to what's happening in education today, both publicly and privately. The metrics we have in place are incomplete and insufficient, and in some cases, these metrics are being misused and worsening pedagogy. Not only does an overemphasis on standardized assessment promote test-centric practices that call for rote memorization and regurgitation; it treats only the symptoms of a virus that has been ailing our school system for decades.

It's now widely accepted that these assessments do more than promote test-centric practices; their results also favor students born to White and/ or affluent parents. Aside from the implicit biases within the assessments themselves, schools that generally serve low-income populations and communities of color are disproportionately under-resourced. They frequently cling to policies and practices that inflict harm on marginalized children over many generations, as opposed to instilling within them the skills and competencies that will allow them to be problem-solvers and otherwise build strong learning habits that move them from dependence to independence (Hammond, 2014). In contrast, parents of privileged children typically have mastered the art of "playing the system." Not only do they have the economic means to provide extra support to their children, but they are able to derive success from teaching their children how to play by the inequitable rules of an education system. As a result, standardized assessments end up revealing more about the degree to which a child can use their privilege to play by the rules than about what they're actually learning at school.

Too often, standardized assessments tell us more about privilege and affluence than they do about academic achievement.

These assessment measures perpetuate a dangerous cycle of oppression and privilege by treating only the symptoms of "failing" schools. When test scores are low, this symptom is treated with test preparation and the standardization of pedagogy, similar to how one might treat a fever with a fever reducer, all the while ignoring the fact that many children in low-income communities with underperforming schools are likely no better set up for an equitable adult life than they were before. Some may even be worse off, becoming dependent, disengaged, and turned off to education entirely. The solution is to continue teaching and assessing in a standards-based manner but to do so in a way that is culturally responsive, counteracting and dismantling the many barriers—related to institutional racism, classism, and discrimination—that prevent many low-income students and students of color from accessing an equitable education.

"Our schools cannot be improved if we ignore the disadvantages associated with poverty that affect children's ability to learn. Children who have grown up in poverty need extra resources, including preschool and medical care," says education historian Diane Ravitch (2016) in *The Death and Life of the Great American School System*. In her book, she criticizes privatization initiatives such as charter schools and school choice, and lambasts high-stakes testing, the general metric by which the success of any given school is measured.

"Accountability makes no sense when it undermines the larger goals of education," she continues, precisely identifying the role high-stakes testing plays as the primary wellness metric for our schools. She even calls on Campbell's Law to support her stance, reinforcing the idea that standardized assessment is a poor barometer for the true success of a school—setting many schools and communities up for failure, perpetuating cycles of privilege, and committing us to the proliferation of inequity.

> "Accountability makes no sense when it undermines the larger goals of education."
> —Diane Ravitch

Conversely, affluent schools are able to tout their success much more easily. While they may experience periods of academic challenges or low achievement, more often than not children in affluent, predominantly White settings come to school with the advantages of privilege. Some of the most commonly cited advantages include early exposure to literacy and other experiences to build a schema that helps them play by the rules of a White supremacist school system.

Conversely, in under-resourced schools that serve predominantly low-income populations and students of color, while there are many dedicated teachers who care deeply for their children, they are fighting the ripple effects of systemic oppression. Parents need to work multiple jobs just to make ends meet; they have little to no access to health care; they struggle to support children academically at home. As a result, many come to school with a different set of skills, many of which don't translate directly into a system that was built in the image of affluent White folks. These skills are *assets*. In fact, they already possess some of the very skills that are valued in a twenty-first century education—skills like bilingualism and resilience. They carry rich "funds of knowledge" (Moll, Amanti, Neff, & Gonzalez, 1992) and may very well be better equipped to navigate day-to-day challenges than are their affluent counterparts and to adapt to a changing modern society. Culturally biased standardized assessments were never designed to measure such strengths, nor are they a valid indicator of a child's potential.

Oftentimes, the push for personalization comes with an intention to reform a broken system. But it's important to note that this push for technology-driven personalization arose from flawed metrics and a biased lens, drawing on low test scores as evidence of the inefficacy of a given school system. In response, education technology companies are building tools simply to raise test scores, when in reality, the test scores themselves are not the problem but, instead, only a symptom of a greater systemic ailment.

Thought leaders in education technology—who are predominantly affluent White men—examine education through a privileged lens. The toxic, cyclical nature of Campbell's Law coupled with this privileged lens of technology's elite has us convinced that the perceived problems related to student achievement can be solved by pairing the right content with the right child, similar to how an assembly line connects the right pieces at the right time.

But teachers know better than to embrace a reductive metaphor that likens teaching and learning to a machine. Instead, we know that teaching and learning are naturalistic, emergent processes that require mindful attention and care, much like tending to a garden. Sure, there are time-tested rules for nurturing a garden, but ultimately, it requires careful attention based on the many variables that can affect its tiny ecosystem. Its care cannot be reduced to reliable inputs and outputs, and likewise, the overall success of the garden cannot be distilled into the number of plants grown or the amount of vegetables produced by harvest.

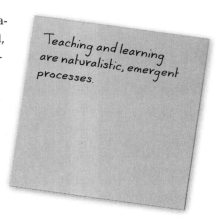

Teaching and learning are naturalistic, emergent processes.

To actualize a vision for democratic education, we must contextualize the metrics through which we measure our schools and change the process by which we analyze academic data. Further, we must change the metaphors we use to understand the complexities of education. Doing so will change our conceptualization of the system, ultimately resulting in a change in our actions. We must expand our perception of what should be measured in schools—by contextualizing academic data with other more nuanced types of data—to make Campbell's Law work in our favor. Should we change our success metrics, then we will be able to change the practices that help us reach them.

What if we found a way to measure connectedness and sense of belonging? What if we found a way to measure inclusivity and equity? What if we found a way to measure the "funds of knowledge" that each of our children bring into the classroom so we might leverage those as assets for future personal growth? These are the metrics that humanize learning and help us better understand how our children, our teachers, and our families *experience* school. If children, families, and educators feel seen, heard, valued, and understood for the assets they bring to a school, the experience will not only feel personalized; it will *be* inherently personalized.

Personalization is a *feeling* more than anything else; it's a matter of perception. To build schools that *feel* personalized, all must be included, and all must feel as though they belong. We can achieve this only if we let go of the shame and fear that cause us to make dehumanizing decisions around assessment collection and curriculum design. Instead, we must build environments where we embrace the uncertainty of the future, remain present in the joy that comes through connecting with one another, and let go of who we think we *should* be as a school system.

"The people who have a strong sense of love and belonging believe they're worthy of love and belonging," Dr. Brown (2010b) tells us. While it's important to make sure our kids are learning to read, to write, and to compute, and while it's important that they are being immersed in a healthy balance of all the sciences, it should not be for the purpose of competition; it should not be for the purpose of getting a job that may or may not exist in the years between now and when they graduate from college. Learning each of these literacies is akin to learning languages. As a result, personalized pedagogy entails teaching children how to connect, communicate, and interact with the world around them. It's instilling within them a sense of belonging to the world through being open to the lessons it has to teach us—becoming one with it. And to do so, they must speak the languages the world has to offer.

The true purpose of education is to expand our perception of what it means to be human and, ultimately, to use this expanded perception to connect to, engage with, and understand the world around us. We should gauge our personalization efforts through these measures, first and foremost, with all other quantitative measures coming second. It's true that standardized and standards-based assessments still have a place in this framework for humanized personalization, so long as we're using them in a manner that is equitable, just, and inclusive.

TRIANGULATING HUMANIZED ASSESSMENT

It's tempting, at first, to pit humanized personalization against the very notion of assessment. The former feels vulnerable and messy, while the latter feels cold and *impersonal*. But it's important to remember that tensions such as these are valuable. They help us see the nuances in education and use them to our benefit.

The negative connotation that accompanies *assessment* and *data* is born from years and years of misusing assessment. In actuality, teachers have always used assessment and data to better understand their students; all human beings use assessment and data to understand *one another*. We are constantly evaluating the behaviors of others, exchanging feedback, and receiving advice on how to grow.

When we humanize assessment, we look for the *story*. And we cannot tell this story with a one-dimensional view. Too many schools emphasize only standardized assessment data, and while these data can be helpful, they need to be contextualized by other data. Triangulating our data contextualizes standardized assessment data and puts the children in the center of our intentions for assessment, in an effort to get to know them better and help them tell their stories. Triangulation also helps us embrace the tensions that exist between individualism and collectivism—between subjectivity and objectivity.

To triangulate effectively, I recommend thinking of the following three assessment types as the three vertices of your assessment triangle: standardized assessments, standards-based assessments, and anecdotal assessments. All three can help us gain an understanding of both the individual and the collective; likewise, by using all three in partnership, we allow ourselves to leverage the objective benefits of statistically valid and reliable assessments, meanwhile creating space for the subjectivity of humanity (see Figure 8.3).

Figure 8.3: Triangulating Humanized Assessment

STANDARDIZED
SERVE AS A VALID AND RELIABLE PROVOCATION, SURFACING POTENTIAL STRENGTHS AND CHALLENGES OF INDIVIDUALS AND GROUPS OF STUDENTS.

STANDARDS-BASED
ALLOW ASSESSMENT TO OCCUR ON A REGULAR BASIS AND WITH A NARROWED SCOPE, INFORMING INSTRUCTION THROUGH FORMATIVE AND SUMMATIVE ASSESSMENTS.

THE INNER DIALOGUE
BY STRUCTURING ASSESSMENTS WITH VALID AND RELIABLE MEASURES AND ENACTING ASSESSMENT PROTOCOLS WITH FIDELITY, THEY SERVE AS A MEDIUM FOR UNEARTHING A CHILD'S INNER DIALOGUE THROUGH ANECDOTAL ASSESSMENT.

WHEN WE UNDERSTAND A CHILD'S INNER DIALOGUE, WE UNDERSTAND BARRIERS RELATED TO EXECUTIVE FUNCTIONING, ENGAGEMENT, AND MOTIVATION.

THE FIRST VERTEX: STANDARDIZED MEASURES

Teachers are sentient human beings, and as a result, we are susceptible to bias. I've met countless teachers, certain that their children are reading proficiently, who realize later that their assessment was based on none other than a flawed perception of the children and their work.

It's not out of malice or ill intent. It's because we are oftentimes unaware of our own biases, and more often, we subconsciously seek information that confirms our biases. We are, after all, human. As a result, it's imperative that we use standardized measures and protocols for benchmark assessments in our classrooms. If we do not use standardized measures to gauge academic achievement, our assessment is too subject to our own subconscious and subjective manipulation. It's like a science experiment. If any of the variables in the assessment are tampered with, it distorts the evidence, entirely undermining the purpose of conducting assessment in the first place.

I can feel it as I write these words—that palpable tension between standardized assessment and humanizing learning. But we must remember that if we embrace the tension, we find ways to balance standardization and personalization, knowing very well that it's not the data themselves that dehumanize a learning environment; it's how we *respond* to the data that either humanizes or dehumanizes a learning environment.

Standardized assessments provide a bird's-eye view of the classroom, shedding light on strengths and challenges even before starting your first unit, and using assessments *as* an indicator of previous learning. They allow us to be curious, to learn about school-wide gaps in achievement, and to propose new ways for addressing the strengths or challenges these assessments surface.

For example, one year I saw that my students' scores in language conventions and writing mechanics from the year prior were low. This showed in their day-to-day work, too. Knowing that language conventions are critical to developing writing fluency and proficiency, I found engaging and authentic ways to work on this. I did not submit to Campbell's Law and engage my students in rigorous test preparation; I found creative ways to make this relevant, such as putting spelling and grammatical mistakes into my morning messages or engaging them in structured word inquiry to get them curious about words. It just so happened that these consistent strategies impacted my students' test scores positively by the end of the year, but if they hadn't, it wouldn't have been a reason to fall into test preparation or test-centric practices; it simply would have been an opportunity to ask why and reflect further on my practice.

Standardized measures can also be a first clue that other factors might be hindering an individual child's ability to learn in school—factors such as learning disabilities or challenges with mental health. Progressive educators are notorious for ignoring standardized measures for fear that these assessments pigeonhole children, but as we learned in the previous chapter, neglecting to establish standards and standardized measures risks allowing children to fall through the cracks.

It's important to note that there are two types of standardized measures: *criterion-referenced* standardized measures and *norm-referenced* ones. Criterion-referenced standardized measures allow educators to assess achievement as compared with benchmarks for proficiency at a given developmental level. Norm-referenced measures, on the other hand, rank children from highest achieving to lowest achieving, generally through percentile ranks.

> *Criterion-referenced assessments measure achievement against developmental criteria; norm-referenced assessments compare and rank students using percentiles.*

I recommend setting up a relatively watertight framework of *criterion-referenced assessments* that provide specific and qualitative insight into what children know and are able to do. I prefer criterion-referenced assessments because they do not entail comparing individual students or putting them in competition with one another. The very nature of a criterion-referenced assessment establishes qualitative criteria for proficiency. These qualitative criteria are not there to pit kids against one another and make them fight for a top ranking but instead to provide a reference point against which educators can see if a child is at risk academically.

Using standardized assessment can be humanizing—so long as we use it in a way that puts the child's humanity first. Standardized assessments *must* be acknowledged for their flaws, including their implicit biases against low-income folks and students of color. All who use standardized assessment for instructional decision-making must use it as only one data point, intended to provide a reference from which we can gauge *potential* strengths or obstacles.

> *We must use assessment in a way that puts the child's humanity first.*

THE SECOND VERTEX: STANDARDS-BASED MEASURES

McTighe and Wiggins's (1998) method for curriculum design entails three stages: (1) identify desired results, (2) build methods for collecting evidence, and (3) establish a learning plan. Coincidentally, these steps align nicely with the four professional learning community questions we covered in Chapter 7 (DuFour, DuFour,

Eaker, & Many, 2010). The first question beckons us to identify what children should know and be able to do—the desired results. The second question asks us how we'll know when children have reached the desired results, imploring us to collect evidence of learning along the way that aligns with the standards we've chosen for a unit of instruction.

Backward design entails three phases: (1) identify desired results, (2) establish assessment criteria, and (3) create a learning plan.

Standardized assessments should be used only as a provocation—an initial data point that beckons us to ask more questions about the child.

The desired results are so critical because they fortify the flexible frame. Without them, personalized, humanized, and autonomous learning will crumble because it becomes very challenging to gauge progress. Sure, you may have standardized benchmark assessments, but using just these allows you to assess children formally only about three times per year. Furthermore, the scope of a standardized assessment is very broad, providing educators with a "mile-wide-inch-deep" snapshot into current proficiency. Standardized assessments are also subject to bias and a great deal of human error, which is why they should be used only as a provocation—an initial data point that beckons us to ask more questions about the child.

By building standards-based summative pre- and post-assessments for the unit, educators may gather more meaningful information on current levels of proficiency, providing data that allow them to gauge progress over smaller periods of time and within a narrower scope. By choosing only a handful of standards that align with your unit, the process of standards-based assessment becomes sustainable, allowing you to leverage *assessment for learning*. This can inform whole-group learning experiences and also help educators create small-group experiences targeting specific skills.

A CLOSER LOOK

STANDARDS-BASED OR COMPETENCY-BASED ASSESSMENT?

Competency-based assessment is yet another buzzword in the personalized learning world. While the word *competency* has a softer connotation than *standard*, the two exist in a mutualistic relationship. After all, *standard* comes from the Old English *standan*, meaning "make or be firm," while *competent* is composed of *com-*, meaning "together or with," and the base *pet*, meaning "to rush, to fly." If anything, after analyzing the etymologies of both words, *standard* has a supportive connotation, unearthing its intention to add structure. *Competent* and *competency*, on the other hand, are relatives of the words *compete* and *competition*, connoting something less desirable.

Competencies and standards really aren't that different, though. They are both statements encompassing what students should know and be able to do. The key differences are threefold:

1. Standards are finite in nature, their breadth smaller than that of a competency. They tend to focus more on the specific bits of knowledge and skill.

2. Standards connote a smaller time frame, partially due to their finite nature but also due to the fact that they are often assigned to a grade level.

3. Competencies tend to share implications for process and implicitly reveal their concomitance with other competencies.

The nuance here is interesting, but at a certain point, the debate between *standard* and *competency* becomes unproductive and semantic. It is, however, clear that it would be very challenging to build a competency-based system for assessment without discrete and finite standards. Likewise, it would be hard to see the whole child without seeing the connections between standards, which is oftentimes what competencies bring us. It seems, then, as though we may just need both.

A 2017 RAND Corporation study showed that one of teachers' biggest hurdles when trying to implement personalized learning was navigating competency-based progressions, ensuring both content coverage and acceptable levels of proficiency in relation to grade level (Pane et al., 2017). Here are some of the questions I often get from teachers who are new to the concept of standards-based measures or competency-based progressions.

Effective curriculum design entails constantly toggling between short-term and long-term vision, as well as between the collective and the individual. To start the year, I map out all the topics and standards that will provide a well-rounded education (see Figure 8.4). Doing so not only helps pace out the year; it also helps prioritize standards. In my first two years of teaching, we didn't do this work ahead of time. Instead, we followed a curriculum manual and attempted to get through as much as we could. Inevitably, we left out critical topics.

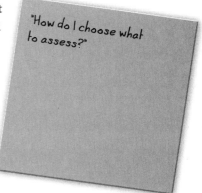

"How do I choose what to assess?"

In Figure 8.5, you'll see an example of a curriculum map my team and I made at the start of our first year working together.

Figure 8.4: Curriculum Map Design Process

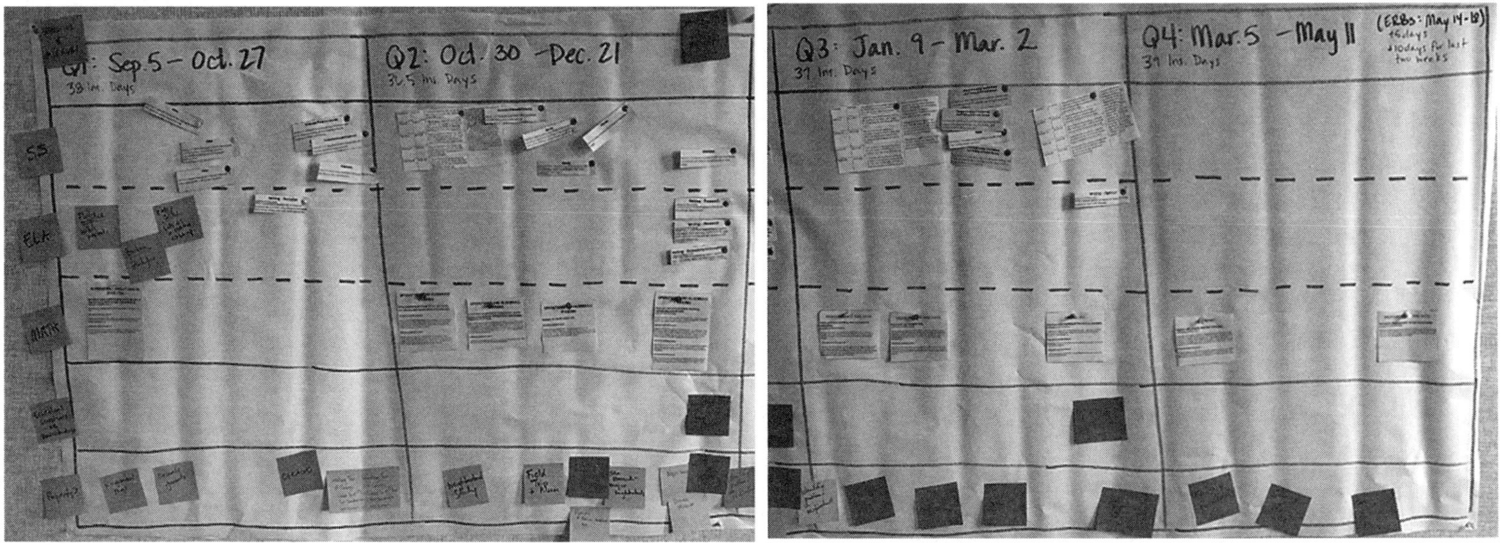

Figure 8.5: Internal Curriculum Map

	The First Six Weeks	Chicago History	Neighborhood Study	Research Projects
	9/5–10/13 32 instructional days	10/16–12/22 44.5 instructional days	1/9–3/2	3/5–5/11
Yearlong	• SS.IS.1.3–5 • SS.IS.2.3–5 • SS.IS.3.3–5 • SS.IS.4.3–5 • SS.IS.5.3–5 • W.3.4 • W.3.5 • W.3.6			
Social studies	First six weeks/identity • Identity 1–5 (Teaching Tolerance) • SS.CV.1.3 • SS.CV.2.3 • SS.CV.3.3 • SS.IS.8.3–5	Chicago history (PAST) • Diversity 6–10 (Teaching Tolerance) • SS.H.1.3 • SS.H.2.3 • SS.H.3.3 • SS.G.1.3 • SS.G.2.3	Peace unit/neighborhood study (PRESENT) • Justice 11–15 (Teaching Tolerance) • SS.CV.4.3 • SS.IS.6.3–5 • SS.IS.7.3–5 • SS.G.3.3 • SS.EC.1.3 • SS.EC.2.3 • SS.EC.FL.1.4	City planning (FUTURE) • Action 16–20 (Teaching Tolerance) • SS.IS.6.3–5 • SS.IS.7.3–5

(Continued)

Figure 8.5 (Continued)

	The First Six Weeks	Chicago History	Neighborhood Study	Research Projects
Reading	Building a reading life • RL.3.1 • RL.3.2 • RL.3.4 • RL.3.7	Reading to learn • RI.3.1 • RI.3.2 • RI.3.5 • RI.3.6 • RI.3.7	Character studies • RL.3.1 • RL.3.3 • RL.3.5 • RL.3.6 • RL.3.7 • RL.3.9	Research clubs • RI.3.1 • RI.3.2 • RI.3.3 • RI.3.7 • RI.3.8 • RI.3.9
Writing	Setting up a writing workshop • Writing notebooks (Fletcher) • Writing strategies (Buckner) Crafting true stories • W.3.3 (narrative writing)	The art of information writing • W.3.2 (expository writing) • W.3.7 (research projects) • W.3.8 (research skills)	Changing the world • W.3.1 (opinion/argumentative writing)	Once upon a time • W.3.3 (narrative writing)

Grammar, word study, cursive	N/A	• Capitalization
		  ○ Start sentences
		  ○ Proper nouns
		  ○ Forms: Titles, addresses, letters, etc.
		• Punctuation
		  ○ Ending sentences
		  ○ Run-ons/fragments
			• Capitalization
			  ○ Continue earlier standards
			• Punctuation
			  ○ Comma usage
			  ○ Quotation marks
				• Capitalization
				  ○ Continue earlier standards
				• Punctuation
				  ○ Apostrophes
				  ○ Contractions

	The First Six Weeks	Chicago History	Neighborhood Study	Research Projects
		• Spelling 　o Differentiated based on needs; see end-of-year expectations 　o Start at early within-word patterns; assess mastery of vowel digraphs, diphthongs, and *r*-controlled vowels • Introduce cursive 　o First third of letters	• Spelling 　o Three spelling rules: double the constant, change the *y* to *i*, replace the *e* 　o Mid within-word patterns and adding affixes • Cursive 　o Second third of letters	• Spelling 　o Assess mastery of vowel diagraphs, *r*-controlled vowels, diphthongs • Usage 　o Subject-verb agreement? • Cursive 　o Third third of letters
Math	Unit 1 • 3.NBT.A.1 • NBT.A.3 (Introduced) • OA.A.1 (Introduced) • OA.A.2 (Introduced) • OA.A.3 (Introduced) • OA.A.4 (Introduced) • OA.B.5 (Introduced) Unit 2 • 3.NBT.A.2 • NBT.A.3 (Introduced) • OA.A.1 (Introduced)	Unit 2 • 3.NBT.A.2 • NBT.A.3 (Introduced) • OA.A.1 (Introduced) • OA.A.2 (Introduced) • OA.A.3 (Introduced) • OA.A.4 (Introduced) • OA.B.5 (Introduced) Unit 3 • NBT.A.3 • OA.A.1 • OA.A.2	Unit 4 • NF.A.1 • NF.A.2 • NF.A.3 • G.A.2 • MD.A.1 • MD.A.2 • MD.B.3 • MD.B.4	Unit 5 • G.A.1 • MD.C.5 • MD.C.6 • MD.C.7 • MD.D.8

Figure 8.6: Parent-Facing Curriculum Map

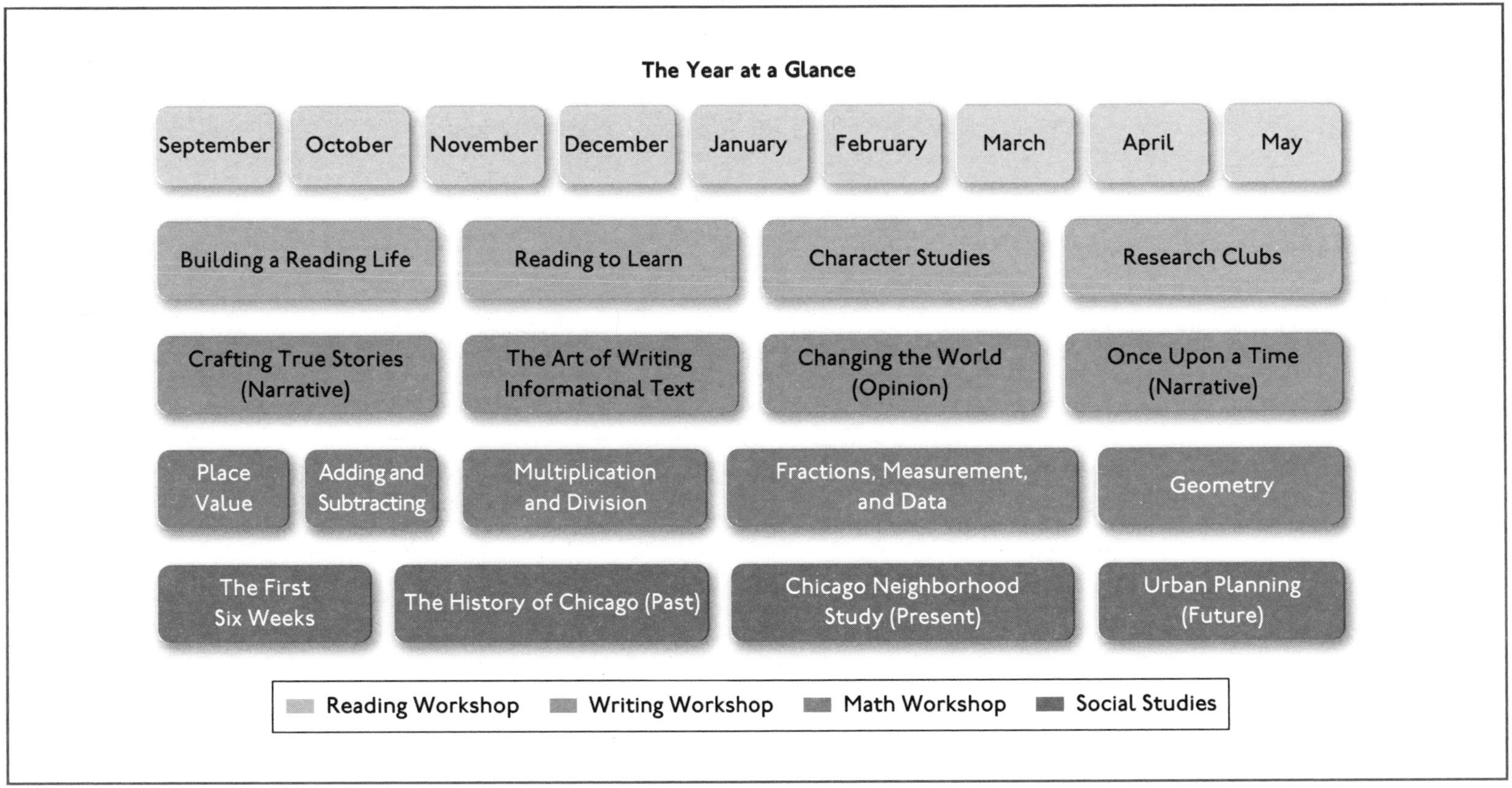

The Year at a Glance

September	October	November	December	January	February	March	April	May

Reading Workshop

Building a Reading Life	Reading to Learn	Character Studies	Research Clubs

Writing Workshop

Crafting True Stories (Narrative)	The Art of Writing Informational Text	Changing the World (Opinion)	Once Upon a Time (Narrative)

Math Workshop

Place Value	Adding and Subtracting	Multiplication and Division	Fractions, Measurement, and Data	Geometry

Social Studies

The First Six Weeks	The History of Chicago (Past)	Chicago Neighborhood Study (Present)	Urban Planning (Future)

Legend: ▪ Reading Workshop ▪ Writing Workshop ▪ Math Workshop ▪ Social Studies

While nothing is ever perfect, and while we found we had to modify the map to meet our needs throughout our years working together, it served as a great reference point for content coverage, ensuring that we emphasized all topics equitably throughout the school year and allowing us to build units and schedule assessments.

It even helped us create a parent-facing curriculum map, helping parents develop a vision for the school year (see Figure 8.6).

Once the standards were mapped out over the course of the year, we began building assessments that were aligned closely to the standards, intended to elicit specific information about both the learning process and the product of learning. We made three types of assessments: (1) summative pre-assessments that encompass all the learning objectives for a given unit, (2) summative post-assessments that encompass those same learning objectives, and (3) formal formative assessments assessing smaller chunks of units, sometimes even single learning objectives. In the next few pages, you can see what this looks like over the course of a unit.

Figure 8.7 shows an example of a unit focused on multi-digit addition and subtraction. We chose to focus on the following standards for this unit, and in each of the following sections, we'll explore how we used those standards to build our assessments.

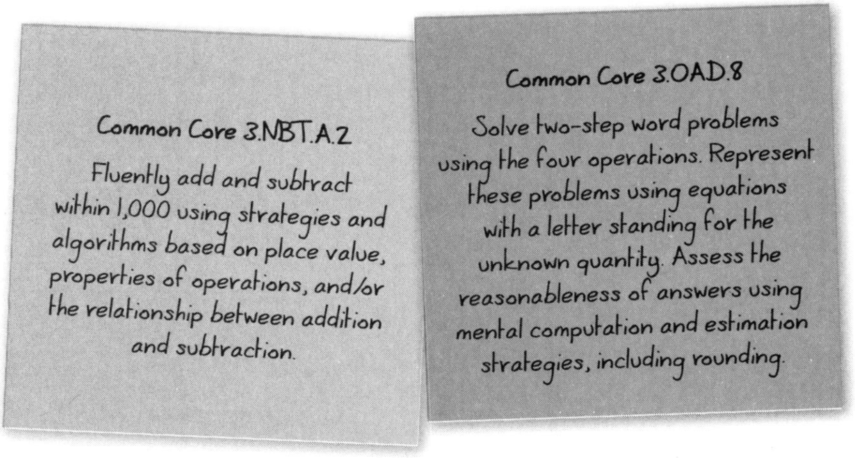

Common Core 3.NBT.A.2

Fluently add and subtract within 1,000 using strategies and algorithms based on place value, properties of operations, and/or the relationship between addition and subtraction.

Common Core 3.OAD.8

Solve two-step word problems using the four operations. Represent these problems using equations with a letter standing for the unknown quantity. Assess the reasonableness of answers using mental computation and estimation strategies, including rounding.

Figure 8.7:
Addition and
Subtraction
Pre-Assessment

Pre-Assessment

In the pre-assessment, we created assessment items that were intended to cover each of the standards we identified for the unit. We also made sure to create assessment items that encouraged students to apply their knowledge in a novel context and apply previous skills (see Figure 8.8).

Name _____ Date _____

Unit 2 Pre-Assessment

Skill	Not yet	Starting to	Got it	Checklist	Feedback
Addition and Subtraction Fluency	❑	❑	❑	❑ I can add and subtract to 5 with fluency. ❑ I can add and subtract to 10 with fluency. ❑ I can add and subtract to 20 with fluency.	
Multi-digit Addition and Subtraction	❑	❑	❑	❑ I can add and subtract multi-digit numbers without regrouping. ❑ I can add and subtract multi-digit numbers with regrouping.	
Journaling	❑	❑	❑	❑ I showed my thinking using pictures or numbers. ❑ I explained my thinking in words. ❑ My work is legible and organized. ❑ My final answer is circled and stated in a complete sentence with units.	

Unit 2 Pre-Assessment

Section 1: Addition and Subtraction

Please add or subtract the following numbers. You may use any method you'd like! You don't need to explain, but please show your work.

1) 23 + 66	2) 89 - 45
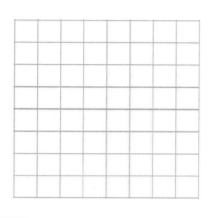	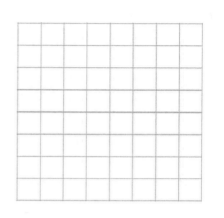
3) 145 + 396	4) 712 - 435
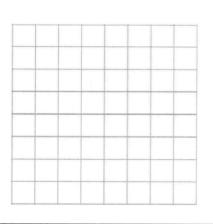	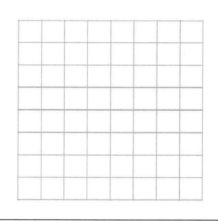

(Continued)

Figure 8.8 (Continued)

Unit 2 Pre-Assessment

5) 402 - 97

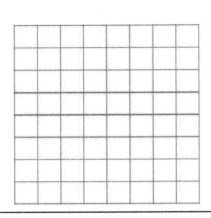

6) 802 - 709

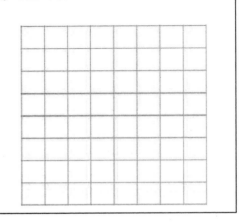

Mr. France sometimes struggles with completing books. He chose a 762-page book that he hopes to complete in approximately one month, or four weeks.
- In the first week, he reads 178 pages.
- In the second week, he reads 242 pages.
- In the third week, he reads 59 pages.

How many pages does he need to read in the last week to meet his goal?

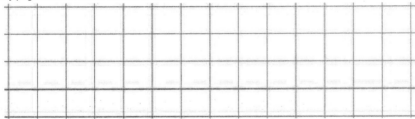

What do you think he needs to do to meet his goal?

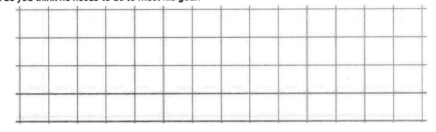

Unit 2 Pre-Assessment

Section 2: Problem-Solving

George has four digit cards.

| 3 | 5 | 7 | 8 |

1) What is the largest four-digit number George can make with his cards?	☐ ☐ ☐ ☐
2) What is the largest four-digit **even** number George can make with his cards?	☐ ☐ ☐ ☐

Please explain your answer.

3) What is the four-digit number closest to 4,000 that George can make with his four cards?	☐ ☐ ☐ ☐

Please show your work.

(Continued)

Figure 8.8 (Continued)

Unit 2 Pre-Assessment

4) Complete this calculation:

$$3578 + \boxed{}\boxed{}\boxed{} = 4000$$

Please show your method.

Unit 2 Pre-Assessment

Section 3: Fact Fluency (Interview-Based)

Use the flashcards to evaluate the child's fact fluency. Start with Math Facts to 20. If the child is not fluent, go backwards until you reach fluency, defined by the rubric.

Math Facts to 5	Math Facts to 10	Math Facts to 20
Ways to Make 5: ❑ 0 + 5 ❑ 5 + 0 ❑ 1 + 4 ❑ 4 + 1 ❑ 2 + 3 ❑ 3 + 2 ❑ 5 - 0 ❑ 5 - 2 ❑ 5 - 3 ❑ 5 - 4 **Doubles/Other** ❑ 1 + 1 ❑ 2 + 2 ❑ 2 - 1 ❑ 4 - 2 ❑ 3 + 1 ❑ 3 - 1 ❑ 1 - 1	**Ways to Make 10:** ❑ 10 + 0 ❑ 1 + 9 ❑ 8 + 2 ❑ 10 - 8 ❑ 5 + 5 ❑ 10 - 4 ❑ 4 + 6 ❑ 3 + 7 ❑ 10 - 9 **Doubles:** ❑ 3 + 3 ❑ 4 + 4 ❑ 8 - 4 ❑ 5 + 5 ❑ 10 - 5 ❑ 6 - 3 **Other:** ❑ 5 + 2 ❑ 6 + 3 ❑ 7 + 2 ❑ 7 - 5 ❑ 9 - 4 ❑ 8 - 2 ❑ 9 - 8	**Ways to Make 20:** ❑ 10 + 10 ❑ 11 + 9 ❑ 13 + 7 ❑ 14 + 6 ❑ 15 + 5 ❑ 18 + 2 **Adding to 10:** ❑ 10 + 2 ❑ 10 + 7 ❑ 18 - 8 ❑ 15 - 5 **Doubles (+/1):** ❑ 6 + 6 ❑ 7 + 7 ❑ 14 - 7 ❑ 8 + 8 ❑ 16 - 8 ❑ 9 + 9 ❑ 13 - 7 ❑ 7 + 8 ❑ 8 + 9 ❑ 17 - 9 **Applying Facts to 10:** ❑ 13 + 3 ❑ 17 - 6 ❑ 16 + 2 ❑ 15 + 4 ❑ 18 - 6 ❑ 19 - 7 ❑ 18 - 3
Check all that apply: ❑ Instant ❑ Automatic (within 3 seconds) ❑ Counting on ❑ Counting back ❑ Related facts ❑ Using fingers ❑ Other (write in notes)	**Check all that apply:** ❑ Instant ❑ Automatic (within 3 seconds) ❑ Counting on ❑ Counting back ❑ Related facts ❑ Using fingers ❑ Other (write in notes)	**Check all that apply:** ❑ Instant ❑ Automatic (within 3 seconds) ❑ Counting on ❑ Counting back ❑ Related facts ❑ Using fingers ❑ Making 10s ❑ Other (write in notes)
Overall Fluency Score:	Overall Fluency Score:	Overall Fluency Score:
Additional Notes:	Additional Notes:	Additional Notes:

Post-Assessment

In the post-assessment, you'll see something very similar (see Figure 8.9). There are assessment items that attempted to elicit knowledge through tasks children had previously seen, but also in a novel context where they'd have to interpret the problem and figure out what it meant on their own. You'll also notice an extra assessment item and lane on the rubric related to place value. While this wasn't on the pre-assessment for the unit, it was a part of the previous unit on place value. At the end of Unit 1, which encompassed standards related to place value, we noticed many students who still had not fully mastered the concepts. Because multi-digit addition and subtraction lent themselves so nicely to reviewing and reinforcing place-value concepts, we decided to reassess the standards with our Unit 2 assessment. It wasn't necessary to include on the pre-assessment, as we'd recently collected data on those standards. However, by the time the Unit 2 assessment had come around, I had already pulled small groups for review and reinforcement of the skills, allowing for a quick reassessment of the skills with the Unit 2 topics.

Name _____ Date _____

Unit 2 Post-Assessment

Skill	Not yet	Starting to	Got it	Checklist	Feedback
Addition and Subtraction Fluency	❑	❑	❑	❑ I can add and subtract to 5 with fluency. ❑ I can add and subtract to 10 with fluency. ❑ I can add and subtract to 20 with fluency.	
Read and Write Numbers	❑	❑	❑	❑ I can write numbers to the 100s in expanded form. ❑ I can write numbers to the 10,000s in expanded form. ❑ I can write numbers to the 10,000s in word form.	
Multi-digit Addition and Subtraction	❑	❑	❑	❑ I can add and subtract multi-digit numbers without regrouping. ❑ I can add and subtract multi-digit numbers with regrouping.	
Journaling	❑	❑	❑	❑ I showed my thinking using pictures or numbers. ❑ I explained my thinking in words. ❑ My work is legible and organized. ❑ My final answer is circled and stated in a complete sentence with units.	

(Continued)

Figure 8.9 (Continued)

Unit 2 Post-Assessment

Section 1: Addition and Subtraction

Please add or subtract the following numbers. Please show your work. You must try at least two different methods in total.

1) 35 + 42

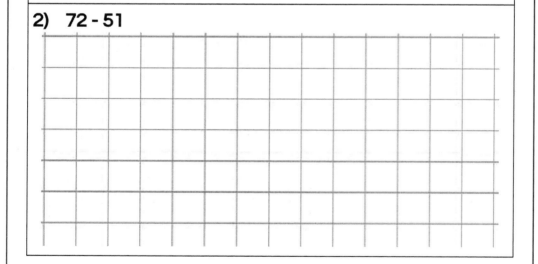

2) 72 - 51

Unit 2 Post-Assessment

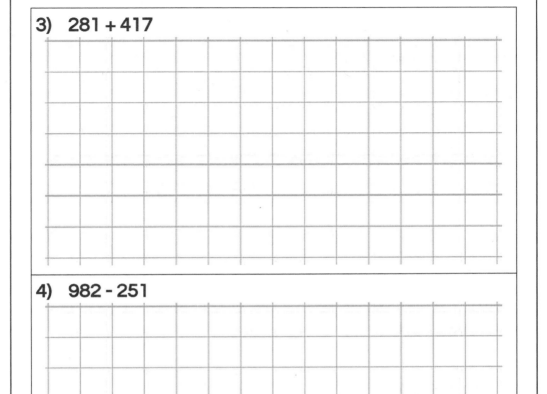

3) 281 + 417

4) 982 - 251

(Continued)

Figure 8.9 (Continued)

Unit 2 Post-Assessment

5) 419 - 149

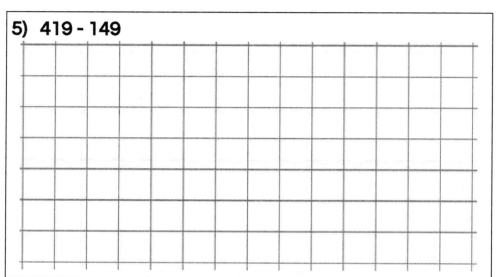

6) 902 - 209

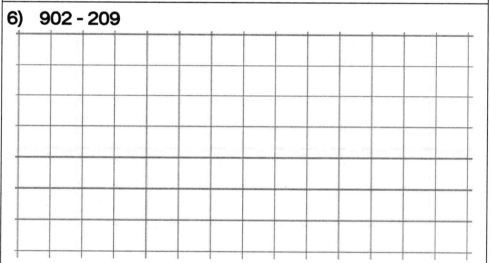

Unit 2 Post-Assessment

Section 2: Place Value

The spaces are blank. Fill in the spaces using numbers 1-4. Then answer the questions.

1) Place a 2 in the hundreds place.
2) Place a 7 in the tens place.
3) Place a 4 in the ten-thousands place.
4) Place a 0 in the remaining places.

Please write the number in **words**.

If you added two **ten-thousands**, how would you write the number in words?

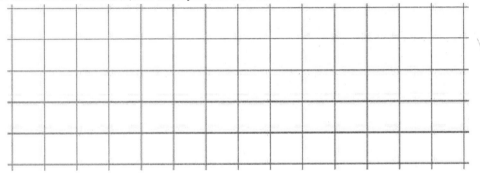

(Continued)

Figure 8.9 (Continued)

Unit 2 Post-Assessment

Section 3: Problem-Solving

Ms. Northover was collecting baseball cards.

- When she counted them in September, she had 312 baseball cards.
- Now, in October, she only has 279 baseball cards.

It turns out that Ms. Fallert was playing a joke on Ms. Northover. She took some of her baseball cards and hid them.

How many did Ms. Fallert hide from Ms. Northover?

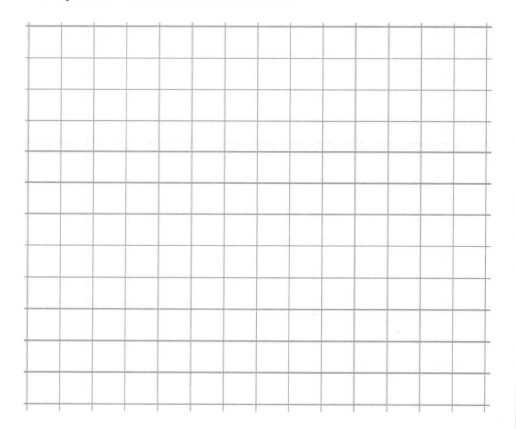

Unit 2 Post-Assessment

Section 3: Fact Fluency (Interview-Based)

Use the flashcards to evaluate the child's fact fluency. Start with Math Facts to 20. If the child is not fluent, go backwards until you reach fluency, defined by the rubric.

Math Facts to 5 Kindergarten	Math Facts to 10 1st Grade	Math Facts to 20 2nd Grade Benchmark
Ways to Make 5: ❑ 0 + 5 ❑ 5 + 0 ❑ 1 + 4 ❑ 4 + 1 ❑ 2 + 3 ❑ 3 + 2 ❑ 5 - 0 ❑ 5 - 2 ❑ 5 - 3 ❑ 5 - 4 **Doubles/Other:** ❑ 1 + 1 ❑ 2 + 2 ❑ 2 - 1 ❑ 4 - 2 ❑ 3 + 1 ❑ 3 - 1 ❑ 1 - 1	**Ways to Make 10:** ❑ 10 + 0 ❑ 1 + 9 ❑ 8 + 2 ❑ 10 - 8 ❑ 5 + 5 ❑ 10 - 4 ❑ 4 + 6 ❑ 3 + 7 ❑ 10 - 9 **Doubles:** ❑ 3 + 3 ❑ 4 + 4 ❑ 8 - 4 ❑ 5 + 5 ❑ 10 - 5 ❑ 6 - 3 **Other:** ❑ 5 + 2 ❑ 6 + 3 ❑ 7 + 2 ❑ 7 - 5 ❑ 9 - 4 ❑ 8 - 2 ❑ 9 - 8	**Ways to Make 20:** ❑ 10 + 10 ❑ 11 + 9 ❑ 13 + 7 ❑ 14 + 6 ❑ 15 + 5 ❑ 18 + 2 **Adding to 10:** ❑ 10 + 2 ❑ 10 + 7 ❑ 18 - 8 ❑ 15 - 5 **Doubles (+/1):** ❑ 6 + 6 ❑ 7 + 7 ❑ 14 - 7 ❑ 8 + 8 ❑ 16 - 8 ❑ 9 + 9 ❑ 13 - 7 ❑ 7 + 8 ❑ 8 + 9 ❑ 17 - 9 **Applying Facts to 10:** ❑ 13 + 3 ❑ 17 - 6 ❑ 16 + 2 ❑ 15 + 4 ❑ 18 - 6 ❑ 19 - 7 ❑ 18 - 3
Check all that apply: ❑ Instant ❑ Automatic (within 3 seconds) ❑ Counting on ❑ Counting back ❑ Related Facts ❑ Using fingers ❑ Other (write in notes)	**Check all that apply:** ❑ Instant ❑ Automatic (within 3 seconds) ❑ Counting on ❑ Counting back ❑ Related Facts ❑ Using fingers ❑ Other (write in notes)	**Check all that apply:** ❑ Instant ❑ Automatic (within 3 seconds) ❑ Counting on ❑ Counting back ❑ Related Facts ❑ Using fingers ❑ Making 10s ❑ Other (write in notes)
Overall Fluency Score:	Overall Fluency Score:	Overall Fluency Score:
Additional Notes:	Additional Notes:	Additional Notes:

You'll also notice that the format of the post-assessment is a bit different. After giving the pre-assessment, we noticed a few things. First, we hadn't given the children enough space to show their thinking. For many, they were in a developmental stage where they needed to use number lines or pictures to show their thinking. The space we had originally provided was insufficient. Moreover, we noticed that the problem-solving task was a bit too much of a stretch for them. We had misinterpreted what the standards meant originally, and our students' work prompted us to reflect and realize we'd made the pre-assessment far too rigorous, to the point that it was developmentally inappropriate for the average third-grader. This information helped us modify the post-assessment to make it reasonably rigorous.

I share these mistakes and missteps in assessment design because they're necessary to becoming skilled at building assessments. Just as we expect our students to take risks, make mistakes, and be vulnerable with their process, we educators must do the same. We must be willing to jump in and learn from our mistakes—just as my team did.

Formative Assessments

In the formative assessments, you'll notice the focus narrow quite a bit (see Figure 8.10). While addition and subtraction are complementary skills, they do require vastly different conceptual knowledge. As a result, it was important to give separate formative assessments related to addition and subtraction to elicit isolated information on each of the skills. This informed my instruction over the course of the unit, allowing me to address needs that arose in small groups.

Name _____ Date _____

Formative Assessment: Addition

Please solve the problem using three different methods. **You may only stack in one of them.**

The third grade is trying to figure out how many books they have on the whole team.
- Mr. France has 240 books in his library.
- Mrs. Northover has 267.
- Mr. Paynter has 318.

How many books does the whole team have?

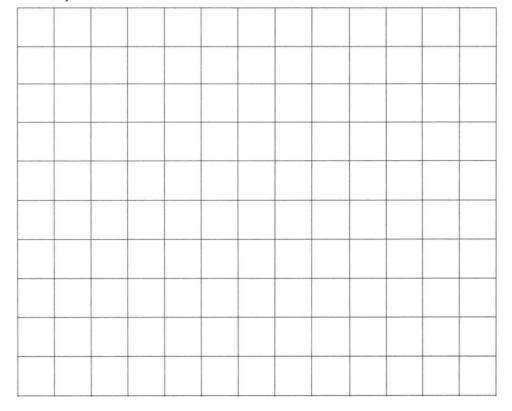

(Continued)

Figure 8.10 (Continued)

Name _____ Date _____

Formative Assessment: Subtraction

Please solve the problem using at least two different methods. **If you'd like, you can stack for the third method.**

Anna has a total of 300 Pokemon cards split between two separate boxes. In one of her boxes, she has 175 Pokemon cards.

First, draw a **bar model** to represent this situation.

How many does she have in the other box?

Standards-based assessment necessitates a forgiving model for mastery. If we're working in a classroom that values humanized personalization, we cannot expect all children to master all skills on the same timeline. This means that you will certainly get to the end of a unit or assessment period without all students having secured or mastered the content.

"What if my kids don't show mastery by the time I've decided my unit is over?"

This doesn't necessarily mean you just pick up and move on. Instead, it means that you find ways to review and reinforce these skills in small groups, reassessing them as the year goes, much like I've demonstrated with the series of addition and subtraction assessments. Another option is to create cumulative assessments that encompass multiple units. These cumulative assessments can be used to reassess the same standards in a reliable way, after providing instruction or intervention.

This requires you to think very far ahead, which is why I want to reinforce the idea of making a curriculum map before the year starts. Doing so allows you to embrace the fact that all students will not master on your timeline and, as a result, will help you identify points in the year for cumulative reassessment, when necessary. Because standards are con-comitant—meaning they naturally accompany or align with other standards—you might also notice places in future units to review skills, allowing your planning of each subsequent unit to be flexible and responsive to the needs that arise in your classroom.

"But don't standards overlap a lot? How do you manage that?"

You'll know you've found a good standard set when the standards are con-comitant. When siphoning off something like addition and subtraction into only one part of the year, it's easy to forget that those skills are closely related to place-value concepts. Likewise, when siphoning off multiplication and division, educators tend to forget that multiplication and division lend themselves to a seamless review of addition and subtraction, as well as an intentional preview of fractions.

Narrowing the scope of assessed learning objectives simply makes it more sustainable for educators to gauge progress over the short-term, but it should not be at the expense of creating meaningful and authentic assessments. Part of my problem while working in Silicon Valley was that I wasn't consistently narrowing the scope of my assessment. At times, my approach lacked the structure and boundaries to make standards-based assessment sustainable. I was assessing too many learning objectives at once.

Sustainability is critical to humanized personalization. To sustainably assess in relation to specific standards, we must be sure our scope is narrow enough that we can assess reliably, validly, and sustainably. But we must also look for connections between standards so we may find opportunities to reassess standards and pair them with others.

THE THIRD VERTEX: THE INNER DIALOGUE

The final dimension of assessment encompasses the anecdotal, unobtrusive, and informal formative assessments that occur countless times throughout the school day. While these unobtrusive and informal assessments can provide insight into content mastery, the third dimension is most valuable for gaining insight into a child's inner dialogue. In this manner, we see a strong parallel forming between the three dimensions of personalized learning and these three dimensions of humanizing assessment.

> *The third dimension helps us gain insight into a child's inner dialogue.*

To demonstrate this, I'd like to tell you another story.

My third-grade class and I were writing personal narratives—true stories from our lives. To help them get into the writing process, we read some mentor texts and even did some highly structured brainstorming, but in those first weeks, I noticed that many of my students had trouble getting started on their drafts, frequently defaulting to side conversations or attention-seeking behaviors.

I reminded myself that their behaviors were trying to tell me something—that they were communicating a deficit in skills, albeit in a dysfunctional manner. I soon realized that we had a few obstacles we needed to overcome. First and foremost, their writing stamina was low. Many of them were unable to sit for more than a few minutes and attend to their writing. Second, they were unable to see how any given day's lesson was connected to the larger project of publishing a personal narrative to share with their classmates. Finally, and most important, I realized that a vast majority of my students were carrying a great deal of emotional baggage around writing, much like Sydney was. Many would sit idly after my minilesson, looking to me to generate ideas on their behalf. One student in particular looked up at me, the corners of her eyes and lips drooping toward the ground.

"Mr. France, I don't know what to write," Bernie said while trying to brainstorm ideas.

"Just write down anything that comes to mind," I replied. "I'm not looking for the perfect idea. I'm just looking for us to brainstorm some ideas today."

I looked around and saw that Bernie wasn't alone. Many others looked similarly forlorn, unsure of where to start and what to write. It became clear to me that I'd have to modify my original plans. Over the next two weeks, the majority of my instruction focused on nurturing my students' inner dialogues. For the first week, I set a class-wide intention of "letting go," and in the context of writing, this meant abandoning perfectionism and embracing the idea that *any idea* was good enough for writing workshop. In the second week, we used a calendar to develop a vision for the steps for our writing project—to help them see that they'd also need to let go of their desire for perfection to get the work done on time (see Figure 8.11). But we also used the calendars to set volume goals, helping them see that the way we were measuring success was not by the perfect idea but instead by the willingness to be vulnerable and get ideas down on paper.

Figure 8.11: Writing Workshop Calendar

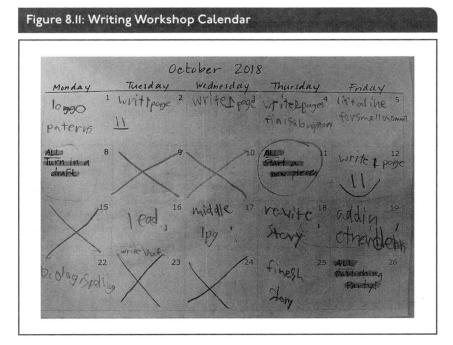

In that situation, no amount of standardized or standards-based academic assessment could have provided me what I needed to help them grow as writers. Using anecdotal assessment helped me address their unique challenges and coach them individually to shift their mindset about writing.

A month later, my writing workshop was transformed, unrecognizable from just four weeks earlier. My students wrote for sustained periods of time, using strategic thinking and a growth mindset to keep themselves working throughout the writing periods, allowing me to meet with students one-on-one and provide individualized feedback about their writing, as Lucy Calkins suggests in conferences. To close our workshops, students would evaluate their progress in relation to the goals they set on their calendars.

I cannot stress the importance of partnership in assessment enough, for it is this assessment of the inner dialogue that adds a great deal of depth and humanity to our assessment practices. It is human connection and partnership that *humanizes* anything, assessment included. It's an emerging but sometimes still unpopular belief that there is a pedagogy for assessment, too. We can, in fact, teach through our assessments and use them *as learning* when our students are able to reflect on them meaningfully and use them for future goal-setting. But this can't be confused with a lack of accountability or permissive teaching. When we use assessment *as* learning, it becomes a tool for cultivating awareness within students—an awareness of their strengths, their goals, and the steps they need to take to build on their assets and continue to grow.

BUILDING THE FRAME TO WEATHER THE STORM

If this sounds like a lot of prep work, it is. This is why I start planning my next unit at least a month in advance, and why I recommend developing a plan for the entire year before the school year starts.

When I moved back to Chicago, I also became the team lead for my third-grade team of teachers. My suggestion to set up this yearlong plan was met with a bit of skepticism but also a willingness to give this method of planning and preparation a chance. For that, I'm grateful. It wasn't until our second year, when it was time to go through the same curriculum with a new group of students, that one of my colleagues said, "I didn't really understand why you were making us do all of this work last year, but now I get it."

In that second year, she saw the benefits of having this flexible frame of standards and assessments. We were able to communicate the curriculum clearly and concisely to families, meanwhile having a clear plan that made us feel safe and supported as we launched into a new year. The flexible frame, while malleable and moldable, is intended to be a strong and resilient structure for your units—to support conversations with families and promote consistency and collaboration on your team. But most important, it's meant to create a structure within which you can understand the inner dialogue of each child even better. Without a medium—in this case, well-designed assessments and a clear plan for using them—it's hard to deepen your understanding of student learning in a valid and reliable way.

It's like building a house to withstand a hurricane, or retrofitting a skyscraper to withstand the force of an earthquake. It takes time, intention, careful thought, and the anticipation of the many variables in a classroom of twenty or more little ones. By investing time and energy into building a flexible frame for standards and assessment, you will see that it can withstand little hands climbing on it, swinging on it, and bending it to meet their needs. It can also support you when things don't go quite as planned. But it can't do that if you don't spend the time building it well.

In the following chapter, our discussion of humanized personalization as a pedagogy will climax, for what matters most is what occurs in our classrooms on a day-to-day basis. The flexible frame, fortified by clearly defined standards and a three-dimensional approach to assessment, exists in tension with humanized instruction. It is in our instruction that we get to be both artists and scientists at the same time, relying on what we know to be true about teaching and learning but also relying on our intuition to be flexible, responsive, and innovative as our children continuously evolve within and without our classrooms.

CHAPTER NINE

HUMANIZING INSTRUCTION TO PERSONALIZE LEARNING

Researchers have spent decades trying to understand flocks of birds. To the naked eye, it seems that they're following a leader or perhaps even acting out of pure intuition or telepathy. Such assumptions are born out of the way flocks of birds move. They oftentimes look like sleek jets careening through the sky, or tranquil silent waves floating with the rhythms of the wind.

Source: Image courtesy of Pixabay.

But it turns out that it's neither telepathy, intuition, nor following a single leader. Instead, they act out of anticipation. Zoologist Wayne Potts discovered this and published his findings in a 1984 issue of *Nature*. He calls this a "chorus-line" maneuver, comparing it to the way people in a chorus line coordinate their movements with those around them. They don't do it through direct observation but instead through anticipation. Through his research, Potts discovered that birds were able to react three times more quickly when moving with a flock of birds than they would if they were observing a neighboring bird, due to the fact that they were anticipating the movements of the birds around them. As a result, flocks move in synchronicity, acting as one embodied entity. They *sense* emerging changes of the flock's direction through subtle, likely imperceptible movements, ingrained in them through intergenerational experience and evolution.

Likewise, this means that there is no identified leader of the flock, but instead every bird has an opportunity to change the direction of the flock, depending on where it is positioned. Say, for instance, one bird senses a slight change in the wind, causing it to elevate slightly. Other birds may follow suit and anticipate the slight change in wind before it reaches them. All birds in the flock have this capability, and as a result, there is a natural democracy within the group of birds, allowing their individual perceptions to contribute to collective perception.

EMERGENT SYSTEMS

This same phenomenon can be observed elsewhere, too, such as in schools of fish. Russian biologist Dmitriĭ Radakov (1973) observed that schools of fish can avoid predators if they coordinate their movements with those of their neighbors:

> Even if only a handful of individuals know where a predator is coming from, they can guide a huge school by initiating a turn that their neighbors emulate—and their neighbors' neighbors, and so on. Unlike linear flocks of geese, which do have a clear leader, clusters are democratic. They function from the grassroots; any member can initiate a movement that others will follow (Friederici, Audubon, 2009).

But there's even more support for this idea, which David Brooks, *New York Times* columnist, describes in *The Social Animal* (2012). Brooks shares a number of unconventional ideas, from modern humanity's preoccupation with rationalism and individualism to the notion that a great deal of what we do is actually dictated by the unconscious mind, similar to how schools of fish or flocks of birds can anticipate the movement of their pack. This conditioning comes with time, experience, practice, instinct, and a ceaseless evolution. He refers to these as emergent systems, ones that do not "rely upon a central controller" but instead act democratically, allowing any one of their members to initiate a movement that others could follow.

> Once a pattern of interaction is established, it has a downward influence on the behavior of its components.

> For example, let's say an ant in a colony stumbles upon a new food source. No dictator ant has to tell the colony to reorganize itself to harvest that source. Instead, one ant, in the course of his normal foraging, stumbles upon the food. Then a neighboring ant will

notice that ant's change in direction, and then a neighbor of that ant will notice the change, and pretty soon, as Steven Johnson puts it, Local information can lead to global wisdom." (Brooks, 2012)

There are countless examples of this, from air and water coming together to form a hurricane to the way language changes over time. The human race is also subject to emergence. Grassroots movements are how great change occurs, how kindness spreads, and how evil and prejudice can capsize a whole community. This means that our classrooms are emergent systems, as well, shaped democratically by all the individuals in the classroom, not just the teacher. With educators as close partners, children can play a critical role in the co-construction of a rich learning environment, fit for exploration and discovery, balanced with mindful and productive constraints that build a structure in which children can grow and perhaps even change the course of a learning experience.

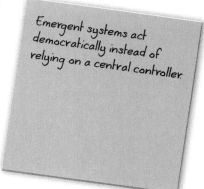

Emergent systems act democratically instead of relying on a central controller.

Our job as educators changes when we view the classroom as an emergent ecosystem of learners. First and foremost, we become responsible for enforcing the boundaries and productive constraints that create structure for an emergent system to grow. This involves building and reinforcing structures for classroom management, effective routines, and curriculum development, as we've discussed in the previous four chapters. Furthermore, our responsibilities as pedagogues change. While we're still responsible for identifying standards, building assessments, and planning for intentional, standards-based instruction, we are also responsible for enacting *responsive instruction*. To humanize personalization, we must make sure learning is a dynamic conversation. This requires a constant exchange between learners and educators, which is why the idea of *responsive* instruction is so critical.

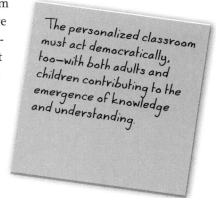

The personalized classroom must act democratically, too—with both adults and children contributing to the emergence of knowledge and understanding.

THE FOUNDATION OF RESPONSIVE INSTRUCTION

Charlotte Danielson (2007) defines responsive instruction as a teacher's ability to "make adjustments in a lesson that respond to changing conditions." Sometimes there is little need for this, and sometimes there is a need for educators to completely change the course of a lesson, depending on how students respond. In my opinion, most lessons lie somewhere in the middle, and this should be by design. Our lessons and lesson structures should be open enough for our students to interact with the content and mold it with their autonomy and agency. Too didactic an experience does not allow for this; it becomes unidimensional and exclusive, disallowing diverse funds of knowledge to be incorporated into the collective conscious of the classroom.

This is, in fact, one of the most commonly misunderstood components of personalized learning. Far too many reduce personalized learning to individualization, attempting to match content with learners, assuming that appropriately rigorous content will personalize instruction on behalf of learners. This creates a great deal of complexity, necessitating digital technology to provide individualized lessons to individual learners. In doing so, we limit educators' abilities to be responsive pedagogues and disallow local knowledge gained in individualized lessons to become part of the collective conscious of the learning environment.

Many progressives would argue that by putting structure in place, we limit our children's ability to be children, that we over-institutionalize school and kill learning for them. But I disagree. It's not the boundaries themselves; it is, instead, how the boundaries are communicated and enforced that affects student agency positively or negatively. In reality, what many progressives unknowingly advocate for is a passive and permissive teaching style, one that relies solely on children's ability to educate themselves from within. This is neither practical nor supported by widely accepted empirical research.

> *It's not boundaries themselves that chip away at student agency; it's how the boundaries are communicated and enforced.*

Education serves a number of purposes, and while we want those purposes to include a bolstering of autonomy, an outlet for natural curiosity, and a means for children to still be children while learning productively, we must also acknowledge that education serves a social purpose, one that goes against inclinations for self-interest and fierce individualism. The process of socialization is not always going to be comfortable, but it can be empathetic, compassionate, and responsive to a child's needs.

Responsive instruction that leverages both productive constraints and learner autonomy can and will address all these purposes. Similar to how viewing the classroom as a complex ecosystem necessitates a change in perspective, so does a change in how we view responsive instruction. While standards frameworks and assessment procedures are sturdy and rigid, instruction is not. Instruction is the climb to the top of the jungle gym: it includes the moment we hang upside down and let all the blood rush to our faces; it embraces the fall into the sandpit far below, the one we laugh off before climbing back up on the bars for another exciting ascent.

HALLMARKS OF RESPONSIVE INSTRUCTION

John Dewey, the father of progressive education, advocated against a permissive atmosphere where children weren't held accountable. While I'm unsure if he would have advocated or even been able to imagine the culture around digital assessment and data we live in now, I feel confident that he'd advocate for a world in which productive constraints are used to promote autonomy, reflection, and responsive instruction. Throughout the remainder of this chapter, I'll outline eight hallmarks of responsive instruction, built on the productive constraints that the flexible frame provides.

BACKWARD DESIGN

Designing responsive instruction requires intentionally identifying desired results and evidence. Without desired results and valid assessments against which we can evaluate learning, there is little to which we can respond and no substantive medium through which feedback can be exchanged. Generally speaking, I default to McTighe and Wiggins's method for backward-designing instruction (see Figure 9.2).

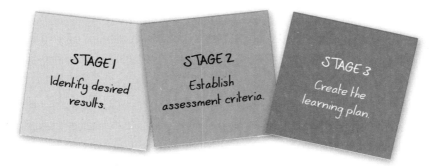

Figure 9.2:
Backward Design

Source: Adapted from Wiggins and McTighe, (2005). *Understanding by Design.* Upper Saddle River, NJ: Pearson Education Inc.

The nature of the third section of a backward design template allows educators to build a learning plan in the way they see fit. It doesn't necessitate educators to plan a lockstep, day-by-day scope and sequence but instead creates space for educators to build a learning plan based on anticipated misconceptions and unanticipated bumps in the road.

My unit plans are usually riddled with idealism, much of which is not actualized over the course of the unit. I may misjudge the amount of time I have, realize that I improperly anticipated a misconception, or write a lesson that I later realize won't be quite as effective as I thought it would be. When teaching responsively, we are always collecting data as we go, even in the first days of a new unit. These data—whether they're anecdotal, formal, or somewhere in between—has the potential to radically change our learning plan. We would be remiss if we didn't embrace opportunities to modify our learning plan to be more aligned with the needs of the children. Therefore, it's sensible to make a learning plan that's malleable, because you have the strong foundation of standards and assessments—the flexible frame, if you will—to catch you if you fall.

Too rigid a learning plan, I've found, can be more disabling than it is helpful—and a lot more work, too. Just recently, I fell into the unforgiving grasp of blindly following a curriculum manual for writing workshop. I did this to be consistent with my fellow teammates. However, as I was teaching the unit, I felt the urge to deviate based on students' responses to my instruction. It wasn't until about halfway through the unit that I realized I'd made a mistake in following the curriculum so closely. It was hard to figure out how each of my students was progressing and responding to my lessons because I was simply plodding through the lessons. My quest for fidelity and consistency with my teammates made me blind to best practice, and I realized that I'd forgotten to teach my kids how to actually write. I quickly changed course based on the results of a formative assessment, and I haven't looked back since.

> To teach responsively means to change our plans in response to student needs.

You might wonder if this was a wise choice, due to the fact that my team was following the manual pretty closely. In fact, one of my teammates voiced the concern that if we didn't follow the lessons with fidelity, our children would go from different classrooms to the next grade with varying sets of skills.

I see the argument here, and it contains grains of truth and reality, but the same would likely be true even if we all followed the lessons in the manual as closely as we could. After all, we're unique human beings, different teachers. Not only that, we have different sets of children in our classrooms. Naturally, unique combinations of individuals are going to bring different sets of experiences, varied background knowledge, and different obstacles to any given unit of instruction. In essence, knowledge, understanding, and experience will emerge in different ways with different combinations of individuals, even if we follow the manual verbatim.

For this reason, I argue that this point is moot. Children may go to the next grade level with moderately varied skills, simply due to the fact that they've learned with differing teachers and classmates, but assuming the flexible frame of standards and assessments has been built mindfully—and from grade level to grade level—the difference in skill sets will be minor, generating new funds of knowledge that will contribute to the natural diversity of the collective conscious of the school. In our case, while I had deviated from the day-to-day monotony of following a curriculum manual, my teaching and the lessons I built still aligned with our team's flexible frame. I was still teaching to the same standards and using the same assessments to gauge student achievement and the effectiveness of my instruction. I was just playing on the frame a little differently than my teammates were.

In fact, I'd argue that this diversity in lessons and learning plans—again assuming that the standards and assessments remain the same for the purpose of validity, reliability, and equity—is actually desirable when trying to humanize the learning process across several classrooms or even an entire school. Diversity and a healthy amount of divergence in lesson planning forms the cradle of pedagogical innovation in our classrooms. Piloting different techniques, exploring different mentor texts, and experimenting with different materials helps us learn from one another. Not only that, it builds agency in individual teachers, as well as confidence when taking risks, making mistakes, and otherwise witnessing their own pedagogical autonomy. To grow, adapt, and constantly learn how to be better teachers—in essence, to personalize adult learning—we must have a mindful degree of pedagogical autonomy.

I voiced this idea to my team, and they were receptive, as they always are. The following year, we changed the nature of our backward-design templates. My teammates had advocated for more day-to-day planning, since we had spent so much time in our first year together building the flexible frame of standards and assessments. To find a happy medium between consistency and autonomy, we began looking through the curriculum manuals together, identifying specific lessons or terms we wanted to keep consistent (see Figure 9.3). This allowed us to find a healthy level of consistency on our team, meanwhile enabling some pedagogical divergence, creating fruitful discussions when we'd discuss student work.

Diversity and divergence in lesson planning allow us to innovate.

Figure 9.3: Must Do/May Do

Bend I (Completed by 9/21)	
Objectives (Acquisition) • I can identify books that are too easy, too hard, and just right. • I can read "long and strong," building my reading stamina. • I can read fluently, with accuracy and expression. • I can orient myself to a text by previewing.	**Key Vocabulary** • Too easy, too hard, just right • Reading "stamina" • Fluency • Preview
Must Do • Modeling selecting books and filling book bins/bags • Anchor chart for "Just Right" books • Reading in the company of partners—establishing routines and expectations for partner reading (Lesson 6) • Establish process/expectations for reading/thinking journal (stamina chart)	**May Do** • Explore systems for book recommendations (Lesson 5) • Read fast, strong, and long bookmarks • Anchor chart for partner conversations • HOW to use thinking journals (Sticky notes? Quick jot each session? Glueing strategies in?) • Reading timeline (+ possible visit to K–2 libraries) • "Mystery Reader" K–I teacher to come read and spark memories
Formative Assessment • Read a passage from a self-selected book. Record I–2 minutes and put it on Seesaw. Ask students to orient themselves to the text.	

ARC-STYLE PLANNING

When building units, I like to plan in terms of arcs, or series of lessons that fit together. Generally speaking, they all relate to the same skill or competency, allowing an opportunity for a formative assessment at the end of the arc. Oftentimes, these arcs occur over the course of a week or two. By planning in terms of arcs, I allow things to get a bit messy from the beginning to the end of the arc. I still choose specific goals, objectives, lessons, and provocations that I plan to introduce to my children over the course of the arc. The only difference is I don't expect myself to follow the lessons in the specific order I've laid out. While I try to stick to a time frame, I don't require myself to adhere to arbitrary pacing. Instead, I try to feel out the pace of my students and work from there.

As a part of our unit on writing informational texts, I planned an arc focused on text structure. Judging from my students' initial writing samples (the pre-assessments for the unit), I saw an overwhelming need to address text structure. As a result, I generated a couple of ideas for lessons, one of which leveraged direct instruction to teach text structure. I introduced the various text structures to the children and then had them pick one to use for their topics. They completed a Thinking Map to make their text structure clear and visible, which served as my formative assessment for the arc before moving on to revising individual paragraphs.

> Planning in arcs allows us to strike a balance between preemptive structures and emergence.

It wasn't far into the lesson that I realized this was not a great way for them to truly grasp the differences between the different structures. Regardless, I had them try to apply it, and while meeting with individuals and small groups during the workshop portion of the lesson, I realized that my minilesson was hardly effective enough for them to be able to apply this independently to their pieces.

I didn't get down on myself, though, and I think this is really important to remember. If we are allowing our children to take risks and make mistakes in our classrooms, it's important that we allow ourselves to do so, too. Our inner dialogues as reflective practitioners must exude kindness, persistence, and constant reflection. Autonomy may be the cradle for pedagogical innovation, but courage, vulnerability, and self-kindness are the fibers that build the cradle itself.

> An inner dialogue must be reflective and critical, but it also must exude kindness and compassion.

My lesson may not have gone the way I intended, but that did not mean it was completely ineffective. It simply meant that I gained some new information about my students and my teaching. I learned that didactically sharing the different text structures and asking them to apply them readily was too much of a leap for third-graders. I considered another one of the ideas from this arc on text structure, where I planned to show them mentor texts that aligned with each text structure. But I knew this wouldn't work due to time constraints. While this would be a great reading activity, I was operating within the constraints of my grade-level team, and it was important to me to finish the unit as close to on time as I could, assuming that this didn't sacrifice deep and salient learning for my children.

It dawned on me that perhaps it might be helpful for my children to see me model my thinking—the type of thinking that might be necessary when evaluating text structures and deciding which one would best suit my topic. This modeling lesson was not in my original plan when I'd developed the arc. However, by picking up on a class-wide obstacle through anecdotal assessment, the idea for the lesson emerged. It allowed me to build on previous lessons, meanwhile targeting specific needs I'd discovered in my children. It also allowed me to model how I think about text structure when writing one of my own pieces. Since I hadn't put too much time into a rigid, lockstep series of lessons, I was easily able to change my lessons over the course of the arc.

Learning this about my students not only served them in the present; it also served my students the following year. The next year, I began my arc with this new lesson, modeling my thinking around text structure and taking two days to allow them to explore different topics and different text structures. By planning in arcs and allowing myself the opportunity to make mistakes the year prior, my pedagogy was forever changed. This would not have happened if I had blindly followed the curriculum manual or planned my lessons in an overly rigid, strictly day-by-day manner. Seeing the big picture, planning in arcs, and taking pedagogical risks helped me get there.

THINK-ALOUDS, DIALOGUE, AND DISCOURSE

Humanized personalization is a pedagogy that values human connection, mediated by conversation. This is why in Chapter 2 we identified dialogue and discourse as a hallmark of a strong second dimension, and why in Chapter 5 we discussed the importance of think-alouds and their role in fostering metacognition. These work together to foster a sense of connectedness to the collective conscious of the classroom, meanwhile nurturing students' inner dialogues.

Likewise, it is through serendipitous interpersonal communication that knowledge and understanding can emerge democratically in a classroom, much like the ecological analogies that sit at the foundation of this chapter. Similar to a flock of birds or a school of fish, the conversations our children have are guided by intuition and anticipation; they are instinctual and built on a schema composed of both the conscious and subconscious.

In describing this, I'm reminded again of Ellie, whom I mentioned in Chapter 5. One day, we were sitting on the front carpet, talking about some of her writing. Ellie struggled immensely with spelling, and frequently when we met, we would talk about strategies for spelling. That day on the front carpet, she asked me how to spell a word.

"Wait," she said, stopping herself almost immediately after asking me. "I know what you're going to say."

I smiled at her knowingly. "What am I going to say?"

"You're going to tell me to see if the word I want to spell is on the page," she said. She would frequently ask me how to spell words that were related to the topic we were writing about or studying. More often than you'd think, it would be in the question written on the page or on a sentence strip posted close by.

"And if that didn't work, you'd tell me to tap it," she finished.

And she was right. That was exactly what I was going to say to her. Ellie was still hurdling the early stages of spelling, despite the fact that she was in third grade. We had begun to scratch the surface of morphology, but she still hadn't quite mastered encoding all her basic sounds. Regardless, the fact that she knew what I was going to say was proof that my words had had a powerful impact on her, so much so that they had become a part of her internal dialogue.

In *Teaching Reading in Small Groups*, Jennifer Serravallo (2010) shares a powerful analogy for think-alouds. She equates them with how artists and art teachers help their students learn how to draw human figures. Drawing human figures is incredibly complex, but with the proper scaffold, ovals, it is possible to teach this complex art form. For a while, art students need these ovals to draw the human form accurately. With time, however, they are no longer needed. The scaffold has built in the artists' minds a more intuitive and direct pathway for drawing human figures. They no longer need the ovals to draw human figures and can instead draw them simply from intuition, no doubt recalling the ovals subconsciously.

We can't always see think-alouds working when we start doing them. In fact, sometimes when beginning, our children stare at us uncomprehendingly. But this is okay, because they're simply processing this new way of learning. We must, however, trust the process of thinking aloud and remember that it's like drawing the ovals for an apprentice artist. With time, the thinking patterns become intuitive and no longer require the scaffold, allowing us to model even more complex thinking patterns afterward.

This is precisely what I did to respond to my children's obstacle with text structure. I used a think-aloud to model how I might play with different text structures in my mind. I showed how my topic might (or might not) fit into a variety of text structures. By modeling my thinking through a think-aloud and asking them to engage in peer-to-peer discourse to evaluate my decision, I provided them the proper amount of scaffolding to apply the lesson to their topics. From there, I was able to capitalize on the second and third dimensions of personalized learning, where I met with small groups and gave feedback to individuals to reinforce the lesson, as needed.

PLAY, EXPLORATION, AND TINKERING

When I hear the word *play*, my kindergarten and first-grade classrooms immediately come to mind. I think of children building with blocks, drawing, or playing make-believe games where they pretend to be different characters. We should be doing everything we can to leverage play in the classroom, because play is the epitome of humanized personalization. Play normalizes failure and inherently teaches grit and persistence. It is also intrinsically conversational; it allows children to go through the Framework for Mediated Action repetitively, constantly conversing with themselves, each other, or whatever medium they are using for play.

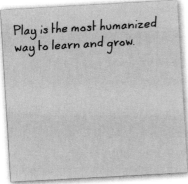

Play is the most humanized way to learn and grow.

The next time you watch a child build with blocks, watch the decisions they make and notice the dialogue that occurs between the child and the structure they're building. I witnessed this time and time again while working in the primary grades, but I didn't have words for it until I watched Devin one day in my classroom.

He was preoccupied with building the tallest tower he could, even though he had not yet fully understood the concepts of symmetry and balance. But I could see him developing an intuition for these concepts each time he built a new tower. The tower would grow, each block perilously placed higher and higher. When the tower was low to the ground, it would appear as if it was saying nothing. It stood there still, allowing Devin to continue adding blocks to it one by one. Its silence was a response all its own.

Keep building, it said to him.

As it grew taller, the tower began to speak to Devin. It would lean one way or the other, depending on the distribution of blocks. As a novice builder, Devin frequently ignored this communication from the tower. He would continue to build in a lopsided manner until he could no longer ignore the tower's message. Alas, his tower toppled time and time again. But eventually, he realized that the tower was trying to tell him something. The tower was telling him to distribute the blocks differently.

When the tower leaned, instead of placing the blocks on the side of the tower that was leaning, he began to place blocks on the opposite side, watching the tower carefully communicate that it had found balance with Devin's decision. This is why play is so magical and potentially valuable. He would not have reached that understanding without the space to engage in a conversation with the tower—and without the time to learn from his mistakes.

Play doesn't always necessitate concrete toys such as blocks or dramatic play centers. Children can play and tinker with all literacies and media, including math, reading, and writing. This means that we can even leverage play in the upper grades.

When meeting with small groups surrounding my third-grade text-structure lesson, I came upon Asher. He had a memory like a steel trap and frequently told me how easy things were, even when I could see that they weren't. I knew he'd always be able to consume and recall information with little to no problem, but his metacognitive and reflective abilities were underdeveloped. He didn't routinely demonstrate an ability to manipulate information and "play" with it to help him learn independently.

> Play doesn't have to stop in the younger grades. Older children can play and tinker with all the literacies—including the printed word and mathematics.

He came to me during workshop with his tablet in hand, unsure of which text structure to use. I could have asked him a series of probing questions, leading him to the text structure that I felt best aligned with his topic, but I knew that would not help him reach his full potential; it would not help him develop the reflective and metacognitive skills I knew he needed.

"All right," I said to Asher, "are there any text structures that you know won't work? Sometimes that's what I do when I need to solve a problem. I figure out what won't work first."

He looked at me, still unsure. "Uh, I think compare and contrast won't work. I don't think I'm comparing anything. I also don't think sequence will work. I'm not telling steps."

"Great," I replied. "What about the other ones?"

He went on to share that he thought it could be either problem/solution or description. Internally, I disagreed with problem/solution, unsure how he would fit his topic, skiing, into a problem-and-solution text structure. But it's important for us educators to remember that we don't necessarily know more than our children, especially about a topic as specific as skiing. Truthfully, I don't know a thing about skiing. So I replaced my skepticism with humility and instead asked him to play with the text structures.

"All right, I have an idea," I began.

Asher nodded.

"Why don't you go back to your seat and just try making two different text structures. Be flexible, and let yourself play with both of them. Maybe by doing that, you'll see which one works better for you."

He still seemed unsure. I knew he was craving an answer from me.

"I know you probably want me to tell you the answer, and I know it probably makes you a little bit *yellow* to be unsure. But I want you to give it a try anyway. Just see what happens. Maybe you'll make a mistake and learn something."

Asher went back to his desk and got right to work. It wasn't long before he came back to me, relieved that he'd found the answer.

"I tried doing the problem/solution text structure, and I realized I wasn't really trying to solve any problems. I used the description text structure and realized I wanted to describe the different levels of skiing. So, I think description makes sense."

I smiled and capitalized on the moment to help him reflect on what had just happened. Coincidentally, what he learned had little to do with writing. Instead, he learned something about himself. He learned that if he was unsure about what to do, he could play; he could try different solutions and use his own evaluative abilities to come up with a solution on his own.

But this would not have been possible had I not encouraged him to go and play.

MAKING SPACE FOR MULTIPLE STYLES OF WORKSHOP

We, too, must allow ourselves to play. It is through mindful exploration of our own ideas, exercising our autonomy, creating an internal dialogue within ourselves, and sharing our practice with others that we push the boundaries of pedagogy. In Chapter 2, we discussed the workshop model and its effectiveness in supporting the first dimension of personalized learning. It allows for didactic, direct instruction but also creates a great deal of space for the children to explore on their own, meanwhile giving the teacher time to meet with small groups and provide formative feedback. The workshop model concludes with a final point of convergence where the entire class is able to come back together and reflect.

In many cases, it makes sense to have the workshop model take on a more didactic form, but there are other possibilities, and to remain flexible and responsive to students' needs, feel free to play with other styles of the workshop model.

Complex Instruction and the Constructivist Workshop

Elizabeth Cohen and Rachel Lotan (1997), professors in the Stanford School of Education, developed an approach to promoting equity in classrooms by de-tracking students and leveraging heterogeneous grouping, all the while ensuring that every child—regardless of socioeconomic status, ability level, or group identity—gets what they need. It's called *complex instruction* (CI), and it's built on three key components: multiple-ability curricula, instructional strategies that promote social learning and human connection, and an enhanced awareness around issues of status in classrooms (see Figure 9.4).

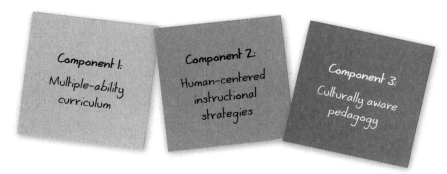

Figure 9.4: Components of Complex Instruction

In complex instruction, children converge around open-ended tasks or common provocations. These provocations are mindfully designed, intended to focus on a specific concept or discipline, but open-ended enough where children of varied abilities can converge around a common task, not only promoting social learning and human connection but also cultivating a sense of belonging among students, countering the stigma that comes from individualizing curriculum based on ability level.

Jo Boaler (2015) also lauds this approach in her recent educational masterpiece, *Mathematical Mindsets*. In it, she preaches an approach for teaching mathematics that grounds itself in complex instruction, using open-ended math tasks with a "low floor and high ceiling." When tasks have a low floor and high ceiling, it means they are accessible to students at various ability levels, once again promoting social learning and preserving a sense of belonging for all students. Her findings suggest that this form of instruction not only enhances student achievement but also changes students' mindsets around mathematics.

To begin her study, Boaler and her colleagues interviewed students in schools that use a traditional approach for teaching mathematics, asking, "What does it take to be successful in math?" Ninety-seven percent of students replied, "Pay careful attention," demonstrating both a fixed mindset and subtle anxiety around mathematical learning. In schools using CI, however, student responses to this question were markedly different, describing more varied behaviors such as "asking good questions" and "justifying methods" make one successful in math.

This deviates slightly from the typical structure of a workshop, which generally involves a focused minilesson, independent or small-group work time, and reflection, because it allows for mid-workshop teaching points where the whole group can converge to discuss methods. It's less didactic in nature, and it's for this reason that I call these *constructivist* workshops. While we are always trying to have children construct their own knowledge, the structure of this workshop is designed so children may discover teaching points, guided by intentional feedback and questions from the teacher.

Taking a constructivist approach requires a great deal of planning. It's a common misconception that constructivism and/or emergent curriculum requires less planning because so much is supposed to emerge from the children. But this isn't the case. Instead, it entails a nuanced understanding of the cognitive demands required of students, as well as an anticipation of the many misconceptions and routes children may take. Through my own professional exploration, I've learned how to create and/or choose math tasks and anticipate responses so I may guide my students through math workshop in this constructivist manner.

In the planning documents in Figure 9.5, you can see just how much thought and intention go into one lesson. Meghan Smith, my colleague and friend, introduced me not only to Lesson Study, but also to this way of planning. The planning document was adapted from her work. Not only do I draw on previous lessons to anticipate as many misconceptions as possible; I also try to create a lesson flow that allows for several points of convergence and divergence, also allowing me to pull small groups of students when necessary and possible. In some cases, I even allow for student-selected support, leaving my kidney table open for those who'd like to learn in a more intimate setting.

11.1.18

Target Objective

I can subtract using multiple strategies (i.e., open number line, base-ten blocks).

Task

Mr. France was doing some research on Chicago history and found this:

- In 1830, the population of Chicago was 98 people.
- In 1833, the population of Chicago was 351 people.
- By 1837, the population of Chicago was 4,470 people.

How much did the population change between 1830 and 1833?
How much did the population change between 1833 and 1837?

Anticipated Responses

Anticipated Response	Questions to Ask	Student Names
Incorrect Bar model	Are you saying that $99 + 351 =$ the amount it has changed?	
I don't know what to do.	Can you draw the problem to help you understand? Which numbers are important in the problem?	
Stacking	Please prove that method worked by demonstrating it in at least two other ways.	
Expanded form	Can you prove it in another way? Can you show those numbers in an open number line? How do you know that's accurate?	
$5 - 9 = 4$ (or small number minus a large number)	Can you prove to me that $5 - 9 = 4$? Can you prove to me that $50 - 90 = 40$?	
Base Ten Blocks	How might you represent this in your math journal?	
Number Lines	How might you make an even more efficient number line?	

(Continued)

Figure 9.5 (Continued)

Lesson Flow

Math Game (11:00 am)

- Bring whiteboards and markers to the rug

- Subtraction Top-It

Introduce Task (11:15 am)

- Create bar model for the task

- Introduce "Models for Subtraction" anchor chart—comparison and part-part-whole

Independent Work on Task (11:20 am)

- Small group: Alex, Neil, Darren, Greta, Jackson, Lilly

Mid-Workshop (11:30 am)

- Share Methods (5 min per method)

  o Method 1: Base Ten Blocks

  o Method 2: Open-Number Lines

  o Method 3: Adding with equations or an open number line

Finish Independent Work (11:45 am)

- Circulate and give feedback

Reflection (11:55 am)

- What was a mistake you made today? How did it help you learn?

- Which method makes the most sense to you?

Other reflection questions:

- Which method helped you learn something new?

- A question I still have is . . .

- Something someone said that helped my thinking was . . .

- Whose solution made the most sense to you?

- My idea changed from the beginning to end of the lesson because . . .

- A mistake I made was. . . . What I learned from this mistake was . . .

Source: Adapted from Jo Boaler, *Mathematical Mindsets*, Jossey-Bass (2015) and from Meghan Smith.

During these workshops, I routinely witness what Boaler's research has proven. Not only do my students demonstrate substantial growth with regard to academic achievement; their mindsets around mathematics change significantly. Students begin advocating for themselves, getting the learning tools they need; they become more persistent, open to trying different methods and tools to prove the same answer in various ways; they turn and talk with one another, connecting over different methods or even conflicting answers. This atmosphere I describe is humanized personalization realized. It's an environment that shows children motivated and engaged, toggling among all three dimensions of personalized learning and leveraging their own agency to learn in an equitable yet autonomous manner.

Reflective Workshop

Children are blessed with the gift of a present mind. As a result, they oftentimes take the present as self-evident, meaning they're unable to see just how much they've changed over a short period of time. They look at a final summative assessment, frequently unsurprised by their successes because it feels as though they've been like this all along. However, when they're able to see their previous work and compare it side-by-side, they see that this was not always the case. As a result, reflecting builds their confidence and helps them see that their hard work has contributed to their progress. According to Daniel Pink (2009), whom I referred to in Chapter 4, this is the definition of mastery—when we can connect our efforts to our achievement. A sense of mastery is critical to building intrinsic motivation, and structured reflection, built on the flexible frame, can help us achieve that.

Oddly enough, reflection is often the first thing to go when time becomes limited. I've done it time and time again, and it's usually because of my bias toward covering content. We all have a bias toward covering content; it makes us feel as if we're accomplishing more when we move forward and "cover" more. We feel like we're checking boxes and completing a to-do list. It's taken me a long time to try to break myself of this mindset. Even so, I still find myself falling into it regularly.

Reflecting requires us to go back in time, and as a result, it oftentimes feels repetitive and redundant. However, when we engage in reflection, we're not only reviewing and reinforcing already "covered" content; we are also teaching an entirely separate skill. Reflecting is very challenging to do, but by intentionally committing time to the reflection process, we are helping build an internal dialogue within our children. This internal dialogue will compound over time and develop autonomy

> Reflection, feedback, and self-reported progress are not only more humanized than web-based, individualized education; they're also more effective.

within our students, helping them learn, reflect, and make improvements to their work on their own. Moreover, John Hattie (2008) tells us that self-reported grades, feedback, and formative evaluation also have strong effects on learning—all of which are strengthened by student reflection.

The reflective workshop takes on a very similar form to the typical didactic workshop; it simply is used for a more specific purpose: reflection. To structure this effectively, I begin by making a reflection sheet, formulaic enough to provide children the structured scaffold they need to reflect on their own. I model how to use this sheet in a minilesson, thinking aloud while documenting my thinking on the sheet itself. You'll notice the first step is to read through the pre-assessment, post-assessment, and any documented work that's occurred in between. For this reflection in particular, they look through their math journals (see Figure 9.6).

Figure 9.6: Reflection Template

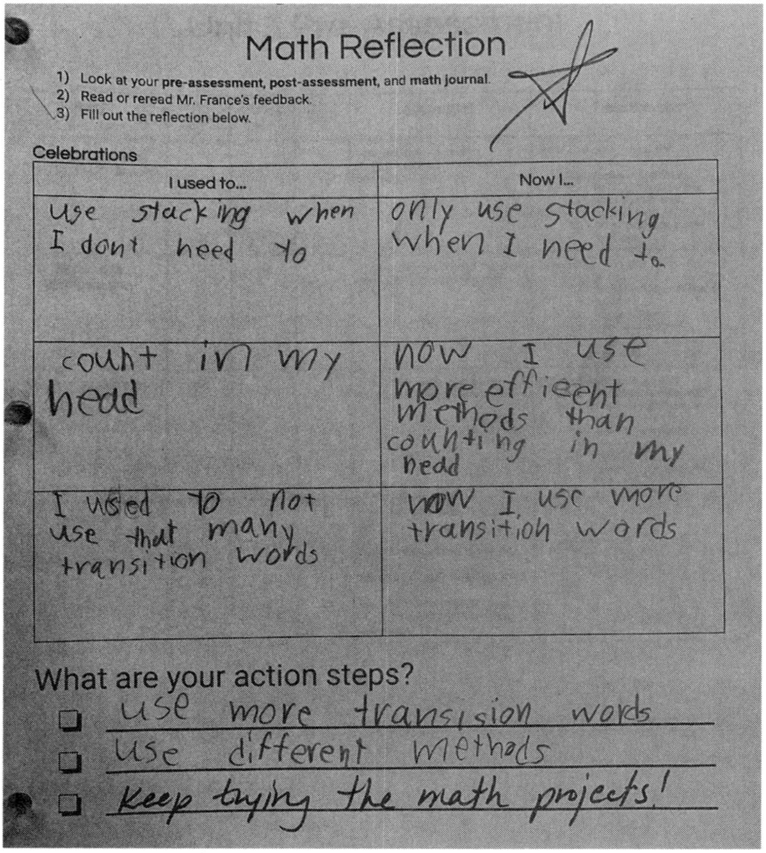

Math Reflection

1) Look at your pre-assessment, post-assessment, and math journal.
2) Read or reread Mr. France's feedback.
3) Fill out the reflection below.

Celebrations

I used to...	Now I...
use stacking when I dont need to	only use stacking when I need to
count in my head	now I use more efficent methods than counting in my head
I used to not use that many transition words	now I use more transition words

What are your action steps?
☐ use more transision words
☐ use different methods
☐ Keep trying the math projects!

After they've gone through this process, they can use multiple pieces of assessments to show what they "used to think" and what they now think or can do after having gone through the process of reflecting, similar to Project Zero's "I used to think . . . Now I think . . ." thinking routine. Shortly thereafter, students identify "action steps." As we all know, children oftentimes get to the end of a unit without fully mastering the learning outcomes. Leaving space for action steps allows learners to set goals for the future.

This is just one more reason why it's so important to build a flexible frame with clearly defined standards and assessment criteria: it aids reflection. Consistency and clarity with regard to learning outcomes provide a strong foundation on which children can reflect later. In math, for instance, the children are able to look at their pre- and post-assessments (as well as the rubrics or checklists on them) so they may use objective evidence to see how they've grown and which goals to set moving forward. Especially with young learners, this is nearly impossible without an immense amount of structure. What's more, the reflection itself is also a great artifact to bring home and share with parents. The reflection sheet, which you can see in Figure 9.6, scaffolds the conversation.

Choice Workshops and Quiet Time

Responsive Classroom (2015), the evidence-based approach to proactively managing student behavior mentioned in Chapter 6, advocates for *quiet time*. Quiet time helps children learn to build autonomy and agency in a scaffolded way. In my classroom, quiet time is reserved for *entirely independent work*. This means that, during this time, my students are not allowed to talk to others. They aren't even allowed to talk to me.

Within the first few weeks of school, I noticed just how challenging this was for my children. They had trouble abstaining from talking with friends or coming up to me to ask questions. While it's important that we create spaces for children to ask questions, it's also important to help them witness their own autonomy and build a sense of self-efficacy. The truth is that sometimes our students ask questions they don't need to ask, and answering them is a threat to their own autonomy. Simply put, sometimes they need to figure it out for themselves.

During quiet time, my students are expected to be completely independent. They choose from a limited number of choices—usually reading, writing, and drawing—and as they grow in their autonomy, I open up the choices even more. During this time, they are expected to problem-solve entirely on their own, without talking to neighbors or teachers. If they finish the books from their book bins, it's their responsibility to transition to a different choice or get a new book. If they complete a drawing, they may transition to writing or another choice they prefer.

"We are building our *still* stamina," I say to them. "We're not necessarily keeping our bodies still, but we're keeping our minds still within ourselves. We're taking time for ourselves, to give our minds what they need. We're taking time to show ourselves that we can solve problems on our own."

This is incredibly challenging for them at first. It's hard for us to go even thirty seconds without someone talking to a neighbor or coming up to ask me an unnecessary question. But with time and practice, we are usually able to achieve fifteen to twenty minutes of uninterrupted quiet time, with most students sustaining their attention to one activity. The impact on executive functioning skills—specifically with regard to self-regulation—is astounding. These behaviors spill over into other times of day, like reading, writing, or math workshop, where they are sometimes asked to sustain their attention to a given task or text for extended periods of time. We even go so far as to chart our progress, to help them set goals around "still stamina" and link their efforts to their achievements in this area (see Figure 9.7).

Figure 9.7: Still Stamina Chart

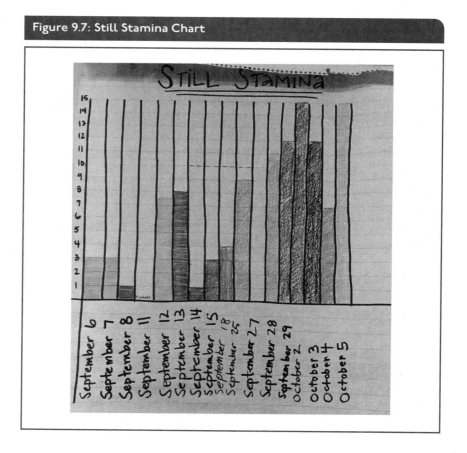

These sorts of experiences also allow us to build awareness around goal-setting. In Figure 9.7, you'll see a dotted line from September 14 to September 25. My class and I identified that as a reasonably high goal for still stamina. It felt as though it was in reach given two strong days on the twelfth and thirteenth, although it wasn't quite realized until the twenty-eighth. But even this allowed us to begin to cultivate an awareness around the purpose of assessment in our classroom. It helped us see just how much we'd grown over the course of the first four to six weeks of school, tangibly documented in our colorful still stamina chart.

And this is ultimately the goal of a choice workshop or quiet time. It's not for the construction of new knowledge, necessarily, but instead for the intentional training of social-emotional and executive functioning skills. It instills within children mindsets that will spill into other times of day and, if necessary, may even give educators time to meet with children one-on-one.

CULTIVATING AWARENESS AROUND THE PURPOSES OF ASSESSMENT

It was time for our first assessment of the year, and it was only the first week of school. I've come to learn that this is quite an unconventional move, but I can't see doing it any other way. After all, without some baseline assessment data, it's next to impossible to understand what the students in my class know and don't know, especially when I've just met them. At the same time, I understand the counterargument. It's tough giving an assessment in the first weeks of school. This can cause anxiety in our children, which is why it's exceptionally important to help our students understand the purpose of assessment in a personalized classroom before giving the first one.

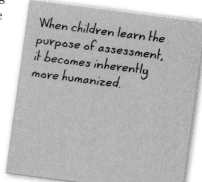

When children learn the purpose of assessment, it becomes inherently more humanized.

"I'm going to let you into my teacher brain," I told my new third-grade class. "But before I do, do you know why teachers give assessments?"

"To know our level?" one student said.

"To tell if we're good or bad at something?" another mentioned.

"So we know what our grade is?" a third said.

I'd expected these responses, and each of them is indicative, in a way, of what the industrialized model has done to our children's ways of thinking—and at such a young age.

"These are interesting ideas," I told them, "but it's a lot simpler than that. I'm not really interested in telling you whether you are *good* or *bad* at something, and I don't see it as knowing your 'level.' I think all of us have great strengths—things we know or are able to do really well—as well as things we can work on. I give assessments because it helps me see what we need to learn next."

There was still a palpable anxiety in the room despite my explanation. I could tell this was new to them, but I also trusted what I knew about persistence, resilience, and a growth mindset, using this as an opportunity to coach them through the uncomfortable feelings they were bringing to the table. Unfortunately, assessment is a necessary evil of modern education. It's one of the structures from the industrial era that will likely be around for quite some time. It is only through assessment that we'll better understand what our children need from us. And in a model of education where there are twenty, thirty, or even more students in one classroom, this unfortunately necessitates paper-pencil assessments.

In an ideal world, we'd sit down with each child and interview them for each assessment, asking questions that probe deeper into their psyches. While I try to do this as often as I can, we live in a world where there is not enough time to do this regularly. While we can work toward a more authentic way of assessing student learning as we explore new methods in our classrooms, in the meantime, we must use paper-pencil assessments as a tool for gauging what our students know and are able to do and helping them explore their own vulnerability and resilience. By opening up conversations like this and letting them into the intention behind assessment, we can help them do just that.

INQUIRY-DRIVEN LEARNING

Working in education technology taught me a lot about what *not* to do; so when I moved back to Chicago, I knew I needed to take stock of what *does* work in the classroom and recommit to pedagogy that puts human beings at the center. I knew that building a culture of agency and autonomy was important to me, and I also knew that helping my kids become independent thinkers and problem-solvers was important. It seemed to me as though I had forgotten just how important asking questions was in building student agency.

As a result, I prioritized teaching children how to ask questions. I wanted to help them see that questions are a means for independent learning. Here are a couple of simple ideas for explicitly teaching children how to ask questions in the interest of helping them become autonomous learners.

When greeting each other in the mornings, I teach my students about asking follow-up questions—about "keeping the conversation going," as I like to call it. They might ask someone how they are feeling or what they're doing later that week, eliciting what I consider to be mainly declarative knowledge. And instead of letting the conversation end there, I want them to see that they have two other options: they may ask more questions that elicit further discourse, or they may ask *thick* questions—nuanced questions that promote dialogue and discourse. We generally work hard on this over the first months of school, using the Responsive Classroom technique of *interactive modeling* to provide feedback on how to do this effectively. I tell the children what I'm going to teach them, and then I model it using only behaviors I hope they'll demonstrate. Finally, I have small groups of children model it for the class, receiving feedback as they go.

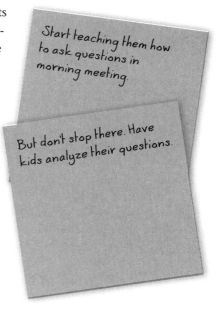

Start teaching them how to ask questions in morning meeting.

But don't stop there. Have kids analyze their questions.

Learning how to ask thick follow-up questions provides a path to inquiry-driven learning and building strong social, emotional, and academic competencies. Asking questions and engaging in productive academic discourse allows for the development of academic language (Zwiers, O'Hara, & Pritchard, 2014), helping remove a barrier that often impacts English-language learners or students whose oral language is not as developed as that of their grade-level counterparts. Collaborative conversations grounded in inquiry provide us not only a path to equity but a path to personalization that's humanized through conversation, connection, and interaction.

I generally begin the year with a unit on personal identity. I do this because it allows the children to get to know each other and themselves better. Inquiry ties in very naturally here, as to learn more about one another, we must ask thick questions. But I frequently notice that many of my students' questions are thin, eliciting only small and shallow bits of knowledge about their peers—such as favorite foods, colors, or after-school activities. To address this, we used iCardSort—one of the iPad applications I love so much for its flexibility—to sort the questions into groups.

We used it very similarly to when we created classroom rules and consequences. After generating questions together, I sent the sort to my children via Bluetooth, and from there, they were able to come up with more questions on their iPads. After, I encouraged them to sort the questions into "thick" and "thin" questions. It didn't take long for most of them to realize that they had asked mostly thin questions, and this was where I was able to model, using think-alouds, how I might come up with more complex questions—questions that asked *why* and *how*.

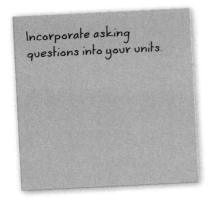

It wasn't long before our identity unit ended, culminating with the children composing their own identity books. In them, they shared bits and pieces about their friends, families, and neighborhoods, as well as reflections on how they viewed their identities and how their understanding of identity changed over the course of the unit. Because we had built a foundation for inquiry in this first unit, I used it to start our next social studies unit about Chicago history. While my team had gone through the process of planning the unit using the principles of backward design and building our flexible frame with Illinois Social Studies Standards and the Teaching Tolerance framework, we wanted to embody our desire to teach the children about asking questions by having them formulate guiding questions for the unit.

Using what we'd learned about thick and thin questions from the first unit, we took our children to the Chicago History Museum, which just so happened to be right across the street from us. While there, the children had one task: they had to generate at least ten "thick" questions, using the exhibits in the museum as provocations. Putting the onus on them created a perception that they had control over what we'd learn, even though we had specifically chosen certain exhibits to elicit specific questions about intentionally chosen content. By creating the illusion of choice, we found a balance between teacher- and student-driven learning. We mindfully set the field trip up as a provocation, one that would cause them to ask questions related to topics we knew we'd study, meanwhile helping them feel ownership over the course of the unit. This, in turn, created an investment in what we'd learn.

Our myths about personalized learning from Chapter 1 remind us that learning is *high-interest*, not necessarily *interest-based*. While we could have simply thrown it up in the air and let them learn about any topic related to Chicago they found interesting, we knew that was neither sustainable, scalable, nor best for the kids. We knew that motivation, instead, comes by instilling senses of autonomy, mastery, and purpose in children. Inquiry helps us achieve all those ends. Generating questions on their own helps them exercise autonomy and lay the foundation for mastery, as they'll be able to connect their efforts to what they'll later learn and recognize that they played the most significant role in deepening their understanding of any given content area. And finally, they'll have a sense of purpose. They'll know *why* they're learning it—after all, they are the ones who asked the question!

It is here we can see how teaching truly becomes an art: we must engineer learning environments and educative experiences for our children that not only elicit the knowledge and understanding we want them to develop but also help them witness their agency and engage with their autonomy.

When we returned from our field trip, we compiled all our questions. We grouped them based on similarities and synthesized more than a hundred questions into guiding questions we could use for weekly learning arcs. Even then, our question-asking didn't stop there. They needed to know that asking questions would continue throughout each of our units, that learning would never stop, and that even at the end of a unit of learning, there would be questions unanswered.

Inquiry starts conversations—conversations that beget even more questions and conversations, perpetuating a sustainable cycle of inquiry that will continue over the course of a unit. It's for this reason that inquiry is the hallmark of responsive and humanized instruction: asking questions is part of the human condition. To question is to be human; it's how our conscious has managed to evolve, and it's how it will continue to evolve until the end of time.

Industrialized models for education pose a threat to this, especially industrialized models that are supported by web-based, adaptive technologies. These technologies accelerate students through content instead of mindfully decelerating students, providing opportunities to move beyond one plausible answer and toward uncertainty and limitless possibility. I've seen this in countless classes—children obsessed with getting minutes on their tablets, infatuated with gamified levels of academic content. Make no mistake, this is neither engagement nor excitement for learning; this is addiction.

As educators, our job is to notice these patterns of digital addiction in our children and counteract them with a pedagogy that rehumanizes our classrooms. It wasn't until partway through the aforementioned Chicago history unit that I recognized the benefits of explicitly teaching my children how to use inquiry to learn independently. While studying early Chicago, we examined a page from the journal of Henri de Tonty, one of the first French people who came to what is now called Chicago. He referred to the natives as "savages," which managed to catch many of the kids' attention.

The week prior, we'd learned about inquiry through a cycle of inquiry, a framework I had chosen to help my children learn how to ask questions. We used this cycle of inquiry to learn more about the various perspectives at play in early Chicago, attempting to answer the question: *To whom does Chicago belong?* Through reading stories and examining primary resources, much like the page from Tonty's journal, children were able to notice, think independently, and engage with their curiosity. In Figure 9.8 is an example of an inquiry cycle, adapted from International Baccalaureate (2014). There are lots of inquiry cycles out there, and I suggest you find one that suits your style and needs.

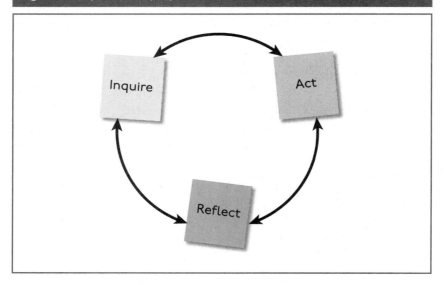

Source: Adapted from Middle Years Programme: Evaluating MYP Unit Planners, International Baccalaureate Organization, 2015.

Shortly after discovering the word *savages* and discussing what it meant, Asher came up to me and said, "Mr. France, maybe we can use the word 'savages' to continue the cycle of inquiry! I'm wondering why they would call them that."

I smiled at Asher, sharing his sentiments, reveling in the fact that the learnings about inquiry had transferred and were so readily recalled in gleeful serendipity, confirmation for me that autonomous learning was bubbling beneath the surface of our unit on Chicago history.

But teaching inquiry doesn't have to start and end with a cycle of inquiry. There are other ways to help children become metacognitive around questioning. I suggest looking into Project Zero's work, as well, as there are many routines that promote inquiry through structured thinking routines, such as See-Think-Wonder, Question Starts, or Think-Puzzle-Explore (see Ritchhart, Church, & Morrison, 2011).

STORYTELLING

To be human means to have a story, and most stories are embedded with lessons that draw connections between human beings. Through our stories of joy, success, failure, pain, and vulnerability, we are able to connect with one another. We're able to break down the barriers that diversity can bring and instead revel in what we can learn from our differences. Stories have that unique power.

Stories humanize the very profession to which you and I have chosen to dedicate our careers, and as a result, stories can humanize the experiences of our little ones, as well. Storytelling is the final hallmark of responsive, humanized instruction that I will share with you—and for a very specific reason. The humanized classroom is shaped by the stories of individuals within distinct and intersectional identities.

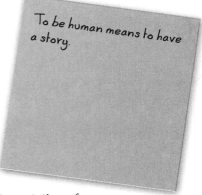

To be human means to have a story.

You could take this quite literally and make space for children to tell their own stories from their lives. But you could also take this figuratively. Telling one's story could mean a lot of different things: it could mean sharing your interpretation of a text; it could mean sharing about a topic that is especially important to you; it could mean reflecting on academic work and telling a story of obstacles and process. What humanizes the learning process and ultimately personalizes it—more than an automated program or list of individualized activities ever could—is the minutiae that come from *telling our own* stories.

Student-driven conferences or portfolios are a great way to help children tell their own stories. After all, what's more personal than being able to document your journey as a learner? While this could be done with the traditional binder, there are technology tools that can support this, as well. It could be something as simple as taking pictures on a camera or tablet. It could become more complex with Google Drive, allowing children to make folders that document their learning. I've also enjoyed exploring Seesaw these past few years, as it allows children to reflect on their learning in all the ways kids know how, from talking about their learning to writing and even drawing about it.

When we make space for children to tell their stories, we see that there is no right or wrong way to learn. While building a flexible frame is important, it's not the individualization of the content or the assessments that makes learning personalized; it's the journey each child takes to get to these ends that humanizes personalization. We must make it a priority to help our kids tell their stories.

ENGENDERING A GROWTH MINDSET IN EDUCATORS

We must make it possible for educators to tell their stories, as well. Industrialization assigns everything a fixed purpose. Anything that could potentially act in opposition to the predetermined product in an industrialized environment is seen as a costly waste of resources. And when trying to scale a pre-molded product out to the masses, this makes sense. But what we are continuing to learn is that education cannot and should not be seen as a pre-molded product that is the result of a mechanistic system. It is not an industrialized process, and as a result, it cannot be mass-produced through purely replicative means. It's messier than that because it involves people.

Making the shift from industrialization to humanization means that we will have trouble immediately finding purpose in everything that our humanized and personalized classrooms create. It means we'll have to find solace in discomfort and invest our trust in the uncertain. It means we have to be willing to watch our students make mistakes and maybe sometimes even watch them "waste time." It means we have to allow knowledge and understanding to emerge democratically, through play, exploration, inquiry, and storytelling—for these are the most intimate and *personal* ways to learn. It means we'll have to make *ourselves* vulnerable to taking risks, making mistakes, and exploring our own autonomy as educators, too.

> Educators, too, must be willing to take risks, make mistakes, and be vulnerable with their practice.

Humanizing personalization not only calls for a change in how we view our curriculum, assessment, and instructional practices; more important, it necessitates a change in how we view *ourselves* in our classrooms. Just as we don't want our children to be mindless consumers of education, we also must take part in the production of education in our classrooms, as opposed to simply following a curriculum manual or reverting to traditional pedagogy that promotes compliance over autonomy. This will be scary and uncomfortable at first, but it will be absolutely necessary to welcome the messy process, to engage with it, and to show ourselves the same kindness and compassion we show our children in a personalized and humanized learning environment.

Storytelling transcends risk-taking, mistake-making, and academic progress; it's more than just an avenue for meaningful reflection. Storytelling is important in a personalized classroom because it cultivates inclusivity and a sense of belonging—both of which lie at the foundation of humanizing personalization. It is impossible to shape the collective conscious or nurture an inner dialogue if children do not make the choice to do so—if they do not enhance their awareness, engage with their agency, and choose to interact with the learners and learning environment around them. When learners do not feel a sense of belonging—when they don't feel included for their strengths, challenges, and idiosyncrasies—they withdraw, become isolated, and shy away from human connection.

A fish will not stay with the school if it believes it's not a fish; a bird will travel astray without the innate and instinctual notion of belonging with the flock. Likewise, our children will not engage in the collective conscious of the classroom if they cannot see and sense themselves within it. I refrained from including cultural awareness and responsiveness within this chapter on humanized instruction, for I felt it deserved more than simply a section within a chapter. I instead wanted to leave you with the idea that diversity, equity, and inclusion are foundational to humanizing personalization—and they are all too often overlooked when discussing personalized learning.

After all, for learning to be inherently personal and meaningful, it must speak to an individual's inner dialogue. Each one of our individual voices is distinct and intersectional—composed of different colors, races, and ethnicities; both gendered and genderless; ranging in ability; possessing different belief systems, impacted by family structures and histories. They come wrought with inextricable experiences and memories—memories of happiness, struggle, connection, trauma—all of which impact the way learners see and communicate with themselves and the world around them.

In the final section of this book, we will unpack diversity, equity, and inclusivity, and develop an understanding for how these are, in fact, foundational to humanizing personalization. You'll notice that I've very specifically chosen the words cultural *awareness* and *responsiveness*, as opposed to cultural *competence*. Cultural competence implies an ending point; it implies that after a certain amount of time, our work will be complete. But within the personalized classroom, we understand that our children are constantly changing and diversifying. This necessitates a constant evolution and diversification of our pedagogy so we may build inclusive and equitable learning environments in which all can participate. This constant evolution means that our work will never be done.

For some of you, this will be your first foray into diversity, equity, and inclusion in the context of personalized learning; for others, this will be a continuation of your journey in exploring your privilege, bias, and identity in the context of teaching and learning. Regardless, for all of us, our work will continue long after you've completed the final three chapters of this book. The purpose for these final three chapters is not to leave you with clear and concrete answers but instead to provide a provocation for the continuous evolution of your practice.

SECTION II

PEDAGOGY

Implications for Humanized Personalization

Humanized pedagogy consists of three major components: building the flexible frame, humanizing assessment to better understand the collective conscious and the inner dialogue, and humanizing instruction so educators may be flexible and responsive to student needs (see Figure II.I).

Figure 11.1: Humanized Pedagogy

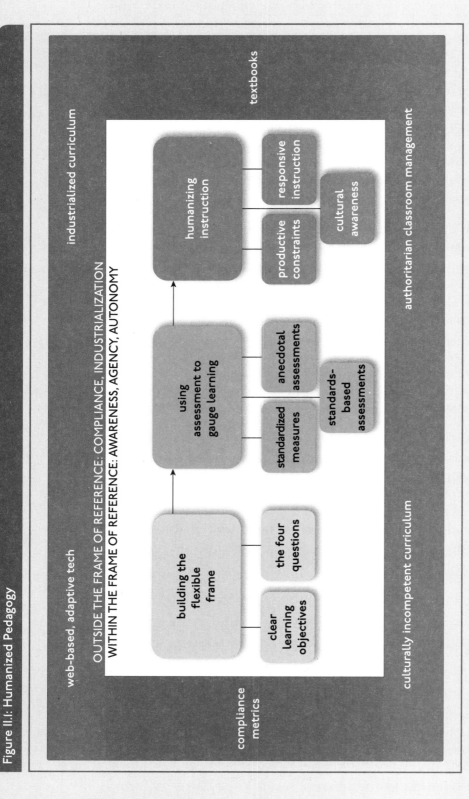

web-based, adaptive tech

industrialized curriculum

OUTSIDE THE FRAME OF REFERENCE: COMPLIANCE, INDUSTRIALIZATION

WITHIN THE FRAME OF REFERENCE: AWARENESS, AGENCY, AUTONOMY

compliance metrics

textbooks

building the flexible frame

clear learning objectives

the four questions

using assessment to gauge learning

standardized measures

anecdotal assessments

standards-based assessments

humanizing instruction

productive constraints

responsive instruction

cultural awareness

culturally incompetent curriculum

authoritarian classroom management

The classroom is an emergent ecosystem, and as a result, it is fueled by the energy of its inhabitants. In the classroom ecosystem, children should be the primary producers of education. To do this, they must access their *agency* and witness their *autonomy*. Remember these tips to help you build agency and autonomy within your students.

Tip	What to Say	What to Do
First impressions are everything.	Make your boundaries clear with your students, and tell them why you've set those boundaries.	Hold true to those boundaries. No exceptions.
Build routines, expectations, and consequences as a class.	"This is your classroom, and I need your help making rules we can all live by."	Use thinking routines and Thinking Maps to make these visible to students.
Praise the journey, risk-taking, and mistake-making.	"Thank you for making a brave mistake. Now we can all learn from it."	Make mistakes and take risks in front of your students. Then show them how you use those to learn.
Let go, and let kids fail.	"Nobody's perfect, and I know you can handle this. I'll be here to help you if you need it."	Give kids space to grapple with complex tasks and sit in the discomfort that comes with struggle and failure.
Reflect, reflect, reflect.	"Wow! You used to _____, and now you are _____. I'm so happy to see that you've taken some risks and grown from it."	Bookend your lessons and your units with focused reflection, even if you feel you don't have time.
Ask if you can give feedback.	"Can I give you some feedback?"	Honor their request if they say no, and give them the option to accept or reject your feedback if they say yes.

Developing *agency* and *autonomy* will be insufficient without explicitly developing a child's self-awareness. Start with these guideposts when cultivating awareness in your classroom.

Guideposts	What You'll Need
Set up a mindfulness practice.	Training on mindfulness Your own mindfulness practice A singing bowl and a morning meeting
Set weekly intentions with your students.	A list of intentions A place to post the weekly intention in your room
Explicitly teach emotional awareness and emotional regulation.	Zones of Regulation by Leah Kuypers (2011) Superflex by Stephanie Madrigal and Michele Garcia Winner (2008) Peace corner
Model the thinking and speaking you expect to hear from children.	Thinking stems Think-alouds Resilience and a growth mindset
Social and emotional learning are not benign subjects.	Opportunities for modeling awareness in the core curriculum Think-alouds and thinking stems
It starts with the adults in the room.	A conscious knowledge of yourself as an educator and human being The humility to learn and grow with regard to your own social and emotional awareness

Curriculum, assessment, and instruction are too often industrialized, making policymakers and administrators the primary producers of education. In reality, children should be the primary producers of learning, constructing their experiences within the laws that govern the classroom ecosystem. It's not always easy to see the difference between industrialized and humanized practices, for they share some characteristics. Use the map in Figure II.2 to help you understand whether your personalized practices are humanizing or dehumanizing.

Figure II.2: Comparing and Contrasting Dehumanized and Humanized Personalization

HUMANIZED PERSONALIZATION

Standards provide **constructive constraints** and **evolve** with the children, and are subject to revision on a consistent basis.

Assessment practice is **multidimensional** and serves as an objective medium for focused **reflection** in relation to agreed-upon benchmarks.

Instruction allows learning to **emerge** through co-construction between educators and students.

Clear standards provide **a structure** and **common language** for learning outcomes.

Assessments are aligned to standards and provide **valid and reliable data** for success metrics.

Instruction is **aligned to standards** and teaches with the end in mind.

DEHUMANIZED PERSONALIZATION

Standards serve as a **rigid structure** that is more confining than liberating. Standards are fixed and not subject to revision.

Assessments generally gauge the **reproduction** or **regurgitation** of material.

Automated instruction adjusts for **pace** and amount of **repetition**, but **does not allow for agency and autonomy** in the construction of knowledge.

SECTION THREE

EQUITY

CHAPTER TEN

A SENSE OF BELONGING

It was a Friday evening in early November 2013, just as the wholesome Midwest began to go to sleep for winter. The lights in the hallways were shut off, leaving them dark and quiet. I looked down to the end of the hallway, out a large floor-to-ceiling window, to see a nearly empty parking lot and an overcast sky.

Just then, my teammate, Markus, left his classroom, also ready to go home for the weekend. He walked excitedly down the hallway toward me in his oversized hipster beanie, bushy beard, and hand-knit scarf. He stopped in front of me with an excited grin on his face, recounting the news that Illinois had just legalized marriage equality; it would be signed into law just a few weeks later and put into effect the following summer. Unbeknownst to me, the brief interaction that followed would change the course of my career— and my life.

"I think we should do a lesson about it," Markus said, the *it* being marriage equality.

I had to think about it, I'll admit. I wasn't sure if I was ready to take that on. I had hardly built up the confidence to be out to my colleagues over the course of my then three and a half years there, much less to host a discussion about marriage equality with fifth-graders. I wasn't sure that I was emotionally prepared to face homophobic and discriminatory remarks from children—not to mention their parents.

That year, we were on a team of six teachers, me and Markus included. We were like brothers and sisters, possessing a love for one another that has yet to be extinguished, despite the fact that we all work in different places and, in some cases, even different states. So when Markus and I brought this idea to the team one night not long after Markus approached me, I was surprised at their apprehension. When they asked if we were planning on talking with our principal first, we mentioned that we weren't, assuming she'd say no. This didn't sit well with the rest of our team. Their discomfort was palpable; so Markus and I continued with the plan on our own, trying to respect our team's wishes.

I empathized, not wanting any of them to risk their jobs for the cause. I understood that they had lives to lead and this could, in fact, put their jobs in jeopardy—or at the very least, their standing with the principal. Had I not been in my situation, I can't guarantee I would have made a different decision than they did, and to this day, I don't blame them for it. I know what it's like—being an already underpaid teacher, afraid to lose a job. My only regret from that time period was not telling them then and there just how much their hesitation and eventual inaction hurt.

The key to building strong relationships—and ultimately to cultivating a sense of belonging in schools—is vulnerability, honesty, and of course justice. Because I didn't confide in them just how much I was hurting, it caused a part of me to disengage and disconnect with them over the remainder of the school year. It wasn't rare for feelings of resentment to bubble up in a team meeting without their knowledge. *To them*, I sometimes thought, *I am taboo. I am controversial.* I was the *other* in the situation, the one who was pitiable but also the one for whom few were willing to advocate.

Regardless, Markus and I pushed forth, intent on our decision to host the lesson. We used what we knew about social justice education to plan it. We found an article from the *Washington Times* that summarized both sides of the issue. We revised it slightly to remove words such as *bestiality*, which we deemed child-inappropriate, without taking away relevant points of the opposing argument, such as defending the sanctity of marriage and family. We also found articles intended to educate about tolerance and the origin of values. After we assembled the resources, we crafted an e-mail to send to families, sharing the articles, identifying some guiding questions for the discussion, and explaining the importance of the topic and its relation to our curriculum specifically in the context of the Common Core State Standards (see Figure 10.1).

Cultivating a sense of belonging in schools necessitates vulnerability, honesty, and advocating for justice.

What is the definition of tolerance?

What does tolerating another person's beliefs look and sound like?

Can you tolerate another person's beliefs without agreeing with them?

Is it okay to not know what I believe?

Do I have to share my beliefs?

Do you believe people should have the right to marry whomever they want? Why or why not?

By this point, we had not yet informed the administration of our plans. While Markus and I had deliberated about asking permission, we ultimately decided not to. We didn't want to put our then principal in a position where she'd have to say no. And we knew she would.

But we also chose not to ask on principle. After all, we were able to discuss barbaric deaths and killings in the Revolutionary War and the Holocaust within our curriculum. Surely the idea of marriage equality was far less graphic.

Justice goes beyond giving every individual what they need; justice entails righting wrongs and leveling the playing field.

Markus and I sent the e-mail to families on a Thursday evening, informing them that we'd be hosting the lesson in just a few short weeks. We copied the principal on the e-mail to inform her of our intent. Hindsight and maturity have granted me some wisdom since then; they have helped me see that my impulsivity was indicative of my own desire to rebalance the scales in favor of the LGBTQ population. I wanted to expose the hypocrisy and homophobia that bubbled beneath the surface of upper-middle-class White America. I wanted justice.

At the time, my then principal claimed that it could have turned out differently had we gone to her first. But if that was true, the following series of events would not have occurred. It was these events that allowed me to see the extent to which homophobia and bigotry had poisoned the wholesome suburb where I taught. The antidote to this poison was exposure and vulnerability, offering me redemption from my own internalized homophobia and that of a heteronormative school system. For that, I'll be forever grateful.

Coincidentally, one of my teammates was getting married that same weekend. The morning after Markus and I sent the e-mail to families about discussing same-sex marriage, we showered our teammate with a celebratory breakfast, decorating her classroom in white, with toilet paper hanging from the ceilings and walls, and adorning the table with a golden cloth and champagne flutes for sparkling wine. It wasn't long before the principal showed up at the school-condoned celebration of our teammate's marriage, her anger and frustration palpable.

"Can I see the two of you in my office?" she gestured toward Markus and me.

We walked quietly down to the office, and the door was closed behind us.

"I'm so incredibly disappointed in both of you," she said, heaping shame on us.

"Well, I've never been prouder of myself," Markus replied. I smiled, honored to have him not only as a friend but as a true ally and advocate for the LGBTQ community.

Markus was—and continues to be—the gold standard for allyship. A cisgender, straight White man, swimming in privilege that more often promotes complacency over action, he was steadfast and true to our original intentions, never wavering. "A good friend would bail you out of jail," he later said to me. "But a best friend is the one sitting there in the cell with you saying, '*Damn*, that was fun!'"

"And, Paul," my principal said, turning to me, "you should know that the classroom is not the place for personal agendas."

It's impossible to engage in a school's collective conscious if we do not belong.

She was, of course, referring to the fact that I was the *gay* person in the room—the one who would so selfishly advocate for his own minority group, similar to how a Black teacher might bring up discussions of racism or how a female teacher might address gender inequality. What she failed to say—but what I heard loudly and clearly—was that our school was, instead, the place for *her* heteronormative personal agenda. My heart sank; my shoulders drooped. I felt defeated, for if the leader of my school was not ready to openly and warmly welcome the gay community into the school, how could I ever feel as though I truly belonged? How could I engage in the collective conscious of the school and build trust among colleagues and students if I wasn't able to be vulnerable, embrace my identity, and be true to myself?

A FORUM FOR CHANGING THE WORLD

When discussing personalization, we oftentimes default to many of the myths I outlined in Chapter 1. We discuss academic level, time on task, and assessment scores. We talk about closing "the achievement gap" and teaching within the zone of proximal development. If we're lucky, we may even talk a bit about socioeconomic status and institutionalized bigotry—and how these factors have contributed to the current status of the education system. But we too often neglect to search for what sits beneath all this: Our education system is not built with everyone in mind. It's not built with the intention of cultivating a sense of belonging for every individual who enters into it.

I know that I'm not speaking for all schools or educators when I say this. In fact, I know it's quite the opposite. I'm not trying to demonize educators or administrators, either, because I've met far too many whose top priority is just that: to cultivate spaces where all are welcomed, loved, and nurtured as is. Instead, I'm trying to convey the extent to which the incentives and structures of the education system inhibit educators and administrators from creating learning environments where all are welcome and feel as though they belong.

In my heart, I believe that my then principal wanted to do good, even in that situation. Months later, she confided in me that she, too, would have wanted her granddaughter in a classroom where the LGBTQ community was talked about openly. She saw a future where that was accepted. Her decision-making in the present, however, was dictated by fear.

"This is not the forum for changing the world," she said as our meeting concluded. In that moment, it became exceedingly clear to me just how dehumanized she had become through years and years in an oppressive system, unable to make a just decision of her own volition. But my anger overpowered my sympathy for her. In this situation, she was in a position of power and privilege. It was her responsibility as an instructional leader— and as a cisgender, straight White woman—to advocate on my behalf and amplify my voice as a member of a minority group.

I crossed my right leg over my left knee, rested my head in my right hand, and looked at her dumbfounded. I was nearly speechless, unsure of how to rebut such ignorance.

She was wrong. She just had to be. The classroom is, in fact, a forum for changing the world—and it will always be. It's a place where we can alter the collective conscious of a group of people, opening their minds to new ideas and new ways of thinking; it's a place where we can nurture learners' inner dialogues, helping them develop an attitude toward learning that encourages them to *act* in the face of adversity and injustice. If not in the classroom, then where?

A few months passed, and I managed to fly under the radar. After the respite of winter break and the renewal of the New Year, I was ready to recommit to my students and find contentment in the relationships I'd built with them. But it seemed I wouldn't be able to escape the fallout from what would come to be known as the "controversial lesson incident" of the previous November. In early February, about three months after, I heard from the superintendent for the first time since the incident.

> The classroom will always be a forum for changing the world.

> Whenever addressing issues of discrimination, make sure to have a strong ally with you.

"I was going to stop in to see how you're doing," he said to me in an e-mail, "learn of any iPad insights you've gained so far, talk about the controversial lesson incident you were a part of this past fall . . . learn how the Common Core implementation is faring, see how your leadership aspirations are developing, etc. As you can see, there is a lot I wanted to check in about."

Suspicious of his true intentions, I called on the union president immediately, as I would suggest all teachers do in these sorts of situations. I agreed to meet with the superintendent, but only if the union president was there. Months later, at my final evaluation, my principal mistakenly told me that *she* had actually asked the superintendent to meet with me, to see if I had "learned my lesson" regarding the marriage equality lesson. It turned out that my suspicions were warranted.

It's true that I *had* learned a lesson, just not the one they hoped I'd learn. I'd learned to be vulnerable, to "draw deep on my courage," as Brené Brown (2015) would say, and to speak truth to power—even though it was terrifying.

"Frankly speaking," I said to him, "I'm incredibly disappointed that our district would ban a discussion about this."

He provided the same rationale my principal had. He noted it "wasn't the right time" to be discussing this issue, and that perhaps sometime in the future the community might be ready for a discussion about marriage equality. I attempted to rebut and debate, but it was clear that his stance was immovable.

"It sounds like you're taking this personally," he replied, "but this isn't personal."

He was right. I *was* taking it personally. And I had every right to.

"What you're telling me," I retorted, "is that I can't talk about people like me in school. I can't help but take that personally."

He responded, expressing his concern that I was imparting my own values on my students, conveying the very same message my principal had just months prior—that I was acting out of a personal agenda, instead of in the best interests of my students. The superintendent was asking me to teach *without* my personal values, to put a boundary up and block out this very important part of my identity—and all for the sake of the children.

Youthful defiance shot out of every pore of my body. I felt my face flush with anger and my heart begin to race. It became obvious that the district and its administration would not be changing any time soon. Shortly thereafter, our conversation ended, and I learned that the superintendent had chosen to meet only with me. Markus was my *straight* and equal counterpart in this situation, yet the superintendent had felt it necessary to have a discussion only with me—to see if the *gay man* had learned his lesson, allowing the straight man to continue on with his year, not needing to learn a lesson or reflect any further.

To me, it was more evidence that their decision was discriminatory in nature; it was more evidence that the culture of the school was not designed with all in mind. I retraced my steps, looking at old e-mails, intent on proving that the world was, in fact, ready to welcome the LGBTQ community into the classroom and that the district had acted discriminatorily.

Markus and I had sent the e-mail to fifty-four families. Of those families, eleven replied to our original e-mail or the follow-up e-mail the district sent communicating the banning of the discussion. Three of those replies supported the district's decision to ban the discussion, while eight of them replied in emphatic support of bringing the LGBTQ community into the classroom openly and proudly. The remaining families did not feel strongly enough to reply either way.

The data spoke for itself. Institutionalized homophobia, fear, and shame—not the will of the families—guided the decision-making of the district's administration. The administration acted in the name of preserving the status quo, but they did so at the expense of the LGBTQ population.

When we act in opposition to diversity, equity, and inclusion, we act in opposition to humanizing personalization. We do so because, for children to learn meaningfully—to access their agency, witness their autonomy, and otherwise play on the flexible frame of standards, assessment, and humanized instruction—they must know deep down that they belong. This is a precursor not only to agency and autonomy but to *vulnerability*. They must be able to sense their belonging in every way possible: from the words their teachers speak right down to the stories teachers choose to share within the classroom. Creating a culture of belonging necessitates acceptance, representation, and most of all *pride* in all identities.

Expressing pride in all identities is critical to cultivating a sense of belonging.

THE THREAT TO BELONGING

I had my final evaluation that year in March, about one month after my meeting with the superintendent and about five months after the principal called Markus and me into her office, accusing me of pushing a personal agenda. Two observations had occurred since November, both touting my thoughtful planning, responsive pedagogy, and reflective practice. I say this not to toot my own horn but instead to add a layer of context that will help you understand the full impact of this discriminatory "controversial lesson incident."

The year prior, I was rated *excellent*, a new evaluative level in Illinois, intended to incentivize teachers to innovate in their practice. Shortly after my *excellent* rating, I learned that the district had established an unofficial quota for *excellent* teachers. Of the roughly four hundred teachers in my district, about ten of them were rated *excellent* that year. They had decided, behind closed doors and without transparency, that only so many teachers could be rated *excellent* within one school or one given year. To determine this, each principal would pitch various cases to a room full of principals, most of whom had not even seen these educators in action. I was one of those chosen that year.

Not only did this pose ethical issues; it posed a threat to evaluative validity and reliability, too. The very nature of criterion-referenced evaluation is that, should an individual meet the criteria as determined by the evaluation tool itself, said individual should be rated as such. In that district, however, it is reasonable to infer that the *excellent* rating was used as a compliance metric—to otherwise dehumanize the process of professional growth by making teachers compete for a coveted ten spots—give or take a few. As we now know from Chapter 8, assessment that intends to compare and rank individuals instills a culture of compliance, competition, and shame. It is dehumanizing. Professional evaluation that compares and ranks teachers does this, as well, and the effects of it trickle down to our students.

Much to my surprise, my final evaluation was glowing that year. "Mr. France continues to exhibit numerous strengths in all aspects of his teaching," read the evaluation, written by my former principal. "This year, his participation in the National Board Certification Program, has served to enhance his practice to even higher levels." These words alone connoted that my practice had, in fact, risen above the levels necessary to earn me an *excellent* rating the year prior. She went on to identify seven additional components of the Danielson Framework for Teaching in which I rated in the *distinguished* category, including my contributions to the professional community, such as planning professional development for the community, effectively implementing our one-to-one initiative, participating in curriculum mapping, and demonstrating my team's use of incorporating instructional technology "to enhance curriculum, instruction, and assessment."

Her evaluation of my performance ended with this.

I have identified the following area as one in which Paul can continue to reflect and grow. This year, Paul and a colleague engaged in a decision-making process that resulted in a significant error in judgment, one that compromised a District 34 policy, that put his principal in a position that required her to make other decisions that polarized our parent community, and a decision that did not include the rest of his team—a team that has, in the past, been held up and highlighted as THE standard for teamwork, effective collaboration and cohesion. The opportunity for growth, comes in the reflective process that [led] Paul to respond in a manner that inhibited the growth and progress that can come from such mistakes.

Once this situation was brought to his attention, Paul could have responded by coming back to his principal and seeking support in formulating a plan to affect change in curriculum or policy that could have [led] to realizing his original intent for developing his lesson on empathy and tolerance using the Gay Marriage Act.

This process, using proper channels to properly vet all perspectives and develop a systematic, District-wide approach to teaching children about controversial but important topics, could have benefited children everywhere. Instead, Paul expressed frustration and resentment at the decision and professionally withdrew from the situation.

Despite the fact that these were her words, she attempted to relieve herself of taking responsibility for them. She stated that she originally brought my case to the room of administrators as an *excellent* teacher and that the superintendent, as well as the technology director, voiced their disapproval of an *excellent* rating for someone who demonstrated such an "error in judgment." After that, she stated that she concluded on her own that I was undeserving of an *excellent* rating that year, giving me no choice but to accept this act of discrimination and injustice.

Even then—even in that very moment of outright discriminatory behavior—I still didn't believe my former principal to be a homophobe or a bigot. I instead more acutely saw what connected us. We were both victims of an oppressive system, one that aims to control through vertical power structures, comparative evaluations, and shame-based tactics that coerce individuals into strategic compliance. What made us most different from each other wasn't our opinions about homosexuality or marriage equality. Instead, what made us differ the most was what we had to lose (or gain) through welcoming the LGBTQ community into the curriculum.

I had a lot to lose. My silence would have been treasonous, complicit in the school's discriminatory exclusion of the LGBTQ community from our curriculum. On the contrary, my former principal had more to gain by shielding herself with her privilege. Through her inaction, she protected the status quo and avoided dealing with angry parents, some of whom would have voiced homophobic sentiments toward her, accusing her of acting against the best interests of the children in the school.

I say this neither to defend nor judge her; I say this because we can all identify with her. Just one year prior, when I had received my *excellent* rating, I said very little about the unfair practices. I spoke to my principal about it once in passing, and other than that, I spoke about it only behind closed doors, afraid to discuss it further with my superiors and risk losing my good standing. It wasn't until it affected me significantly that I became louder and more confrontational about it, ultimately filing a grievance against the principal.

Complacency and mindlessness are the largest threats to diversity, equity, and a strong sense of belonging in our schools. We are all guilty of being complacent and mindless, me included. I don't mean *mindless* in the haphazard and erratic sense; I mean *mindless* in a way that is the opposite of *mindful*. When we are mindless, we neglect to consider bias and context; we neglect to act with intention and purpose. When we act mindlessly, we too often dehumanize our schools, our classrooms, and learning without even realizing it.

I share these stories of disconnection, exclusion, and discrimination because they have a great deal in common with the detrimental effects of dehumanized personalization. Discrimination of any kind, even if it seems to exist only within the adult culture of a school, is a threat to equity and inclusion for children, too. Discrimination, inequity, and exclusive practices impact the collective conscious of the school, engendering institutional discrimination through overt acts of racism, sexism, homophobia, or the like, but also through silence, complacency, and an unintentional curriculum that ignores the many group identities that fill our schools.

> Complacency and mindlessness are dehumanizing.

> Discrimination does lasting damage that can never be fully repaired.

> When we perceive scarcity, we think we are not and won't ever be enough.

Without a doubt, there were children within our classrooms that year who would soon identify as members of the LGBTQ community. To not bring this conversation into the classroom was to act without a sense of equity, belonging, and justice—in opposition to what's best for children and inclusive learning environments. It was, by all measures, a missed opportunity we would never be able to rectify.

A CULTURE OF SCARCITY AND FEAR

Scarcity, by definition, is the state of being in short supply. In layperson's terms, it simply means that there is *not enough* of a given commodity. In economics, this means that a good, service, or product is in short supply. Culturally, scarcity plays a slightly different role. Brené Brown (2015) refers to this as "perceived scarcity."

"We spend inordinate amounts of time calculating how much we have, want and don't have, and how much everyone else has, needs and wants," Brown says in *Daring Greatly* (2015). "We are often comparing our lives, our marriages, our families, and our communities to unattainable, media-driven versions of perfection, or we're holding up our reality against our own fictional account of how great someone else has it."

As a result, scarcity lies at the root of many issues related to diversity, equity, and inclusion, and likewise, it lies at the root of many of the myths related to personalized learning. It is for this reason that I've delved so deeply into my own struggles as a member of a minority group—for I believe that my experiences as a gay teacher and my experiences working in personalized learning are inextricably connected. They are connected through education's pervasive culture of scarcity and fear.

Scarcity certainly played a role in the "controversial lesson incident" that defined my final year teaching in public school. I believe wholeheartedly that my former principal might have made a different decision if not for education's culture of scarcity and fear. While I can't be sure, I believe she was afraid of losing her job.

I was, too. But as a gay man in a school, I was already operating in opposition to another form of scarcity. No one could truly see me because of the black cloud of fear I lived under every day, worrying that if I was outed to all the parents— or for that matter, if the children found out—my professional standing would change, people might view me as a lesser educator, I might be seen as ineffective or, even worse, as a pervert or pedophile, as many gay teachers are still seen.

When we examine both of our perspectives in the context of scarcity, we see that there is so much about us that is similar—so much about our feelings that is united. They're really just two sides of the same coin—unable to see each other because they're facing opposite directions. Both are dehumanizing, and both are a threat to building equitable schools where all are welcome. In retrospect, I wonder what would have happen if we had just turned around—turned inward toward one another—to see what we were both turning our backs to.

Likewise, humanized personalization and dehumanized personalization represent two sides of the same coin. They are inextricably connected in their intention to make learning personal to individual learners, but operating in opposition to different forms of scarcity. Dehumanized personalization—oftentimes manifesting as a technology-driven pedagogy focused on individualizing curriculum—operates through a perceived scarcity of academic achievement, initiated by a fear of falling behind other students, other schools, or other countries. Humanized personalization, on the other hand, operates in response to a scarcity of the very things that make learning an innate human condition. Now more than ever, we see rates of anxiety rising in schools, with children afraid to take risks and make mistakes; we see teachers and students alike turning toward screens more than they are turning toward one another, prioritizing the accelerated consumption of academic content over dialogue, discourse, and inquiry; we see racism, sexism, and homophobia ever present in our schools, in need of focused attention from mindful educators.

Despite the fact that these are inextricably connected, they should not be given the same attention and weight. Dehumanized personalization is littered with privilege, built in the image of technology elites, intent on capitalizing on the competitive nature of education in the United States. Technology-driven personalization provides only short-term benefits for a select minority population, which is ultimately bad for the education system. Humanizing personalization, on the other hand—by prioritizing human relationships, human connection, and equity—provides a sustainable solution to making learning meaningful and personal in our schools, serving as a mechanism not only for bolstering empathy and human connection but also for increasing achievement in schools. The research is clear that the many aspects of humanized personalization have a significant impact on student achievement, including but not limited to enriching student-teacher relationships, enhancing awareness through self-regulation, setting clear learning goals, providing meaningful feedback, and teaching using classroom discussion and intentional reflection (Hattie, 2008). Humanized personalization is, in every sense of the word, a *healthy* response to a scarcity that is likely to continue eroding the original intentions for a democratic education—a scarcity only exacerbated by the practices of dehumanized personalization.

> Perceived scarcity goes hand in hand with dehumanized personalization.

It would be reductive to claim that a simple change in pedagogical approach—moving away from technology-driven pedagogies and toward human-centered pedagogies—would solve all of education's woes. There are systemic factors at play here that must be unpacked further—factors related to race, ethnicity, and class that we'll discuss in Chapter 12. Likewise, it would be equally reductive to claim that simply cultivating a sense of belonging in classrooms will solve all of education's problems. The fact of the matter is that American *culture* is not a place where all belong, and due to the fact that the education system is situated within American culture, it is nearly impossible to build an education system where all children belong if we don't first make changes to the collective conscious of American society.

We need to recognize that all American citizens are not, in fact, created equal. The colors of our skin and our zip codes provide some of us more privilege than others, impacting our ability to access an equitable and rigorous education. This necessitates a nuanced dialogue about the differences between equity and equality.

EQUITY VERSUS EQUALITY

Equality is a romanticized ideal, rarely, if ever, existing in pure form. *Equality*, by definition, means "having the qualities of being the same." Conversely, by definition, *equity* refers to "fairness and impartiality." While both words may share the base *equi-*, meaning *equal* or *even*, these are again two sides of the same coin, related in many ways but separated by the directionality of their perspectives.

We do not live in a fair and impartial world. Instead, our worlds are inherited, bestowed on us by chance. While it's true that social mobility is possible, that it is *possible* for Americans to live some semblance of the quintessential American Dream—it's becoming less and less likely.

"If Americans want to live the American Dream," says social epidemiologist and Professor Emeritus at the University of Nottingham Richard G. Wilkinson in his 2011 TED Talk, "they should go to Denmark." His comment came some thirty years after the beginning of a sharp decline in social mobility in the United States (Aronsen & Mazmuder, 2007).

In a world like this, where individuals inherit their destiny only by chance, with a low likelihood of mobility, striving for equality makes little sense. Striving for equality in a society where all do not come into this world as equals is like giving a one-year-old child and their 180-pound father the same portions of food to sustain them through the day. It's like watering a six-foot houseplant with the same amount of water you'd spray on a succulent.

However, striving for equity and justice *does* make sense. When we strive for equity, we provide each child what they *need* from the education system, and when we strive for justice, we attempt to right the wrongs bestowed on children and families who have been raised in a systemically oppressive society.

The fact of the matter is this: what's fair, impartial, and just is not always equal. It's not the same for everyone because we all come into this world differently—with different circumstances, privileges, and obstacles. The same goes for our classrooms. Mainstream theories on personalization—ones that are often technology-driven and dehumanizing—will beckon you to believe that for learning to be personalized, each child's learning must be individualized. But this simply isn't true. It's a falsity perpetuated by technology companies that prey on the aforementioned perceived scarcity, creating a perceived *need* in families and capitalizing on their vulnerabilities to turn a profit. It's bad enough that it's happening to any

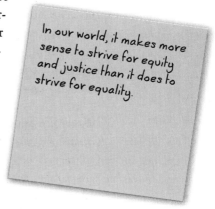

In our world, it makes more sense to strive for equity and justice than it does to strive for equality.

family at all—and I regret the role I played in it over the course of my time in Silicon Valley—but it's even worse that it's happening to vulnerable communities, specifically low-income urban communities.

Nowadays, companies that promote personalized learning technology oftentimes use equity as a marketing tactic, promising that their technologies will "close the achievement gap" or "help all learners reach their full potential." But providing all children with the same digital tools and simply varying the pace or combination of activities is, at best, a reductive and dehumanizing way to attempt to achieve this end. Worst of all, it doesn't have the empirical research to prove its efficacy (Pane, 2018; Pane et al., 2017; Steenbergen-Hu & Cooper, 2013). Furthermore, operating under the assumption that all children need a high degree of technology-driven individualization is likewise narrow-minded, unsustainable, and unscalable. It disembodies the human experience of learning, breaking it into unrecognizable pieces.

Make no mistake, children in so-called "failing" schools are not failing due to poor teaching or even a lack of access to these digital technologies; they are instead "failing" because the American education system is not built for all to succeed. The American school system is built on the systemic oppression of working-class families and families of color. This pattern persists now and finds its roots in the segregation and post-segregation eras that were intended to level the playing field for students of color. But the problem with the desegregation of schools during this time period was that it operated off of an unconscious bias toward White saviorism, as opposed to a conscious effort to dismantle institutional White supremacy.

White saviorism refers to the assumption that White folks should be saving or providing aid and charity to working-class folks and/or people of color. It's a way of thinking that aligns with Manifest Destiny, the spreading of Christianity, democracy, or capitalism to indigenous parts of the world. It operates off the assumption that certain groups of people require civilization by Western, White cultures that value Christianity, democracy, and capitalism. This way of thinking is inextricably linked to the desegregation policies of the *Brown v. Board of Education* era and likewise has dragged on into the twenty-first century. At the time of *Brown v. Board*, the problem wasn't necessarily that there was something wrong with the quality of teaching or teachers in predominantly Black schools; the problem was that Black schools did not have access to the same systemic and economic resources as White schools. To many, integrating schools was an act of cultural assimilation; it was done in an effort to make Black students assimilate into White culture.

The problem was (and still is) the White supremacist lens through which we view the issues plaguing education. When we view our schools through a lens of White supremacy—when we decide that our students must *be* and *perform* in a historically White way—we operate in opposition to equity and justice in our schools. To build equitable learning environments where learning is inherently personal and meaningful, our classrooms must reflect the natural diversity of the world around us. This means we must take very active and intentional steps to dismantle White supremacy in our classrooms because when we operate from a place of White supremacy, it becomes impossible for people of color to find a sense of belonging in schools.

The current personalized learning movement is strikingly similar in terms of this unconscious bias toward White saviorism and White supremacy. As opposed to effectively dismantling White supremacy in the education system and beyond, technology elites assume that by placing personalized learning technologies in urban schools, we will save our schools and "turn them around," referring to schools that usually serve low-income students and students of color.

The reality is, though, that urban schools are too often denied access to the resources to support families, students, and teachers in providing an equitable education because of *who* they serve. It's not necessarily a pedagogy issue, but an issue of *access*. Inundating schools with personalized learning tools that are intended to "close the achievement gap" presumes that urban schools and students of color need to be saved by tools, created mostly by affluent White people, that digitize learning and provide students access to content. But this content will neither dismantle White supremacy nor remove the many systemic barriers that often prohibit working-class folks and people of color from participating in American society as their authentic selves.

When we examine personalized learning technologies in this context, and when we evaluate their ability to restore equity and humanity in our classrooms, we easily see that the threat they pose to human connection and a sense of belonging is greater than the supposed academic benefits technology companies will have you believe they provide. Instead, they send a message to students that, to fit into our (White) society, you'd better catch up on these skills—and you'd better do it quickly. It sends an implicit but incredibly powerful message to working-class students and students of color that they, in fact, don't innately belong in a White and upper-middle-class education system and that if they want to fit in, they had better overcome the many barriers we've placed in front of them.

As we learned in Section I, personalization must be multidimensional. When we personalize in three dimensions, we shape the collective conscious; we foster small-group dialogue to allow learning to occur in more intimate settings; we nurture inner dialogues to build intrinsic motivation and executive functions; and now we also see that personalization must make identity and equity central to its priorities, effectively dismantling White supremacy, heteronormativity, and ableism. Technology companies offer a unidimensional approach to personalization, one that abandons the relationships formed between human beings through the personal process of learning. These relationships are the way most people can *sense* that they belong. And it is through these relationships that we can dismantle toxic biases in American society, helping all find a sense of belonging in our schools.

TECHNOLOGY IS NOT THE SOLUTION

Sarah always had an inquisitive glow in her eyes. She had a big heart, and she wore it on her sleeve. When she felt joy, it was boundless; when she felt sadness, it was palpable.

"Mr. France," she said to me one day, "I'm worried that if I don't learn how to listen at school that I won't be able to go here anymore."

It was true that Sarah struggled with sensory regulation and attention. It had been a challenge for her over the course of the school year, and it persisted even into our final months together. While I was glad she had cultivated an awareness around her obstacles, her words and her shame hit me like a ton of bricks.

"Well," I replied, "I know that you have trouble focusing sometimes, but I don't think that means you don't belong here. Everyone has a challenge, and this is yours."

"Do other people struggle with this?" she queried so poignantly.

"They do," I replied. "And other people struggle with lots of other things. They're just not always things you can see."

I paused and looked into her eyes, brimming with tears and seemingly ready to burst from behind her eyelids.

"If anyone ever asked me if you should stay at this school, I'd tell them that you absolutely should. And if they're going to ask anyone, they're going to ask me because I know you the best."

Her face, which had been taut as a tightrope, relaxed. Her shoulders returned to a resting position, and I could see a cautious smile creep onto her face. Temporarily, her shame and fear had been assuaged. But that moment in time helped me see why it was unsurprising that her struggles with focus and regulation had worsened. It's hard to be vulnerable with our challenges and work toward improving them if we're constantly worried we don't belong.

It's too challenging to take risks and make mistakes when constantly feeling as though we don't belong.

That night, I reflected on my time with Sarah. I'd be lying if I said I'd always been the perfect teacher for her. I'd become frustrated with her off-task behaviors, and in a few instances, I even coerced her into compliance through illogical consequences or a short and impatient tone. Instead, I needed to nurture her inner dialogue.

The next day, Sarah and I had a meeting one-on-one where I asked her what she thought might help her learn some new strategies for staying on the group plan and keeping herself organized. We created a chart that she hid inside her desk that helped her identify her feelings and some strategies she could use when she needed a break. The intervention was moderately successful in terms of helping her learn new behaviors, and incredibly effective in enhancing her awareness. By the end of the year, she would frequently come up to me and ask how I thought her day went, to which I would immediately respond, "How do *you* think your day went?" She would then give me a list of specific behaviors she thought were either on or off the group plan, clear evidence that her awareness was greater than it once was.

The next fall, she came to see me in the first week of school.

"Whoa, it looks really different in here!" she said, referring to the new setup of the classroom, which she took in with the bright and whimsical eyes I knew so very well.

"It is," I replied to her. "Do you like it?"

She replied in the affirmative, told me she missed me, and then went on her merry way to fourth grade. While I'm sure her obstacles persisted into the following year—and will for quite some time, as obstacles tend to do—her sense of belonging spoke for itself.

I'm proud of that—and of her.

Dr. Brené Brown (2010), whom I've now mentioned several times for her work with vulnerability and shame, said in her now famous TED Talk,

"When you ask people about love, they tell you about heartbreak. When you ask people about belonging, they'll tell you their most excruciating experiences of being excluded."

I share these stories of belonging and disconnection because I carry them with me every day. They guide me in a way that few other things do. That is why I'm grateful for all my students, especially students such as Sarah who've pushed me to be a more mindful, more empathetic teacher. I'm also grateful for what happened with the "controversial lesson incident," for I now know just how important it is that we all feel as though we belong— and that we advocate for those who don't.

No degree of technological intervention could have helped Sarah. In fact, I saw firsthand how the web-based and adaptive technologies only exacerbated her anxiety through their emphasis on leveled learning that accelerated her through content. Likewise, no degree of technological intervention will help low-income students, students of color, or LGBTQ students overcome the systemic barriers they're faced with every day. Unfortunately, discrimination and inequity are sown into the very fabric of our nation and our education system—and to assume that the same technological intervention will meet the needs of every child, regardless of race, class, or any other group identifier, is misguided, shrouded in an ignorant privilege that is likely to do more damage than good.

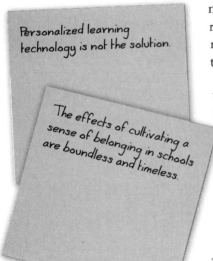

Personalized learning technology is not the solution.

The effects of cultivating a sense of belonging in schools are boundless and timeless.

We can instead make steps toward remedying this problem by reclaiming the term *personalized learning*, redefining it as a humanized pedagogy that embraces identity and actively works to right the wrongs of an unjust system. This will happen only if we start investing in the people who create the pulse of the education system—the learners and the educators. Only they can counteract this with intentionally inclusive practices and school cultures that humanize learning—fostering a sense of belonging for all and a path to equity in schools that will compound over time.

INCLUSIVE CLASSROOM PRACTICES THAT HUMANIZE LEARNING

We must start by changing the collective conscious of our classrooms. Our classrooms *are*, in fact, forums for changing the world, and by incorporating inclusive practices and curricula into our classrooms, we can shape the collective conscious of the future. Even if you teach in an affluent area where the majority of children come to school with strong executive functioning and oral language skills, know that you play an important role in this, too.

When we are in a position of privilege—and we all are at some point in our lives, as privilege is relative and intersectional—it is our job to act in a manner that is fair, impartial, and just—to build partnerships with, advocate for, and amplify the voices of marginalized groups and individuals. We must do it in the name of making learning inherently personal, meaningful, and visceral to a generation of young people who are lucky to be alive in a time when much of the country is waking up to the realities of systemic inequity and institutionalized discrimination.

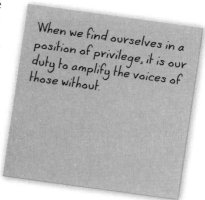

When we find ourselves in a position of privilege, it is our duty to amplify the voices of those without.

LEVERAGE COMPLEX INSTRUCTION TO ENCOURAGE HETEROGENEOUS GROUPINGS

The intention behind equitable practices is to ensure that every child is getting what they need in the classroom. This aligns with the intentions of both differentiated instruction and humanized personalization. This does not, however, entail individualizing curriculum on behalf of each child. Conversely, it entails broadening the scope of any given instructional task, allowing for multiple entry points into any given task, lesson, or unit.

While our examples have largely focused on mathematics, complex instruction need not be limited to that. In reading, this could entail providing children with a common text in which they all can integrate in *some* way, even if not with 100 percent comprehension. In writing, this entails having children converge around a common genre or teaching point, allowing children to mold the teaching point in a way that works with their ability level. This can even work for spelling and word study.

In third grade, it's common for students to learn about various vowel patterns, from vowel digraphs to diphthongs and *r*-controlled vowels. This means we focus on single-syllable words such as *toad* and *mind*. The challenges here are rather obvious when it comes to personalization. There are many third-grade children who have already "demonstrated proficiency" in these single-syllable words, while others grasp them rather quickly due to a strong visual memory. Others struggle altogether, not quite ready to retain the various spelling patterns.

In these lessons, my primary objective is for students to master the spellings of these single-syllable words and words like them. Similar to how we might pose a task in math workshop and invite children to ask questions, we do the same in spelling. When we study long vowels, I generally begin by offering all students the same word sort, typically pulled from Words Their Way. Children sort the words in a way that makes sense to them, receiving feedback from me as they go if their sorting seems illogical or unproductive.

"Tell me how you're sorting," I'll say to them.

"Well, I noticed that *a* was the second letter in most of these words," some of my less sophisticated spellers will reply.

"Let's try another way," I suggest. "I know that logical spellers use sounds and word patterns to spell words. Will you try sorting by sounds or word patterns, instead of the position of the letter?"

After they've done that, I invite them to brainstorm more words with Neil Ramsden's Word Searcher or confirm their spellings with Dictionary. com. While they've all begun with the same sort, this process of sorting and generating new words allows for diversity to emerge within the work products, making the children agents of the personalized work products they've created.

Some do not need this level of support with sorting and word generation, and for those students, there are other options that do not over-individualize the content. Over-individualizing and accelerating them through content is not only a threat to deep and meaningful learning; it's a threat to equity, too, creating more points of divergence among students in the classroom, isolating students and dehumanizing learning through disconnection. Just because a given child has sorted the words efficiently and accurately doesn't mean their journey with exploring long-vowel words needs to end. Those students can explore homophones, too, completing what I call a visual dictionary (see Figure 10.2).

In one instance, a group of students was curious about other possibilities for homophones, replacing rimes with other homophonic rimes. They tried replacing vowel-consonant-*e* words like *gate* with its vowel-vowel counterparts (*ai*).

"Oh, *gait* is a word!" one of my students said.

"Whoa, I had no idea there was a homophone for *gate*!" I replied with excitement.

They discovered that it referred to "a person's manner of walking," allowing them to create a visual dictionary and build their vocabulary, despite the fact that previous assessments stated that they'd already "mastered" long-vowel patterns.

_____ 's Visual Dictionary

_____	_____
Picture:	Picture:
Part of speech: noun verb adjective other	Part of speech: noun verb adjective other
Mini Word Matrix	Mini Word Matrix
Make a word matrix on the next page!	Make a word matrix on the next page!

Some choose to make word matrices (Bowers, Kirby, & Deacon, 2010) using some of the long-vowel words as bases. Take *use* for instance. There are more than forty words that have *use* as a base, including words such as *used*, *abuse*, or *usually* (a commonly misspelled word in elementary school). By building a word matrix and generating word sums, students are able to affix word parts to the base, navigating spelling changes and otherwise building their understanding of how long-vowel words are really just generative bases that will expand our vocabulary and provide for us a foundation on which to spell lots of words. In Figure 10.3, you can see an example of a word matrix we made when exploring long-*a* words, allowing students to explore spelling changes that occur when adding suffixes.

By exploring equity in the context of spelling, it becomes clear that acceleration is not

Figure 10.3: Word Matrix for *Take*

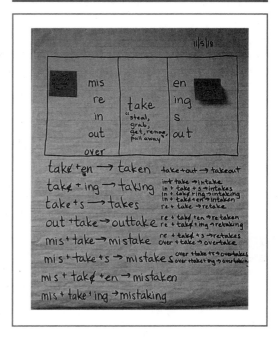

the answer. Instead, choice, autonomy, and teacher feedback are all critical to giving students what they need in terms of spelling instruction. When we do so, we leverage inquiry and student agency; we grant students the opportunity to engage with the content in a rich and generative manner, simultaneously practicing spelling, expanding their vocabulary, and deepening their knowledge of English orthography. In an instance like this, we find a harmonious balance between convergence and divergence. Students are getting what they need while still connected to the collective conscious of the classroom. *That* is equity. *That* is humanized personalization.

USE COMPETENCY-BASED ASSESSMENT PRACTICES TO DELIVER FEEDBACK AND STRUCTURE LEARNING

Personalizing learning in a manner that is fair, impartial, and just requires a great deal of intentionality and thoughtful planning. Many falsely believe that student-driven learning or emergent curriculum is associated with minimal planning or "letting the kids take the lesson where they will," but this is more likely to result in chaos and non-educative experiences.

For quite some time, I subscribed to the methodology that Words Their Way recommends for personalizing spelling. In their methodology, students are grouped based on their spelling proficiency, generally resulting in three to five spelling groups within a classroom. Each group uses a different set of spelling words for their spelling instruction, which in theory provides each child with what they need in terms of spelling instruction. While this level of individualization still fosters collaboration and connectedness between small groups of students, it's unsustainable for the educator. I know this because I've tried it, and I find that I can't keep up with this for more than a week without feeling drained. But it turns out that this level of individualization is not necessary, either, and we must remember that classrooms that embrace humanized personalization must also embrace sustainable workloads and teacher wellness.

To structure learning like this and make my work more sustainable, I try to anticipate levels of proficiency ahead of time. Here is how I think of spelling in the context of long-vowel patterns.

	Level 1	Level 2	Level 3
PROFICIENCY	Students sort based on position of letter.	Students sort based on vowel patterns with few errors.	Students sort based on vowel patterns efficiently with no errors.

	Level 1	Level 2	Level 3
ACTIVITIES	Students create word webs or word families using Dictionary.com or Word Searcher. If students begin to show proficiency, move them to Level 2.	Students create word webs or word families using Dictionary.com or Word Searcher. Add visual dictionary for homophones, if applicable.	Students have the option to explore homophones (using the visual dictionary) or create word matrices that add prefixes and suffixes, using Word Searcher and Dictionary.com as supports.

I even let the kids into this, explaining to them how to become more efficient with their spelling as they learn more.

"It's too much to remember the order of all the letters, so as you learn more words, I want you to look at the *parts* of the words and how we can use those to make lots of words," I'll say to them.

I notice this most often with my high-achieving students. They've gotten by for so long on their strong visual memories and expansive oral language that they've missed ample opportunities for feedback on the process by which they learn. That was certainly the case with Penny.

Penny frequently reversed and mixed up letters in words, spelling a word like *usually* as *usaluly* or something similar. It was clear to me that her inner dialogue told her to memorize the order of the letters when spelling. Somewhere along the way, she had pieced together that this was the only way to spell—by committing the millions of words in the English language to memory. But this is incredibly inefficient and cognitively demanding.

"Can I give you some feedback?" I said to her in a writing conference. She nodded in reply. "I notice that you flip letters around a lot, and I think it's because you're trying to memorize all of the words you're spelling. But if you use word parts to spell, it actually gets a lot easier and a lot more efficient."

I reviewed the word matrix tool with her and showed her how to use that to spell more efficiently. I shared this with her parents at her conference, too. A few days later, Penny came to school thrilled to show me the homework she'd assigned herself. She'd created a word matrix for *work* (see Figure 10.4).

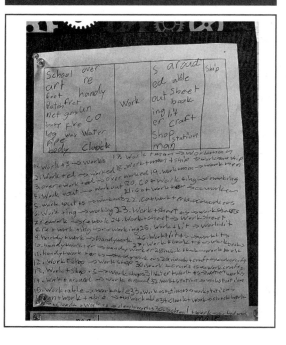

"Mr. France! I made like fifty-six different words using *work*!" she exclaimed. Through her study of *work*, she found words such as *workable* and *overworked*, allowing her more exposure to common word parts. Truth be told, Penny wasn't in need of intervention. It's likely that, with time, her visual memory would have become even more sophisticated, remedying her spelling. Or perhaps it wouldn't have, and she might have become a high-functioning adult who makes self-deprecating jokes about how poor of a speller she is. Regardless, I was thrilled to see how excited she was to leverage this new tool to improve her spelling.

Penny's excitement was a sign of her agency and autonomy—and it served as a success indicator for me as a teacher. Instances such as these illuminate the degree to which humanized personalization is a partnership between teacher and student. The teacher's assessment and feedback, supported by a flexible frame of standards and assessment, encourage the learner to change something about their behavior or the way they think, allowing the learner to personalize on their own behalf.

ENSURE EQUITABLE REPRESENTATION IN CHILDREN'S LITERATURE

Our conscious is constructed through the stories we're told as children. These stories serve as a medium through which we construct our mental models of the world. Children's literature has been historically dominated by cisgender White characters who experience the world in a heteronormative way. To be more inclusive and to grant children the opportunity to diversify their mental models for characters and their obstacles, we must diversify the literature we bring into our classrooms. This goes beyond choosing stories that simply have LGBTQ characters or characters of color; it entails acknowledging the intersectionality of identity and ensuring that the stories we tell of one group identity are neither monolithic nor stereotypical.

Too often, stories of individuals who come from marginalized populations succumb to stereotypes. For instance, teachers will choose stories with Black characters relating to the civil rights era or overcoming poverty; teachers may choose stories that feature LGBTQ characters where their coming out is central to their story and therefore their identity. While these stories are important to tell, choosing *only* these stories limits the stories of communities of color and the LGBTQ community, when there are innumerable stories to tell where oppression is not the central obstacle. The key is *balance*. Here are some of my favorite titles:

- *A Family Is a Family Is a Family* by Sara O'Leary

- *All Are Welcome* by Alexandra Penfold

- *I Am Human* by Susan Verde

- *The Last Stop on Market Street* by Matt de la Peña

- *Whoever You Are* by Mem Fox

- *The Name Jar* by Yangsook Choi

- *Peter's Chair* by Ezra Jack Keats

- *Red: A Crayon's Story* by Michael Hall

- *Strictly No Elephants* by Lisa Mantchev

- *Lovely* by Jess Hong

- *George* by Alex Gino

- *Fly Away Home* by Eve Bunting

- *This Is the Rope* by Jacqueline Woodson

- *The Keeping Quilt* by Patricia Polacco

Teaching Tolerance has an excellent rubric on their website (www.teaching-tolerance.org) for evaluating children's literature. When choosing books, remember to ask yourself the following questions:

- How might I use this book in a way that *does not* reinforce a stereotype?

- Does this book diversify my students' knowledge and experiences of a minority or marginalized group?

- Which other books might I use this year to show a different experience for someone with a similar group identity?

This is only the first step in actively dismantling White supremacist thinking and fostering a sense of belonging in our classrooms. By representing as many types of people and stories as we can, we change the narrative, sending an implicit message that all people and all stories belong in our classrooms. The next step is to teach children how to advocate for this when it's *not* happening in the classroom.

EXPLICITLY TEACH ABOUT RACISM, SEXISM, AND HOMOPHOBIA

"They're doing Chinese cuts!" Alex said to me one day, tattling on some of his friends in line.

"Oh, my goodness," I replied to Alex. "What is a Chinese cut?"

"Oh, you know," he replied, "it's like when you let someone cut in front of you, and then you cut them right back. Then they're behind you in line without cutting someone else."

"Got it," I replied. "Do you know why those are called Chinese cuts? That seems like an odd name for something like that."

It turned out that he didn't know. He'd just used the name because he'd heard it from his peers.

"Well," I continued kindly and empathetically, "I know you didn't mean it this way, but that sounds like a really *racist* thing to say. It sounds like you're saying that Chinese people would do something sneaky like that to cut people in line. I'm not saying that *you're* a racist, but I am saying that language is racist. Is that what you're trying to say?"

> We must resensitize our children to racism to right the wrongs of the past.

Of course, that was not his intention. It rarely is with young children. They've simply been shaped by a world whose collective conscious is too desensitized to racism and racist rhetoric.

"I wonder if we could come up with a different name for that. Maybe we call it *back cuts* or *sneaky cuts* or something, because that is what you really mean, right?"

He agreed, his eyes ripe with the realization that his words were quite powerful—that they *mattered*.

"You know, Mr. France, I think we should talk about this at closing circle today and tell other people about it. A lot of kids say *Chinese cuts* and I don't think they know it's racist."

I replied, "I think that's a great idea. Can you remind me at the end of the day?"

Alex did, and we had a great conversation about it with the remainder of the class. It's true that I could have simply extinguished the term by saying, "That's racist. Stop using it." But I instead took the time to help Alex see the impact of his words, building his empathetic capital and perspective-taking. Racist terms such as *Chinese cuts* are a threat to equity and a sense of belonging in our classrooms, similar to homophobic phrases such as "That's so gay!" These phrases send microaggressive messages that certain identities can be appropriated to label undesirable behaviors or our own discomfort.

The power of this story lies in *empathetic accountability*. To take active steps in dismantling White supremacy, we must bring our students *in*, meanwhile holding them accountable to using inclusive language. And this is especially true in predominantly White classrooms where racist, sexist, and homophobic jargon is often easily glossed over. In my case, doing so helped my entire class see that it's important all students in our classroom feel that they belong and that an identity is never a means for appropriation. What's more, it made us even more prepared to continue to have courageous conversations about identity as the year continued.

REMOVE GENDER MARKERS

We are living in a world that is increasingly diversifying in terms of gender, so much so that we've gone beyond two or even three gender identities. There are now students who choose not to conform to a gender at all, allowing endless possibilities for identity development. While our world is becoming more sensitive to and understanding of the nuances of gender identity, the process of schooling can still be a painful one for those who feel that their identity is undervalued, marginalized, or in some schools, under siege.

As a result, I do my best to remove any sort of gender markers in my classroom as a means for actively dismantling the gender dichotomy and counteracting the privileges afforded to the cisgender population. While this begins with simple actions such as removing gender markers on bathroom passes or ceasing the use of girls' and boys' lines, our language can be even more impactful.

Instead of . . .	Try this . . .
Good morning, boys and girls! or Good morning, ladies and gentlemen!	Good morning • scholars • mathematicians • learners • writers • readers • everyone

(Continued)

(Continued)

Instead of . . .	Try this . . .
The boys may go take a bathroom break.	If you use the boys' bathroom, you may go take your bathroom break. (Note: This is only useful if your school has gendered bathrooms.)
The girls may line up first for PE.	Line up if your birthday is in October. Line up if your last name begins with the letter A through K. Line up if you are wearing purple today.
Alternating in boy-girl order or grouping students in girl-girl or boy-boy partnerships	Group students based on friendships, personalities, strengths, and challenges, making sure to group heterogeneously when appropriate.
Assigning colors or certain images (bows in hair, bowties, etc.) to students who present as female or male	Allow students to choose their own colors or activities. Allow students to write their names on name plates and their belongings, too.
Assuming gender in picture books	Ask students how they know how the character identifies.

In actuality, these changes are rather small adjustments to make, but the return on these investments in our students' emotional safety pay off in large dividends when they see that they, too, *matter* in the classroom.

ACKNOWLEDGE SEXUALITY AS AN INTEGRAL PART OF THE HUMAN CONDITION

When we analyze the etymology of *sex*, we see it comes from the Latin *secare*, originating from the Proto-Indo-European *sek-*, both of which mean "to cut." It wasn't until the fourteenth century that the term *sex* arrived, in close relation to the Latin *sexus*, meaning "state of being either male or female." Modern attitudes have baked intergenerational bias and sensitivity into the words, oftentimes making parents and educators alike cringe when they have to discuss sex and sexuality with young children. With younger students, this usually surfaces when they begin to have crushes.

"It's perfectly normal to have crushes," I told my third-grade class after I found out they had been discussing crushes at recess. "Almost everyone has them. Does anyone know what a crush is?"

A student raised their hand, classifying a crush as when you "like someone in a different way" and adding that "you sometimes don't tell them about it."

"Sure," I replied, "and sometimes you do tell them. But we have to remember that when someone has a crush, they have the right to keep it a secret or share it with someone who they feel safe with. It's no one else's job to share that information."

With older students, sexuality becomes more complex. They begin to become more open with crushes and may even identify as someone else's boyfriend or girlfriend. Overt homophobia also begins to show its ugly face. They begin to use same-sex vocabulary as pejoratives, as in this instance.

"Mr. France, Oscar called me a bad name," Henry said to me.

"Oh, what did he call you?" I replied.

"Well, he called me . . ." He paused, lowering his voice and spelling out the word, "G-A-Y."

It wasn't long before the other student walked up, ready to defend himself.

"Did you call him gay?" I asked.

"Well, he was making kissy faces in the mirror!" Oscar replied. "And I thought it was *weird*, so I called him *that word*," he said, afraid to say it aloud.

"Do you know what *gay* means?" I replied.

Henry said, "It's when two people who are the same gender like each other."

"Exactly," I said, "and it's a real thing—not a swear word. It's not bad to say someone is gay if they really are and they call themselves that. Henry making kissy faces at himself in the mirror doesn't make him gay—even if it's a bit narcissistic." I smiled and winked at him, referring to our recent study of Greek allusions. "But you have no right to use the word *gay* to make fun of someone. Got it?"

They nodded and walked away—empowered with new knowledge and desensitized to a word that is often overly sexualized and tainted by fear.

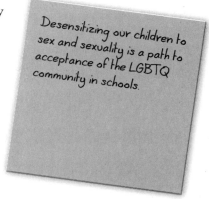

Desensitizing our children to sex and sexuality is a path to acceptance of the LGBTQ community in schools.

There are countless moments throughout the school year that offer us opportunities to send inclusive and accepting messages about sex and sexuality, and it doesn't require discussing genitalia or the physical act of sex. We can talk about sex and sexuality in lots of ways, relinquishing the shame that so many of us adults carry around in relation to sex and sexuality, meanwhile empowering our students with an inclusive attitude and new knowledge.

This inclusive attitude compounds with time. Most children are indoctrinated with heteronormative messages from birth. A disproportionate number of the stories we tell both in our classrooms and in mainstream media reinforce a narrative that praises heterosexuality. And while children are too young to grapple with the way adults experience sex and sexuality, they are not too young to see that heterosexual relationships are the norm. Because children are a product of their environments, they begin to develop biases that are inherently exclusive. As a result, our students become active threats to equity and a sense of belonging in our classrooms. By explicitly teaching about the nuances of sexuality, we normalize it and make it possible for more to know that they can find belonging as their authentic selves, regardless of their emerging sexual identities.

LIMIT WEB-BASED, ADAPTIVE TECHNOLOGIES

Putting anything but people at the center of the education system is a threat to equity and a sense of belonging. Education technology's definition of personalized learning is oftentimes dehumanizing, putting technology at the center of education systems. Technology elites presuppose that to sustainably personalize learning, a digitized algorithm must assign content and collect assessment data. We've repeatedly disproven this flawed hypothesis over the course of this book. Doing so puts people at the periphery. It dehumanizes learning.

While nascent, the research on the impact of digital technology and screen time on young children is unnerving. The research is so convincing that technologists themselves are reluctant to use digital technology with their own children. Even technology elites such as Tim Cook and Bill Gates have limited the use of screens in their homes due to the impact they have on child development. Ironically, these technologists and their technology companies continue to push technology onto schools and children, despite the fact that many studies show little to no significantly positive effects on student learning (Hattie, 2008; Organisation for Economic Co-operation and Development, 2015; Pane, 2018).

The situation becomes even direr when we examine *who* is being inundated with digital technology. Many see web-based, adaptive technologies as scalable and sustainable solutions for personalizing learning, as they provide students with activities, based on the results of digitized assessments. Because the technology assigns content, teachers do not have to manage the complexity of individualizing instruction on behalf of the children—or so it is presumed. As a result, we're seeing web-based, adaptive technologies make their way into urban schools that predominantly serve working-class folks and communities of color, where test scores tend to be lower than in suburban or predominantly White areas.

Many hope these tools will raise test scores, when in reality, the true issues plaguing low-achieving school districts are often associated with systemic oppression manifesting as underfunding and limited access to equitably rigorous learning experiences. Many see digital technology as a sustainable and scalable solution, when in reality, the overuse of digital technology poses a threat to social-emotional and executive-functioning skill development.

The children who struggle the most academically are oftentimes students who also struggle socially and emotionally. They struggle academically not because they are incapable of mastering academic content but likely because there are unaddressed barriers to their learning that have reinforced dependent learning habits. In fact, John Hattie's effect sizes tell us many factors related to social-emotional skills and executive functioning have a much larger impact on student achievement than web-based, adaptive technologies (.18), including the strength of a child's working memory (.52); concentration, persistence, and engagement (.56); and even reducing anxiety (.42).

This disproportionately affects students in low-income communities and communities of color. In part, this is attributable to structural inequities; almost invariably, the highest-need schools tend to also be the most under-resourced. But, more important, while the children who attend such schools bring many assets to the classroom, it's important to keep in mind that the system was never designed to serve them. Rather, it was intended as a sorting factory that favored children of privilege despite its pretense of meritocracy.

As a result, it would be misguided to believe that web-based adaptive technologies can fix this—but these most vulnerable populations are more and more inundated with web-based, adaptive tools intended to personalize learning. It's ironic, then, that technology-driven personalized learning tools are being increasingly pushed into large urban school districts that often serve low-income students. Technology is seen as a means for solving achievement problems at scale. It is presumed that by matching individual students with academic tasks through digital means, controlling for pacing and monitoring progress through mastery learning practices, students will gradually remedy discrepancies in achievement and equity—and without a major investment in teacher training or expensive changes in programming. Personally, I'd like to see education technology used to provide more free resources to teachers, and I'd like to see educators and administrators alike using social media to ban together and advocate for equitable funding between schools and school districts, in an effort to bring justice to schools that have been underfunded for so long.

Disconnection is not only bad for the soul; it's bad for equity, inclusion, and a sense of belonging. When we attempt to individualize through digital means, children become isolated in their studies; they work in silos and are unable to interact with their peers over common content or common learning experiences. After all, it's hard to feel as though you belong when you are so frequently alone, with so few instances to converge with peers. What's more, this disembodied methodology for making learning personal has the potential to track students—only on a more granular level than in years past. Tracking used to be done at the class level, with students grouped by ability, similar to what I discussed in Chapter 3. With new technologies, tracking is now possible on a granular level, with personalized learning technologies that put children on predetermined tracks for learning that accelerate them through content.

> Too much divergence breeds disconnection, and disconnection chips away at belonging.

That's not to say all technology is bad. There have been technological advancements that make learning more personal. Some technologies break down the barriers of space and time, allowing educators the ability to minimize the complexity of learning that is personal; some even have the capacity to enhance human connection and preserve a sense of belonging in the classroom. In the next chapter, we'll identify a few examples of these tools and how they *humanize* technology integration.

A WORK IN PROGRESS

We are all works in progress, and as a result, we must grant one another space for making mistakes, even in relation to equity, justice, and a sense of belonging. My former principal oftentimes said that I put her in an untenable position, and many who criticize my role in the story of the "controversial lesson incident" argue this, as well.

I argue that we were all already in an untenable position—our silence making us complacent, exclusive, and unjust.

But wasn't she a work in progress? Aren't we all just works in progress?

We are. But to earn this title of a "work in progress," we must commit to actually *doing the work*. My former principal, the superintendent, and the school district did not commit to unpacking their privilege or evaluating their roles in the situation. In my last meeting with my former principal, where I resigned to accept my new job in Silicon Valley, she neither acknowledged fault nor offered an apology; she simply asked me to lift the grievance and was resentful when I refused.

We mustn't pity the privileged; we mustn't relieve them from their discomfort. They must dutifully *earn* the title "work in progress." For it is a disservice to their autonomy—and a disservice to equity and justice—if we grant them yet another undeserved privilege.

CHAPTER ELEVEN

HUMANIZING TECHNOLOGY INTEGRATION

It was the first month of school. My students were repeatedly asking me if they could use one of those adaptive technology tools intended to individualize academic content. You know the type: when children answer questions correctly, the technology moves them through more content; when they answer incorrectly, the tool prompts them with extra visual supports, barring them from progressing until they've answered the questions correctly. Once they've answered enough questions correctly, the program assumes mastery.

Deep down, I knew the tool was perpetuating a culture of shallow and meaningless learning. After all, I'd just spent three years in Silicon Valley exploring these technologies—only to find out that every single one of them failed to meet my personalization needs. But I let my students use it anyway. I thought that it could just be the emotional baggage I'd brought with me from Silicon Valley—that maybe these kids would respond to it differently. They were *asking* to use it, after all.

Within moments of pulling out iPads, the entire tone of the classroom changed. A competitive spirit permeated the air. Despite the fact that each child was given individualized content, children needed privacy shields so they wouldn't look at each other's screens, attempting to see which level their neighbor was on; they needed to be reminded countless times that their level did not matter and what mattered instead was that they were learning something new.

"Am I on third-grade level?" Sarah asked, fixated on completing grade-level content and moving on to the next grade level.

"This is too easy for me," Asher said, despite the fact that he was getting questions wrong.

"Mr. France," Carl added, "I'm doing sixth-grade math!"

Meanwhile, Matthew sat with his tablet, his eyes shifting back and forth, shoulders slouched, his affect listless and uncomfortable.

"How's it going?" I whispered to him.

He looked at me sullenly, unaware of how to move on even though he was repeatedly answering the question incorrectly. I worked with him for a minute, explaining to him why his answer was incorrect and getting him on his way, hardly having time for proper intervention.

Matthew was not alone. While about two thirds of my class seemed to be working on their tablets, buzzing through question after question, a substantial portion of my class was not. The students who were most in need of intervention were all working on different problems or tasks, disconnected from an altogether absent collective conscious, left to fend for themselves in this digital desert that provided them little to no educative sustenance. It was, instead, a mirage of learning, meeting only psychological needs of content consumption and competition.

> Web-based, adaptive technologies oftentimes proliferate a learning culture of consumption and competition.

The tool was hardly "closing the achievement gap" in my classroom. That much was clear. If anything, it was widening it. The students working on above-grade-level content were flying through at an ever-accelerating pace, while the students working on below-grade-level content were moving glacially atop a shaky foundation. Many struggled with executive functioning and resilience, unsure of what steps to take in the face of uncertainty. Others had a poor conceptual understanding of mathematics, relying purely on rote or procedural knowledge to answer questions. The computer program itself was not capable of seeing the depths to which their inner dialogues needed to be nurtured; it could see only the extent to which they were answering incorrectly.

Contrary to popular belief, this wasn't even giving my high-achieving students what they needed. Sarah needed to find the intrinsic value in math, evident in the fact that she was hyper-concerned with her level. The tool was only exacerbating her perseveration on this decontextualized number—what we colloquially refer to as a "level"—that was implicitly telling her how much her mind was worth in math.

You're level three, but not quite good enough for four, it told her.

Asher was missing out on the opportunity to think deeply and flexibly about mathematics. His complaints that the content was "too easy" signaled a lack of humility. To him, learning meant answering a sufficient number of problems correctly so he could move on. He was measuring his own success quantitatively, much like Sarah.

And for Carl, one of my highest-achieving students, the tool seemed to soothe him, speaking to and worsening his haste and impulsivity. *The faster the better*, the tool said to him, providing him hits of dopamine each time he answered correctly, keeping him addicted to it.

While Carl was able to answer questions correctly within fifth- and sixth-grade-level content, he lacked firm conceptual understanding and an ability to articulate his mathematical thinking. I'd often sit with him during math workshop, attempting to help him articulate his thinking, frequently coming up short. It wasn't until one day months later, when I was conferring with Carl over a method he used to solve a division problem, that I managed to get through to him.

He had been using the standard algorithm for division—the one where you divide, then multiply, subtract, and bring down a digit (see Figure 11.1). He had memorized the procedure when learning math from his older siblings. This method worked pretty reliably for Carl, as his working and long-term memories were strong, allowing him to process multiple steps at once and retain them after executing them only a few times. But the problem was he didn't actually understand *why* he was executing the method or *how* it was working. He failed to see that what he was actually doing was dividing parts of the number and then piecing them back together to get a quotient.

Figure 11.1: Standard Algorithm for Division

$$3\overline{)126} \quad \frac{42}{}$$

42	Divide
3⟌126	
−12	Multiply
06	Subtract
−6	Bring Down
0	

"Do you know why this method works?" I asked him.

"Yeah, because you divide, then you multiply, then subtract, and then bring down the number," he replied, reciting the procedure to me.

"I understand *what* you're doing," I continued, "but I want to know *how* you know it works. Can you show it to me in pictures? Or with base-ten blocks?"

He looked at me, puzzled, his silence deafening. A smile crept across his face. He knew that I'd found something—something he *didn't* know. This was a new feeling for him, I could tell.

"Can you teach me?" he asked, a wave of humility overtaking him, signaled by his relaxed shoulders and calm smile.

I did teach him (see Figure 11.2), and this became a theme in Carl's and my relationship over the course of the year—a pattern of interaction through which Carl and I developed a strong bond. I knew that he could retain and regurgitate content relatively easily, and as the year went on, my feedback was mostly related to the *process* by which he reached an answer, the quality of his work, and his impulsivity.

Figure II.2: Visual Algorithm for Long Division

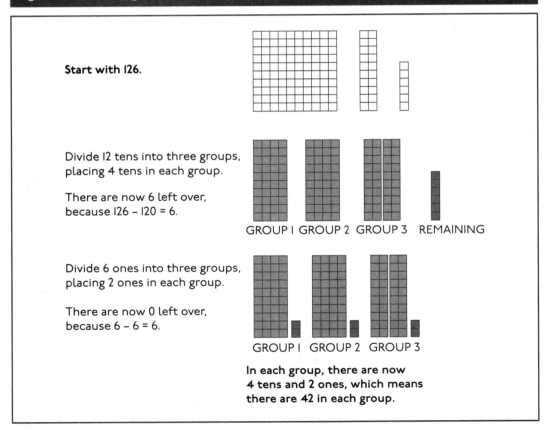

Start with 126.

Divide 12 tens into three groups, placing 4 tens in each group.

There are now 6 left over, because 126 – 120 = 6.

GROUP I   GROUP 2   GROUP 3   REMAINING

Divide 6 ones into three groups, placing 2 ones in each group.

There are now 0 left over, because 6 – 6 = 6.

GROUP I   GROUP 2   GROUP 3

In each group, there are now 4 tens and 2 ones, which means there are 42 in each group.

In the case of Carl, yet again, we see that individualizing the curriculum was not actually helping him in the long run. In fact, it's much easier to see the ways this technology-driven methodology for personalization was actually harmful to him, only exacerbating his impulsivity, mindlessness, and accelerated consumption of content in school. Despite the fact that I had no plan for curriculum individualization, Carl's parents reported a new and revitalized excitement to come to school, which was much different than years past. In school, I noticed an increased mindfulness in his work and a connectedness to his peers as we worked through math tasks, book clubs, and projects. Humanizing personalization worked to help Carl and my other high-achieving students—not through a digitally curated and accelerated curriculum but instead by slowing them down and helping them reconnect with their classmates and me.

THE PURPOSE OF TECHNOLOGY

If technology isn't preserving or enhancing connection between individuals in the classroom, then we *must* reevaluate its use. Note, this doesn't mean it should be tossed out entirely, but we need to always remember to ask ourselves if the technology is working in a manner that truly preserves our humanity as teachers and learners.

After all, the most revolutionary technologies have done this for us. Monumental advancements in technology—ones that withstand the test of time—have been connecting individuals, building relationships, and increasing the empathetic capital of the world since the beginning of time (Rifkin, 2009). Inventions that today seem archaic, such as the telephone or printing press, were once revolutionary. They allowed humans to communicate over long distances and share information with the masses like never before. These technological systems have allowed for user-driven personalization, and they have enhanced human consciousness, extending empathy across space and time.

> If technology isn't preserving or enhancing connection between individuals in the classroom, then we must reevaluate its use.

The printing press employed twenty-six unique letters and a handful of symbols, arranged in infinite ways that allowed users to create an unlimited number of personalized messages; the telephone has allowed human beings to create an expansive and connected network, enabling us to send personalized messages through word of mouth. And now, with the advent of Internet and social media, the possibilities for user-driven personalization seem to have grown even more. We can send videos, post pictures, like and comment on friends' activities, and even communicate and collaborate with people around the world using communicative technologies such as Skype and Google Docs.

It becomes clear when we examine technology long-term that the most impactful technologies are communicative, and this is important to note because communication and human connection go hand in hand. The very nature of what we have to say is indicative of the utterly *personal* and intimate thoughts that exist within our minds. When we communicate these, we are being vulnerable, opening ourselves up to the opportunity to be molded and changed by others. This communication allows for a serendipitous exchange of information, resulting in the emergence of new ideas, feelings, or conclusions. As a result, advances in communication advance humanity because they make us more aware, more efficient, and more connected.

In this way, learning in the twenty-first century is dependent on *connection*. Classroom technology should be supporting human connection in the classroom, not taking away from it. It should be making it possible for us to have more conversations. More conversations mean more chances to be vulnerable, take risks, and make mistakes; more chances to engage in the collective conscious of the classroom and have our inner dialogues be changed by the human beings around us.

WHERE EDTECH FALLS SHORT

There are obvious challenges to each of these technological advancements. Social media has a dark side, encouraging users to engage in obsessive behaviors and compulsive thought processes around image and personal branding. It has the potential to isolate users in echo chambers or make large groups of people vulnerable to psychological warfare through the obfuscation of facts. At the advent of less modern technologies such as the telephone and television, people were concerned about less face-to-face communication and the need for unsightly wires that soon covered cities around the globe. Even the printed word had environmental consequences, necessitating an increase in paper goods. Education technology is no different, and in a vast majority of cases, the costs of most education technology outweigh the benefits.

We must remember that the majority of education technologies are products of for-profit companies. Companies are driven by a corporate and capitalist mentality, measuring success in terms of money made and products purchased. In the technology industry, the metrics are similar. While they likewise measure their success in terms of money made and products purchased, they also measure their success in terms of usage. Technology companies have been known to study addiction in an effort to keep users engaging with the platform as much as possible. Sean Parker, Facebook's founding president, explained to *The Guardian* in November 2017 that they knew very well they were exploiting "a vulnerability in human psychology" when they created Facebook. Their goal was to give users "a little dopamine hit" by adding features such as the "like" button, keeping them engaged with the platform, allowing usage rates to rise and Facebook to profit from ad sales and other revenue streams (Solon, 2017). Gamified technology exploits the very same vulnerabilities in human psychology.

I went to Silicon Valley blissfully unaware of this. I saw education technology as a panacea, and more specifically, I thought that technology-powered personalized learning was a silver bullet—the answer that the education system was waiting for. I succumbed to the many myths I've shared throughout this book—that personalized learning meant pairing children with individualized content and that many of our problems could be solved if we aligned curriculum with a child's interests.

It took me more than two years to arrive at the idea that personalized learning was far more complicated than complexity minimization. And it was then in my third year working in Silicon Valley that I came to a professional impasse—nearing the end of a long road, unsure which way to go next. For more than two years, I had built digital curriculum and consulted with technologists on the tools we were using in our classrooms; I had opened three microschools with the company, learning the ins and outs of operations and logistics; I had helped build three teams of teachers, rebuilding child-centered visions for personalization each year; I had worked with almost sixty children and their families, getting to know their idiosyncrasies, interests, strengths, and obstacles. And it never got easier. It never became more sustainable as the technologists said it would, slowly minimizing the complexity of personalization as the tools became more sophisticated. Overall, it didn't help parents feel more at ease about their children's education; instead, the reverse was true.

By the end of my second year, I had run myself ragged. This was mostly my own doing, as I made the choice to overwork myself, partially because it's in my nature but also because the company told me, should I take on extra responsibilities and contribute to the thought leadership of the company, I could continue to be promoted and earn raises in my salary. My salary wouldn't be defined by the pay scales that dominate the public school system, where salary is determined by the number of years of service and the number of degrees one has.

Personalizing learning entails so much more than minimizing the complexity of individualized curricula.

This was only true to a certain extent. By the time I finished working there (and after one raise), I was earning about $65,000 for a ten-month position, having to work over the summers to earn my full salary of $79,000. This may sound like a pretty good deal, considering the average ten-month teacher salary in the United States hovers around $60,000, but when we account for the staggering economics of Silicon Valley and the sheer amount of money that funnels through the technology industry, it's really not much. In fact, according to a 2018 report from the Department of Housing and Urban Development, any individual earning under $82,000 in San Francisco is considered "low income" (Martin, 2018).

And to think I was one of the highest-paid educators at the company.

I knew the educators' work and knowledge base was driving the company. After all, we were the ones using the tools in the classrooms; we were the ones giving engineers ideas on what to change and how to make the tools more user- and child-friendly.

I used this logic each time I attempted to negotiate my salary. I knew that I'd contributed a great deal to the development of tools the company aimed to monetize. While the educators in the company, most of whom earned *far less* than I did, were considered "low income," the technologists and engineers were taking home six-figure salaries, with many earning double my salary, if not more.

"We aren't capable of changing the market value for educators," the COO said to me at one point toward the end of my time there.

"There is no market value for what we're doing. Our jobs are categorically different than the average teacher," I retorted, knowing full well that my words were falling on deaf ears. I knew because I'd had many conversations like it before, such as the one I'd had with the CEO of the company nearly a year prior. It revealed just how much the company valued educators—and it wasn't too far off from how much American society values educators.

"You see, Paul," the CEO said to me while I was trying to negotiate my salary, "most of what you do is one-off. The engineers build code, and when that code works, it's immediately replicable."

He was referring to the fact that engineers build code that can—for all intents and purposes—be immediately copied and pasted, replicated instantaneously, allowing any and all users interacting with the program to immediately benefit from the changes to the program. It's like when your phone updates. When it does, it requires little to no effort from the user, and automatically, millions have benefited from the work of a relatively small group of engineers.

He wasn't wrong—in the sense that an engineer's work is incredibly valuable for that reason. I don't want for a second to undermine the fact that engineers do incredibly important work. During my time in Silicon Valley, I worked with a number of engineers who earned every penny of their salaries; they listened intently, they valued what educators did in the classroom, and they worked tirelessly to try to make the task of personalizing learning easier for us. But he was wrong to claim that an educator's code is *less* valuable than that of an engineer.

While educators may not be well-versed in Python or SQL, we are well-versed in a different type of code. Our code is the human code. It is quite possibly more replicable and more permanent than any line of code an engineer enters into a computer.

The code we write—this human code—is perhaps one of the *most* replicable forms of code out there. It is a code of kindness, it is a code of joy, and it is a code that fosters self-confidence and self-love. It is a code that literally alters the course of human consciousness and inspires children to grow into the best versions of themselves. It's a code that beckons them to be vulnerable, to reach out to others, and to interact with the world around them. It is a code that brings justice to young children who've had the deck stacked against them. In fact, it is *this* code—the code that we teachers write—that has inspired the digital one that lies beneath all these complex programs you and I use every day. And while it may not replicate as quickly or efficiently as an engineer's, it has the potential to sow seeds that will blossom for generations and withstand the test of time, unlike most education technology.

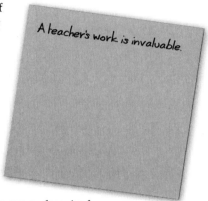

A teacher's work is invaluable.

But we must remember that the goals of education technology are not the same as a teacher's goals. Their goals are not to alter the course of human consciousness. The goals of a for-profit education technology company—even a "certified B Corp" that "balances purpose and profit"—is to make money. Profits are what keeps Silicon Valley's world turning, and as a result, they're what motivates the decision-making of those in power in education technology. This quest for profits is what makes CEOs literally tell educators that their work is less valuable than the work of an engineer—because an educator's work is more expensive and won't make the CEO money as quickly as an engineer's will.

It may seem odd to make such a passionate statement on salary in a professional book about personalized learning, and if you are unsure why I've chosen to do this, I'd like to make my intentions especially clear. Personalized learning has little to do with technology integration. Personalized learning is the art of making learning personal and meaningful to children; it uses the science of instructional design and developmental psychology as a flexible frame for the co-construction of knowledge. Instead of technology, *equity* lies at the heart of personalizing learning for groups of small human beings. And if we want to bring equity to our children, we *must* invest in our educators, for we are the artists, scientists, and keepers of equity within our classrooms. We hold such immense power within our hands—with the ability to shape consciousness, motivation, and the tender inner dialogue of a child. And we do this with a forceful delicacy that pushes on children just hard enough to mold them without breaking them.

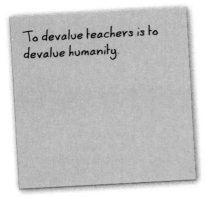

To say that a teacher is less valuable than an engineer—or to say that the teaching profession is less valuable than any other, either in words or in actions—is to devalue our children, the future, and the collective conscious of humanity.

The problem isn't intention, though; it's a lack thereof. Remember that complacency and mindlessness are oftentimes the biggest threats to equity. Much like the words of my former principal from the previous chapter, the CEO's words were not *intended* to hurt or dehumanize; his words were *intended* to rationalize the systemic oppression of educators. To him, this was simply a matter of fact: *You are worth less than an engineer, and that's just the way it is.*

This truth has been part of our society for quite some time now. It has grown from a misogynistic history that devalues female-dominated professions; it has grown from an economic pattern of exploiting educators for prosperity, much like our company did; it has grown from an American culture scared of its own vulnerabilities—resulting in a society that attempts to control and predict the outcomes of its students so it might have a chance at controlling, predicting, and preserving a perceived sense of exceptionalism.

The truth of the matter is that education technology is not revolutionizing learning as technology evangelists will tell you. It's not helping every child reach their full potential or empowering students for a limitless future. Since the exaggerated hype around education technology hit, we haven't seen a marked change in test scores or a restructuring of the oppressive systems that institutionalize racial and class segregation. We've only seen our scores flatline and inequity worsen.

After years of working sixty or more hours per week in Silicon Valley—serving predominantly well-supported, high-income students—I noticed that my results were no better than those of my public school years. In some cases, they were worse, the demands of the technology and the school limiting the impact I could have on my students, ironically making learning less impactful, meaningful, and personal. But it wasn't just the hysteria of personalized learning technology that created an unsustainable workload, arguably making me less effective as an educator; with technology at the center of our vision for education, it also negatively impacted the culture, dehumanizing the process of learning.

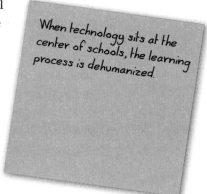

When technology sits at the center of schools, the learning process is dehumanized.

Too often, education technology and its associated ventures fall short because they do not inherently and intuitively put humans and humanity at the center of their strategic plans. Due to the nature of for-profit technology ventures, education technology companies *must* put profits and technology usage at the center of their strategic plans to stay afloat. It's hard to blame them for that given the sources of their funding and the nature of their business models. It's no surprise, then, that many technology companies measure their success in terms of technology usage, the number of users engaging with a given platform, or the number of clicks made on a website; they have no other option.

These goals act in opposition to the goals of a democratic school system. Instead, these goals exist for the advancement of an Americanized form of obsessive capitalism that only widens achievement and economic gaps in our country. It is fueled by competition, self-interest, and privilege, and unbeknownst to the American population, it's causing us to build a new education system in the image of technology elites who are so far out of touch with a majority of the American population and the problems real children, families, educators, and schools are facing on a day-to-day basis. And once you zoom out and see this big picture, it becomes clear that the notion of technology-driven personalized learning as a panacea is at best laughable—and at worst uninformed and naïve.

REFORMING EDUCATION IN THE IMAGE OF TECHNOLOGY ELITES

In August 2015, Willie L. Brown Jr. Middle School opened in San Francisco's Bayview neighborhood, known for its marginalized, low-income population, high levels of industrial pollution, and loss of industry and infrastructure. Bayview's population has historically been diverse, and it still is. According to 2010 Census data, Bayview is about 34 percent African American, 31 percent Asian, and 12 percent White. The area is known to have higher rates of unemployment, poverty, and crime.

To many, the opening of Willie Brown Middle School seemed like a step in the right direction for the neighborhood. According to a 2018 feature in *Wired* titled "How the Startup Mentality Failed Kids in San Francisco," Willie Brown Middle School opened at a cost of $54 million, garnering funding from both public and private entities (Duane, 2018). The private funders and philanthropists came from the likes of Twitter, Salesforce, and Summit Public Schools, an organization of charter schools directed by tech elites such as Meg Whitman (CEO of Hewlett Packard), Priscilla Chan, and none other than Mark Zuckerberg.

The new school was to be focused on science, technology, engineering, and mathematics (STEM), with an emphasis on health and wellness. Students would learn in a state-of-the-art school, with "laboratories for robotics and digital media, Apple TVs for every classroom, and Google Chromebooks for students." There was even an "on-campus wellness center" providing "free dentistry, optometry, and medical care."

"We had a lovely building," one teacher recounted in the *Wired* article, "but it was like someone bought you a Ferrari and you popped the hood and there was no engine," despite the fact that an entirely different story was sold to visitors and affluent donors. Not only did the school have few policies and procedures in place, but they had numerous issues with student conduct and discipline, including kids throwing things at teachers and other sorts of violent behavior. It took the principal about a month to resign his position and many teachers not much longer to do the same. While future administrators would claim that the behavior was not enough to seriously injure other students, arguing that students throwing pens is just what happens in a middle school, that is entirely beside the point.

The point here is that integrating technology, updating curriculum, and building new facilities does not unequivocally lead to education reform. By acknowledging only the superficial, short-term solutions, we ignore what lies at the root of education's greatest challenges. Daniel Duane, the author of the *Wired* article, goes on to share:

> Eric Hanushek, a Stanford professor of economics who studies education, points out that among all the countless reforms tried over the years—smaller schools, smaller class sizes, beautiful new buildings— the one that correlates most reliably with good student outcomes is the presence of good teachers and principals who stick around.

These few lines capture the essence of the article and the essence of the problems that sit beneath the surface of superficial education reform: the problems are cultural and systemic. Few are willing to look under the hood of the car; few are willing to engage with the humanity of the education system to reform it in a way that addresses real human needs.

There are true problems of scarcity in our schools, where the education system is not meeting the basic needs of educators and students. Far too many children come to school without the proper nutrition and wellness; educators are forced to work multiple jobs, all the while using their own salaries to fund their classrooms. Technological scarcity is not one that needs to be prioritized, because it will not solve the problems that pose the largest threats to educational equity.

Technology elites have done a great job convincing us that technology is, in fact, the solution. They've managed to buy a spot at the table where critical conversations are happening about the future of education, all because of the privilege and power they've garnered through success in business. The unprecedented successes of companies such as Amazon, Google, and Facebook have made them the envy of a modern capitalist economy. They have, for all intents and purposes, played a critical role in redefining success and shaping the collective conscious of our country, trickling all the way down to our schools. We currently see this in education reform, with an overemphasis on infusing education technology into the classroom, claiming that it provides students with computer science and/or STEM skills. But it's important to remember that a well-designed computer science or STEM education and frivolous technology integration are two very different things. They've done such a good job at pushing this technology-rich agenda—at making it the envy of the average American—that they have now begun to build schools in their grandiose and out-of-touch image, pushing flawed reforms such as open floor plans, a version of flexible seating that is more about aesthetic than pedagogy, and an otherwise permissive and unstructured style for running schools that is labeled as "child-centered" or "student-driven."

I identify strongly with the reflections in the *Wired* article because I saw them firsthand in my experience in Silicon Valley. I, too, witnessed parades of high-powered technology elites traipsing through my classroom, the executive suite of the company capitalizing on ideas of mine that were born neither out of the company's mission nor out of the vision for technology-driven personalized learning. I constantly listened to members of the executive team attempt to sell a vision for personalized learning, similar to the "Ferrari with no engine" analogy. They painted a picture for personalization that was at best a hyperbolic vision for student-driven learning and at worst a fabrication of what was truly occurring in the schools. It frustrated me so much that I eventually asked them to stop visiting my classroom—to no longer include me in their pitches to future investors, for I did not wish to be involved in the proliferation of the corporately driven hyperbole my classroom was becoming.

It was devastating to realize what I had gotten myself into. I had not only lost my way and lost sense of my own pedagogical vision and educational values; I had allowed myself to become a tool for technology elites, helping them build schools in their image.

A CLOSER LOOK

FLEXIBLE SEATING

The case for flexible seating is relatively straightforward. Advocates for flexible seating suggest that it empowers children through choice, meanwhile offers different spaces that allow for varied types of learning, and provides more options for self-regulation. But I argue that flexible teaching must come before flexible seating.

Does flexible seating really empower kids through choice?

Flexible seating has the potential to empower kids through choice, but it's not a must-have for student empowerment. Sometimes the costs of flexible seating outweigh the benefits, especially if choice becomes less about equity and access—and instead more about preference. Choice is useful in a classroom when it helps all children get what they need; it becomes a threat to equity when it is used to fulfill preferences that are not essential needs.

In a 2015 study at University of Salford Manchester, Professor Peter Barrett and his team identified that well-designed learning spaces do, in fact, correlate with higher academic performance (bear in mind that this accounts for myriad factors such as lighting, color, temperature, air quality, etc.), but Barrett himself subscribes to the old adage that form follows function (Barrett, Zhang, Davies, & Barrett, 2015). In essence, it all begins with a commitment to flexible and responsive pedagogy and a conscious decision to build choice into the culture of the classroom.

What about all the different types of learning that can occur with flexible seating?

Some progressive educators make flexible seating more about aesthetic than about equity and access. They make their classrooms look like a coffee shop or technology start-up without considering the purpose behind various types of learning spaces. Sure, it's beneficial to have different types of spaces in the classroom—a classroom library, a space for whole-group gatherings, and clusters of desks that allow for both small-group learning and individual work. It's possible to achieve this with traditional furniture, all the while giving children the structure and reliability that individual desks or assigned table seats can offer. Ultimately, the pedagogical choices a teacher makes will have a much greater impact on the types of learning that can occur in the classroom, as Barrett and his team suggest.

But doesn't flexible seating allow for a more active learning environment?

It can if it's done correctly, and if teachers take the time to educate students in the process of incorporating flexible seating. Mindful teachers build active learning environments when they humanize their classrooms. And this is not limited to the furniture in the classroom. They build curriculum that is collaborative, they explicitly teach self-awareness and self-regulation, and they partner with their students to better understand their physical needs throughout the day. Again, it's all about the choices an educator makes to build community and set up a learning environment where all children's needs are met. At the end of the day, if your classroom looks like a coffee shop, but your curriculum is still composed mostly of passive activities like worksheets and other consumables, flexible seating will do little to increase activity in your classroom.

Instead, it's a better idea to find balance with seating in the classroom. Provide students with their own home base (an assigned seat at a desk or table), build self-awareness and self-regulation within them, and talk to them to make sure their physical needs are being met during the day. Just remember that it all starts with flexible teaching.

The problem with this is that the interests of technology elites and the interests of the American population are not one in the same. Contrary to popular belief, children do not function well in unstructured environments, with open floor plans that resemble a technology company's office and individualized curricula that allow them to operate with unbridled independence. In fact, few people in the world are truly able to work with such unbridled and unregulated autonomy. The vast majority of us—dare I say, the 99 percent of us who are living the average American life—operate within a relatively narrow range of constraints. To us, the American Dream is more of a tall tale than a reality. And for a large number of Americans, the American Dream is no more than an unattainable myth that no state-of-the-art facility or education technology will help them actualize. This was the case for the students at Willie Brown Middle School and is the case for far too many schools in the United States.

As a result, raising historically underserved students in the image of wealthy technology elites, assuming that a STEM education in a fancy school is going to right the wrongs that society has bestowed on them, is ignorant and taunting. The same goes for personalized learning. To think

> Education technology companies must prioritize consumer desires over student needs. They have no choice.

that we can scale personalized learning technologies that have been tested on a small sample size of elite private school students to meet the needs of an entire nation swimming in economic disparities is not only naïve; it goes against the time-tested techniques of empirical research. But through this examination, it becomes clear that education technology companies are not interested in fulfilling needs identified by empirical research; they are instead interested in fulfilling perceived needs brought about by consumer-driven capitalism.

This is not to say that all classroom technology is bad. There is a striking difference between educating our students in computer science and inundating them with personalized learning technologies. Quality STEM education and modern classroom technologies are important to a modern education, so long as they're not pushing a corporate agenda. In fact, there are some places where education technology is effective, especially if we're certain to put empirically based human needs first. We educators must be prepared to evaluate technology with a keen and informed eye, to ensure the education technology we are supporting is preserving the humanity of our classrooms, our schools, and our learners.

FOUR PRINCIPLES FOR HUMANIZING TECHNOLOGY INTEGRATION

Education technology should serve a few distinct purposes, significantly regulated and coming in second to solving problems of equity and justice in our schools. Effective technology should take the role of seemingly monotonous jobs, allowing human beings to focus on the jobs that human beings are truly needed for. While the execution isn't always simple, and while it may be riddled with trial, error, building, and rebuilding, it can be guided by a few principles (see Figure 11.3).

Figure 11.3: Four Principles for Humanizing Technology Integration

- Minimize the complexity of learning that's personal and meaningful.
- Maximize the power and potential of individuals in the classroom.
- Reimagine learning within and beyond the classroom.
- Preserve or enhance human connection within and beyond our learning spaces.

MINIMIZING COMPLEXITY

First and foremost, technology is useful because it minimizes complexity. Take, for instance, the advent of the smartphone. It's no surprise how popular it is. With a smartphone, we can store all our contacts, surf the Web, and even pay our bills. While costly, the benefits of a smartphone outweigh its expenses by significantly minimizing the complexity of our lives and allowing us to do more with our time.

Classroom technology should function similarly. Teachers' lives are immensely complex, and it's mainly due to the complexity of a classroom where we have twenty to thirty students in one room. In my first year of one-to-one iPad implementation, I remember being unsure of what to do with all the files my kids were producing. They'd open up word-processor documents or take pictures of their work, e-mailing it to me so I could assess it. I ended up with a flooded inbox each week, with student e-mails piling on top of parent and teacher e-mails. It actually ended up making the classroom a *more* complex place, with no relief in sight.

But this is the case with anything new. Technology can temporarily increase complexity at first. With time, our team realized that we could leverage other tools such as Dropbox and Evernote to manage document sharing. We eventually used Google Docs, too, creating folders into which children could drop pictures and documents. Now I use Seesaw, allowing kids to take pictures of their work and share it not only with me but with their parents, too.

In my experience, education technology minimizes the complexities of personalization using tools that function behind the scenes. Younger students are better off managing the complexity of their learning using analog tools such as colored folders, visual checklists, and other concrete tools that promote executive functioning. In fact, should young children overuse technology to minimize complexity, it could hinder the development of executive functioning skills, engendering a mindlessness and learned helplessness that will make functioning as an adolescent and an adult more challenging.

> Education technology benefits teachers mostly behind the scenes.

In my classroom, technology has proven to be most useful for collecting student work, managing student data, and enhancing partnerships with parents. To streamline the collection of student work and assessment data, I use Seesaw. Its interface is simple, student-friendly, and student-driven, allowing me to send student work to parents to keep them in the loop on their children's progress. To organize academic data, my team and I use Google Sheets, keeping track of both standardized assessment scores and summative assessment scores.

This makes it easy for us to identify children for intervention, when necessary, and reflect on our practice as a team. Finally, technology allows me to streamline communication with parents. I am able to send quick notes about curriculum and keep lines of communication open with regard to strengths, challenges, and parent education around topics that parents want to know about.

MAXIMIZING INDIVIDUAL POWER AND POTENTIAL

Minimizing complexity and maximizing human potential go hand in hand. Oftentimes, when we minimize the complexity of a given task, we maximize human potential, allowing people to be more efficient. But this does not begin and end with organizing files. Technology can also minimize the complexity that accompanies abstract thinking, allowing young learners to reach deeper levels of understanding.

Oftentimes, what holds children back from reaching more complex levels of thinking is the abstraction necessary to think in a complex manner. This is why tools such as concept maps and word sorts are so helpful for children. In a concept map, children can draw tangible connections between ideas, allowing them to see how concepts are structured, how they break down, or how the pieces fit together. This is challenging to do in a notebook, as many teachers know. Young children, generally speaking, have trouble navigating space on an 8½″ × 11″ piece of paper. They cram words and sentences into circles and boxes that are far too small; they draw lines without precision, either making roundabout circular structures or cacophonous webs that are hard to follow.

There are a number of concept-mapping tools that help minimize the complexity of abstract thinking, including MindMap and Popplet. While it's true that we should be teaching children how to make mind and concept maps in a notebook, using digital tools can scaffold visuospatial skills, formatting the size of boxes for children and allowing them to move the boxes around digitally. This grants educators the opportunity to develop mind- and concept-mapping skills in both digital and analog settings, minimizing the complexity of deepening abstract thinking and maximizing the potential of each child by removing some unnecessary obstacles.

"Mr. France," Chase said, "look, I made a new thinking map!"

I looked down at Chase's iPad. I saw an arrangement of colors, lines, and words, all in reference to an opinion piece he was working on (see Figure 11.4). We had been using Popplet to explore text structures for opinion pieces. I used Thinking Maps to demonstrate a couple of ideas for how an opinion piece could be structured, then allowed my children to apply one of them to their topics. Using Popplet for this minimized the complexity of a personalized experience, as children were able to explore a universal lesson in the context of their own topics.

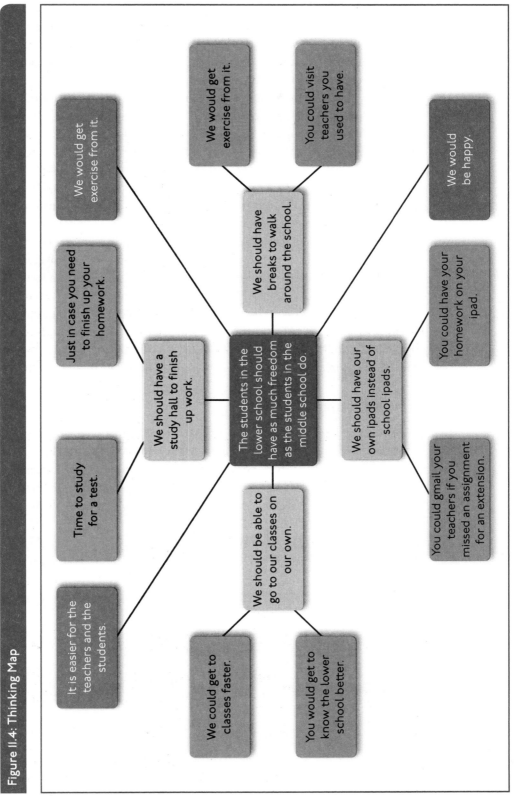

The students in the lower school should have as much freedom as the students in the middle school do.

We should have breaks to walk around the school.
- We would get exercise from it.
- You could visit teachers you used to have.
- We would be happy.

We should have a study hall to finish up work.
- We would get exercise from it.
- Just in case you need to finish up your homework.
- Time to study for a test.
- It is easier for the teachers and the students.

We should have our own ipads instead of school ipads.
- You could have your homework on your ipad.
- You could gmail your teachers if you missed an assignment for an extension.

We should be able to go to our classes on our own.
- We could get to classes faster.
- You would get to know the lower school better.

Chase's Thinking Map wasn't as "new" as he thought it was, per se, but it was definitely a more complex adaptation of the Bubble Map. The Bubble Map usually has two layers to it: the first layer is one bubble in the center that houses the topic; the second layer consists of all the bubbles that "describe" the topic. Chase added a third layer to his. It had additional subtopics under his already identified subtopics. This was not something I'd taught him, but Chase leveraged his autonomy and came to this conclusion on his own, allowing him to play on the flexible frame supporting this lesson.

Most of the children in my class were not ready for this, but there were a few others like Chase who were. By creating the space to have children make their own Thinking Maps with technology, as opposed to using premade maps with circles and lines already decided for them, Chase's individual power and potential was unlocked. Too often, teachers do not realize how restrictive scaffolding can be if it does not suit the child and the task. Had I provided the class with premade concept maps or taught them how to create one in a rigid and linear fashion, I would have lost too many teachable moments. Moments like Chase's would not have come about democratically as they should in an emergent system. And in a time when we are trying to reimagine and reclaim personalization through humanized practices, we must keep this intention of maximizing human potential at the center so moments like these may emerge.

REIMAGINING LEARNING

Developed by Dr. Ruben Puentedura (2015), the SAMR model aims to guide teachers in integrating technology into their classrooms. SAMR is broken up into four levels: substitution, augmentation, modification, and redefinition. SAMR can be visualized as a ladder with *substitution* (S) situated at the bottom of the framework and *redefinition* (R) toward the top (see Figure 11.5).

Figure 11.5: The SAMR Model

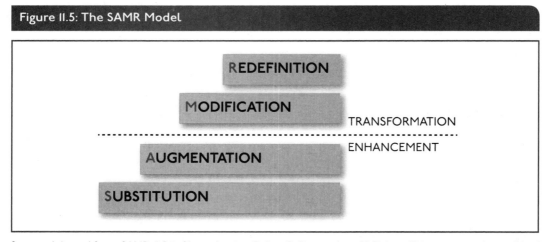

Source: Adapted from *SAMR: A Brief Introduction*, Ruben R. Puentedura, PhD, http://hippasus.com/rrpweblog/archives/2015/10/SAMR_ABriefIntro.pdf

As we climb the ladder, technology integration becomes increasingly sophisticated. Technology as *substitution* entails directly substituting analog technology with digital technology. Turning a worksheet into a PDF is an example of *substitution*. While there is little functional change, it makes sharing more efficient and less wasteful.

As we ascend on the SAMR framework, we reach *augmentation* (A). In the *augmentation* stage, technology still serves as a substitute for analog tools, providing more functional improvement, such as a PDF that includes hyperlinks to external websites. There is now functional improvement that wouldn't be possible without technological intervention.

A great deal of technology lies within *augmentation*. Even Microsoft Word, which is now likely considered an archaic tech tool, provides functional improvement in relation to its predecessor, the typewriter. Google Docs does the same. There is significant functional improvement with Google Docs: it's stored online, and users can access word-processing documents anywhere.

Google Docs also shows elements of *modification* (M) and *redefinition* (R). The very idea of sharing documents via Google transforms the user's experience. Now users from all over the world can witness and participate in the evolution of a given document. Individuals no longer have to send multiple copies of a document as it evolves, which saves time and storage space, also minimizing complexity and maximizing individual and group potential.

But Google Docs doesn't stop there. Google Docs has also redefined collaboration as we know it. Never before were two individuals in separate places—whether across the office or across the world—able to collaborate on the same document simultaneously. With Google Docs, users can collaborate in real time, without locational constraints. This has provided a significant functional change to something as simple as word processing, allowing people to accomplish something previously inconceivable.

It's important to remember that this is all relative. In fact, Google Docs is starting to feel so commonplace that it doesn't seem like it's redefining much anymore. It's fun to imagine what advanced technology might replace Google Docs someday; it's fun to wonder if or when it will become obsolete. But just because it may become commonplace doesn't mean we should find replacement technologies only for the sake of advancing technology. Above all else, what's most important is that we are living by the aforementioned four major principles of technology integration: minimizing complexity, maximizing individual power and potential, reimagining learning experiences, and preserving connection between human beings. Living by these will help us remember that technology should allow us to access more of our humanity, not take us away from it.

Oftentimes in education technology, reimagining learning entails outlandish projects involving augmented reality or complex data-powered algorithms that provide individualized activities to kids. Sure, this is learning reimagined, but it's not necessarily reimagined for the better.

As we evaluate new technologies, we *must* stay in touch with both reality and our humanity. We must ensure that technology preserves or enhances connection between individuals within and beyond the four walls of the classroom. If we don't, we risk taking the humanity out of learning, which is happening in too many schools that value hyper-individualized, technology-driven personalized learning.

PRESERVING OR ENHANCING CONNECTION

It's true that there are two sides to this coin. With any advancement in technology, there are both benefits and costs. While dangerous politicians now have the ability to misguide millions, digital technology and social media have maximized the power of individual voices, allowing stories to surface that likely would not have been told before. This is the case for classroom technology, too, which is why preserving or enhancing human connection is a necessary item on our checklist for humanized technology integration. If the use of any given tool begins to chip away at human connection, we must reconsider its use and find an alternative.

> Reconsider your choice if any education technology tool seems to be chipping away at human connection.

It's hard to think of many tools that actually *enhance* human connection within the classroom, which is one of the reasons why I limit screen time in my classroom. After all, dialogue, discourse, and face-to-face feedback are the most humanizing ways to personalize learning. But this is another one of the reasons I love to use Seesaw. Using Seesaw, my students are able to send pictures of their work to their parents efficiently. This strengthens the home-to-school connection, allowing conversations about learning to become more fruitful.

THE INTERSECTION OF EDUCATION TECHNOLOGY AND SOCIAL JUSTICE

Corporately driven education technology ventures are just as much of a threat to the health and wellness of our schools as any number of institutionalized inequities, including funding disparities. This is because for-profit education technology ventures are, by and large, worsening inequity in schools.

The schools that most need these practices of humanized personalization—practices that enhance self-awareness, bolster agency and autonomy, and establish equity in the classroom through complex instruction that offers rigorous content to all students—are often the least likely to get them, as Zaretta Hammond shares in *Culturally Responsive Teaching and the Brain* (2014).

Digitally driven personalized learning tools more often increase complexity and minimize human potential by dehumanizing learning. They reimagine learning like a dystopian novel, where children are receptors of knowledge, programmed by artificially intelligent programs. Schools with low test scores and minimal resources, often home to low-income students and/or students of color, are increasingly inundated with technology-driven personalized learning initiatives, all the while unaware that these tools are only widening inequity.

In our final chapter, "Justice," we'll explore the systemic constraints that have made high-quality education altogether inaccessible for a large portion of the population of the United States of America. It is the by-products of these constraints—a widening of achievement and the flatlining of standardized assessment scores—that have created a demand for personalized learning. But these by-products are merely the symptoms of a disease that must be treated accordingly—not through the management of superficial symptoms but instead by targeting the cause of the disease itself.

CHAPTER TWELVE

JUSTICE

We began our journey with *foundations*, intended to help you debunk many of the myths promulgated by self-proclaimed progressive educators and technology elites and solidify a strong theoretical foundation on which we could build a definition for humanized personalization. In the middle section, on *pedagogy*, we explored examples of humanized pedagogy, placing self-awareness, student agency, and structured autonomy at the center of our classroom practices. And in this last section, on *equity*, we've peeled back the many layers of the modern education system, breaking free of our internalized and subconscious biases to get to the heart of why all this talk about personalized learning started in the first place—to make sure that every child gets what they need to reach their full potential.

It's true that pedagogy is important; it's also true that there is a great deal of empirical research to support the many practices from Section II. But the truth is that both our students and the world will change. As a result, our teaching will need to change, as well, to accommodate an ever-diversifying student population. There is one thing that will help our pedagogy withstand the test of time and help it evolve right alongside our kids, and that is an acute awareness of justice. Justice *must* be built into both models for personalized learning and the education system as a whole.

WHAT IS JUSTICE?

In Chapter 10, we took a moment to define *equity* and *equality*, juxtaposing the terms to understand the nuances between them. While *equality* advocates for all individuals to have identical supports, equity advocates for equal access for all individuals, even if that means they require different supports to gain access. The push for equity is necessary in all societies—but especially in America. Economic divide, a national legacy of White supremacy, and other systems of oppression set only some up for success in education, leaving others to fend for themselves. The inequity, injustice, and exclusivity of the modern American education system is far more of a threat to learning that's inherently personal and meaningful than is a lack of   digital technology or individualized curricula.

When our schools are built in an inclusive and just manner, equity—not technology—is at the heart of our intentions for personalization. We build curriculum in a manner that accommodates the needs of diverse groups of learners; we take active and intentional steps to remove systemic barriers born of implicit bias and institutionalized discrimination. Further, we continuously question and iterate on the curriculum and the pedagogies that shape our classrooms.

> To work toward justice entails the removal of systemic barriers that impact a child's ability to integrate into the collective conscious of the classroom.

Sometimes the quest for justice necessitates radical action. Sometimes it necessitates a more gradual, mindful, and proactive approach. If I've learned anything over the past ten years of teaching, it's that the answer usually lies somewhere in the middle.

To this day, I do not regret my decision to bring the LGBTQ community into my classroom. As a result of many stories like mine—where individuals had the courage to speak truth to power—there is more LGBTQ representation and visibility in our classrooms than ever before. Several states now even require LGBTQ history to be taught in schools. While we still have a long way to go, I'm so proud of the progress we've made. I like to believe that my youthful and rogue act of e-mailing those families without my principal's permission contributed to that progress.

In *The Three Questions*, Jon J. Muth (2002) adapts a short story from Tolstoy, where readers follow a young boy, Nikolai, as he seeks answers to three of life's most important questions (see Figure 12.1).

When is the best time to do things?

Who is the most important one?

What is the right thing to do?

Figure 12.1:
The Three Questions

As the story concludes, we learn the answers to these questions through Nikolai's experience:

There is only one important time, and that time is now. The most important one is always the one you are with. And the most important thing is to do good for the one who is standing by your side.

The Three Questions teaches us that actualizing justice in our schools requires mindfulness. To teach and learn through justice means to be present in the moment; to disconnect from bias and preconception; to see the experiences of others as undeniable truths; to think and act in a mindful and intentional manner, willing to create new categories (or perhaps abandon categories altogether) to ensure that all who enter our classrooms feel an innate sense of belonging; to acknowledge the intersectionality of each learner's and educator's identities and create learning spaces that allow them to live their truths. At the foundation of justice lie vulnerability and the willingness to open ourselves up to the many truths that exist in our nuanced and intersectional world.

As a result, learning that's truly meaningful and inherently personal needs this, as well—far more than it needs technological advancements or individualized curriculum.

INTERSECTIONALITY AND IDENTITY

It is hard to say whether or not the old adage that it is impossible for two snowflakes to be entirely identical is true, but it appears highly likely that it is. According to Joe Hanson (2014), host of PBS's *It's Okay to Be Smart*, even if two snowflakes appear to be the same structurally, it's almost a certainty that they will differ on an atomic level. Why is this? Because the environment acts on each snowflake in a different way. Because they don't exist in *exactly* the same space and form with *precisely* the same external forces, they all turn out just a bit different, their individual identities related but still intersectional, much like a group of humans.

In Latin, the base *sect* quite literally means "a way, road, or beaten path." When the prefix *inter* is added, the direct etymological translation of the word is "between ways" or "between paths." To understand intersectionality means to understand nuance—to find comfort in the fact that there is so much we don't understand. It is in this way that an ever-evolving understanding of intersectionality is critical to understanding personalization, more so than mastering the many pedagogies we've explored throughout this book. Our mindset and intention behind personalization will guide us far more than the empirically researched practices, for if we act within our classrooms in a manner that is inherently inclusive, just, and aware of implicit bias, empathetic humanized practices will emerge much like knowledge does when a learner is emboldened by their agency.

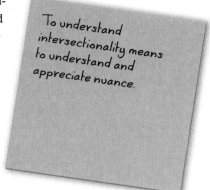

To understand intersectionality means to understand and appreciate nuance.

Technology-driven personalized learning does not understand the role intersectionality plays in actualizing a human-centered vision for personalized learning. Technology-driven initiatives generally explore only one "sect" of personalization, if you will—the sect dedicated to ability and academic achievement—largely ignoring the intersection of gender, race/ethnicity, class, sexuality, ableness, and faith tradition. It's the fundamental flaw in education technology's hypothesis for personalization: there is a lack of awareness around the degree to which identity impacts a child's ability to learn in a school system that is more often exclusive than inclusive.

If technology-driven personalization initiatives demonstrated an understanding of intersectionality, identity, and the role the two play in achieving equity in schools, they would come to the same realization I did after working in Silicon Valley for three years: every child is not in need of the same degree of individualization, therefore negating this perceived need for technology that digitally curates curriculum for students. Curricular individualization should instead be reserved for the students who need it the most, and it should be delivered by human beings.

WHAT IS FAIR IS NOT ALWAYS EQUAL

Technologists and their wealthy funders often hypothesize that the problems afflicting education can be remedied through digital means. It makes sense why they presume this: it is the medium through which their success has been constructed. Their privilege prevents them from seeing that this won't necessarily construct success for all. In their worlds, technology has solved a number of problems related to economies of scale—problems such as access to information and minimizing production costs. But the problem in assuming that these same principles can be applied to the education system is that these are categorically different systems benefiting from entirely different practices.

Technological systems rely on complexity minimization through industrialized practices. These industrialized practices, much like an assembly line, reduce the number of steps necessary to complete a given task. This is the purpose that a great deal of digital technology has served in the late twentieth and early twenty-first centuries. Information is now easier to access because so many can simply open up a digital device and find the information they need. Similarly, social media has minimized the complexity of connecting and communicating with human beings all over the world. These systems are sustainable and scalable because they rely on the agency of human beings to continue breathing life into them. In these digital innovations, a degree of separation exists between the human beings and the technology itself. The technology is the system, and the humans are the users of the system.

The education system is categorically different. In the education system, *the people are the system.* They are, for lack of a better analogy, the wires, connectors, and agents of decision-making. A human's decision-making cannot be neatly placed into a cell on a spreadsheet or traced through an algorithm, no matter how complex. Human decision-making, instead, is governed by the uncertainties of experience, emotion, and cognition. This humanistic component to the education system makes it an entirely different system altogether, subject to bias, privilege, and discrimination.

> Technology-driven hypotheses on personalization do not demonstrate an understanding of the nuances of intersectionality.

Technology companies examine the education system through a narrowed and biased lens, assuming that personalized learning is merely a problem of complexity minimization. Far too many technology executives that engage in for-profit ventures—specifically in the area of personalized learning—come from privilege. As a result, their privilege blinds them; they fail to acknowledge the role that access, privilege, and inequity play in perpetuating injustice in the education system. They instead presume that technology tools that individualize curriculum will "close the achievement gap."

But there are obvious flaws in this hypothesis. Let's say, for instance, that every child is given access to these tools—and that through digitally individualizing education, every child is able to truly reach their full potential each year, experiencing a year's worth of growth. This would not close an achievement gap or counteract inequity in schools. If anything, this would maintain or perhaps even widen said achievement gap due to the fact that all students would theoretically grow the same amount (or more) in one year. The eight-year-old student who has gone from doing second-grade math to third-grade math is no closer in proximity to the child who went from doing fourth-grade math to fifth-grade math.

I've seen this firsthand. Low-achieving students—typically dependent learners who already struggle with regulation, self-awareness, or other components of executive functioning—struggle to navigate these tools on their own and work through challenges. More often than not, they move through these tasks at a glacial pace, shutting down when the going gets tough because they have not learned the necessary skills to work through obstacles and leverage their autonomy to solve problems. They have become objects of education, isolated and alone, burdened by the weight of their failures. They watch their friends around them ascending levels, experiencing success, and otherwise "achieving" at higher and higher levels. These children stagnate unless they receive additional intervention from a sentient educator.

Our high achievers, on the other hand, know how to play the game of education. The skills they bring to school set them up for greater success within this unforgiving system defined by inequitable rules. These personalized learning tools suit them and many of the parents and educators who are willing to invest in them. The tools provide the hits of dopamine necessary to keep high achievers engaged and addicted, all the while accelerating them through content, without a doubt increasing the likelihood that they'll score at higher levels on the flawed and narrowed metrics of standardized assessments.

John F. Pane, senior scientist and distinguished chair in education innovation at the RAND Corporation, claims in two separate reports that the evidence in support of technology-driven personalized learning is very weak (Pane, 2018; Pane et al., 2017). In his 2017 and 2018 reports, he cites the unsustainability of creating individualized lessons for students and the potential negative effects on student collaboration, given the fact that students in technology-driven personalization models are working on individualized content.

Overall, research seems to support some strategies related to individualization, but it is not "due to individualization alone," says the 2018 report, citing a landmark 1984 study by Benjamin Bloom on the effects of one-to-one tutoring. It is, instead, "due to individualization plus nurturing and attention." In Bloom's 1984 report, he shares that tutoring practices delivered by human educators led to what they called a 2-sigma gain in achievement, meaning that it was twice as effective as a conventional classroom (1 sigma). But there are clear constraints here. Economies of scale prohibit schools from building a system where each child has their own personal tutor. It's simply not possible due to cost.

On the other hand, Bloom and his team identified a handful of classroom practices that were nearly as effective as one-to-one tutoring, as Arthur VanderVeen, vice president of Compass Learning, writes in a 2014 *EdSurge* article. These practices include the use of pre-assessment and formative assessment, cultivating ownership in students, building self-esteem through positive reinforcement, and providing corrective feedback to individual students.

"These group instructional practices produced a 1.7 sigma gain in student achievement," he states in the article. "In other words, the average student learning through these classroom instructional strategies performed better than 96 percent of students in a conventional instructional environment—and that's *without* tutoring."

The results of Bloom's study encouraged educators to leverage differentiated instruction and provide regular feedback to students—practices that are encouraged as a part of this model for humanized personalization and backed by replicated empirical research. These practices require sentient educators, not automated or adaptive digital technologies, to enact them.

> Building equitable and just learning environments requires all of us to embrace the fact that different students will require different degrees of individualized attention.

That's not to say there's no place for one-to-one intervention models in schools. Instead of attempting to offer them to everyone through digital means, one-to-one intervention should be offered only to students who present evidentiary need. Students should receive these interventions from expert educators who have a nuanced understanding of how students learn best and who take the time to build meaningful relationships with students. But this necessitates a conversation about how our schools are staffed and funded. We must allot more monies for school psychologists, counselors, paraprofessionals, and other qualified adults who are able to provide intervention when educators identify barriers to a child's learning.

The problem is that everyone wants their child's education individualized—and far too many teachers are afraid to tell parents of high-achieving students that they are, in fact, going to get less individualized attention because they simply don't need it. We are afraid to have a point-blank conversation about equity and what it means for building classroom environments that are *just*. Many families feel it is unfair for low-achieving students to receive more one-on-one attention than their average or high-achieving counterparts. But this point is moot, grounded in privilege and fueled by White fragility, exacerbating the education system's culture of fear.

PERSONALIZATION IS A PROBLEM OF PRIVILEGE

Robin DiAngelo, former associate professor at Westfield University, coined the term *White fragility* in 2011, intending to cultivate awareness around the discomfort and ambivalence many White people exude when discussing race and racism. Through her work, she unpacks the many narratives of White fragility, one of which is *color blindness*—a narrative that encourages White people to "not see color" and to "treat everyone the same."

"You know, actually no one was—or could be taught to treat everyone the same," she says in a 2018 NPR interview, reflecting on the messages she received as a child. "We can't do it. We don't do it. We don't even want to do it in the sense that people have different needs."

This much is true. All people have different needs and strengths, born from intersectional identities, formed through the external pressures of socially constructed experiences. And to assume that a personalized learning tool, delivering individualized content through digital means, will serve every child in the same way is, at best, naïve and uninformed. At its worst, it's a product of White fragility that oftentimes goes hand in hand with issues related to socioeconomic privilege in schools. I say this because the intersection of equity and personalized learning necessitates a conversation about both race and class in the United States.

Personalized learning initiatives are striving for equality in schools, when they should be striving for equity and justice. Inevitably, enacting equity and justice in schools means working in opposition to equality. The data are clear: socioeconomic status and racial privilege have an effect on a child's ability to operate within the constraints of an education system designed to sort students in favor of a hegemonic White upper-middle class. Technology elites only make this worse by attempting to build schools and infiltrate already existing schools, reforming systems in their image—an image that is notorious for its lack of representation of women and people of color. This is what happened at Willie Brown Middle School, and the expectations of the technology industry did not meet reality.

As the life force of reform in the education system, educators must push for classrooms that operate with equity at the center of models for making learning inherently personal and meaningful. This means building classrooms in the image of their populations, differentiating our instruction, and leveraging the three dimensions of personalized learning so that all children may engage with the collective conscious of the classroom, meanwhile receiving the appropriate amount of small-group attention and individualized feedback necessary to nurture each child's inner dialogue. Without a doubt, this means that some children will, in fact, receive more one-on-one attention—and others less—due to a variety of factors related to achievement, executive functioning, and social-emotional skills.

But we can still provide all students *some* one-on-one attention. After all, every child deserves to be known and seen in the classroom; every child deserves to have a teacher who appreciates their strengths and cares enough to provide constructive feedback that helps them grow. For many high-achieving students—those who have already begun to actualize their agency and autonomy—a little feedback goes a very long way. Due to developed executive functioning skills and strong metacognitive abilities, they are often able to evaluate their work while it's in process, making improvements or modifications to it before receiving feedback from the teacher. In some cases, high-achieving students can receive even greater amounts of one-on-one attention if they have underdeveloped executive functioning or social-emotional skills.

This doesn't mean that we simply offer a one-size-fits-all curriculum and say "too bad" if it's too easy for a child. Instead, we build curriculum using a flexible frame that allows for varied entry points and bounded choice. By choosing content that grants all students access to a rigorous education, we build in points of convergence, a sense of belonging, and opportunities for mindful divergence to build agency and autonomy.

Far too many educators and families don't see this. They strive for a form of equality in classrooms that is ignorant to the powers of privilege and institutionalized discrimination, ignoring the fact that certain students come into our classrooms requiring more individualized attention than others. They possess some of these qualities of White fragility—uncomfortable with the notion that their child may have privilege others don't, and bothered by the fact that the school's job is to balance those scales in whatever ways possible. This is where perceived scarcity rears its ugly head, warning parents that their child is not getting *enough* attention during the school day—that they must receive more one-on-one instruction or a more individually curated curriculum. But this is a zero-sum myth. It presumes that, for someone to win, someone must also lose. It's a hallmark of American capitalism and free enterprise, unable to entertain the notion that it is in fact possible to address the needs of different children in different ways—and still have everyone "win."

> We can counteract perceived scarcity by engaging in brave conversations about equity with parents.

Despite the fact that these needs are born of perceived scarcity and White fragility, technology-driven personalization offers a palatable solution for White, upper-middle-class folks—a curriculum that is tailored to the child, modified for pace and content. Because their view is so narrowed, many do not discuss the fact that this palatable solution to personalization offers neither a sustainable nor scalable solution for large-scale education reform due to the many reasons we've explored through this book. These are solutions for problems of privilege, born of perceived scarcity and White fragility and ignoring the fact that the education system tends to work best for those who have amassed the most privilege.

While messier, more nuanced, and more controversial, the answer for this is socially just pedagogy. We must do all we can to remove the barriers in our classrooms that bar certain children from accessing the curriculum and mindfully engineer our learning environments so all children may find a sense of belonging there.

TIPS FOR SOCIALLY JUST TEACHING AND LEARNING

Belonging and social justice go hand in hand. To cultivate a sense of belonging means that we must remove the barriers that naturally exclude children who identify with any historically marginalized population. I differentiate these socially just practices from the inclusive practices I outlined in Chapter 10 because they promote equity through the *removal of barriers*. While strategies such as increasing representation in children's literature, leveraging competency-based assessment, and using complex instruction allow all students to see themselves in the curriculum, the following strategies for socially just teaching actively remove barriers that often limit access to the curriculum or stand in the way of students developing the empathetic capital to advocate for justice in the world around them.

We begin by unpacking our own identities and the privilege associated with the various pieces of our identities. This creates an appreciation for and understanding of the intersectionality of identity, cultivating awareness, and vulnerability. Through an evolving understanding of how identity contributes to learning, we can effectively redefine success in our classrooms, forging relationship-based learning partnerships that allow us to reconnect with our humanity.

START BY UNPACKING YOUR IDENTITY AND YOUR PRIVILEGE

Privilege, by definition, refers to the notion that some individuals are more naturally equipped for success within a social system—and not because there is something about them that is biologically superior but instead because the social system has been built in favor of those with privileged characteristics, affording them more opportunities and fewer barriers. In American society, our social system predominantly favors heterosexual, cisgender White men. This isn't surprising when we consider that the bedrock of our nation— the U.S. Constitution—limited the rights of life, liberty, and the pursuit of happiness to individuals who meet these criteria.

But the world is changing. In Figure 12.2, you'll see a 2018 U.S. Census report that shows the racial demographics of various age groups. In 2017, the school-age population (< 16 years old) was less than 50 percent White, and when compared with a senior population (> 65 years old) that was more than 75 percent White, this substantiates the notion that our country is diversifying. But this diversification doesn't start and end with race and ethnicity. More than 50 percent of public school students now live in poverty. Moreover, a 2016 report from the Centers for Disease Control and Prevention stated that roughly 8 percent of the current high school student population identifies as lesbian, gay, or bisexual. There are no comparative data for this, given the fact that this type of data collection is new. Over the past 30 years, we've seen the percentage of female representation slowly increase in our governing bodies, from a mere 6.7 percent before the 1992 election to about 23 percent in 2018.

We're still not where we need to be with regard to equitable representation in Congress, but these data make it clear that the world is changing and that the

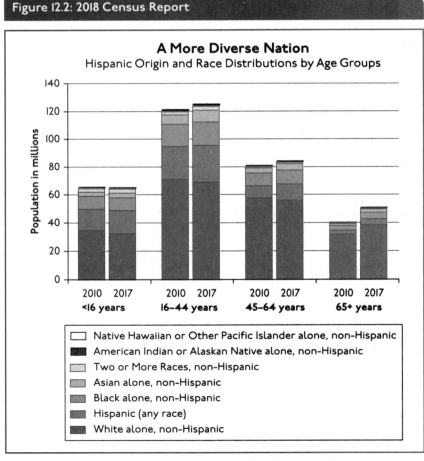

Figure 12.2: 2018 Census Report

Source: https://www.census.gov/library/visualizations/2018/comm/diverse-nation.html

old systems built in the image of the straight, cisgender White male will need to change along with it. America will no longer be a country where rugged individualism and institutionalized discrimination pen the rules. The rule book will be written under the influence of more colors, more genders, and more intersectional perspectives, shaped through an ever-diversifying set of stories.

And this means that people like me—White cisgender males—will have to cultivate a new and empathetic understanding of what it means to exist in a world where we must participate in writing these new rules that favor everyone. To do that, we must first develop an understanding of privilege and start the courageous process of unpacking it, all the while aware that this process will never cease. The work will *never* be done and instead will persist as we meet new people, explore new perspectives, and watch as new narratives reshape the collective conscious of the United States.

My journey with understanding and unpacking my own privilege didn't begin until someone had the courage to challenge it and call it out. When I was in college, I posted an article on my Facebook about affirmative action. At the time, I was opposed to affirmative action. I thought affirmative action policies ignored people like me and how hard I'd worked to get where I was. A former teacher of mine noticed I had shared this article and commented, calling out my privilege and challenging me to think differently about it.

Coincidentally, at the time, I was enrolled in a social studies methods class at the University of Illinois. The class was geared toward methods for social justice education where we learned not only about ways to bring about more equitable representation in the curriculum but also about privilege and perspective-taking as adults. In that class, I learned what privilege meant, aiding my shifting perspective on equity and policies such as affirmative action.

I learned that privilege means not having to worry about *if* you'll go to college but *where* you'll go; it means not having to wonder if you're being followed at a department store or are being racially profiled by a law enforcement officer; it means always being able to find bandages that match your skin color.

Since then, I've learned about the intersectionality of privilege. Privilege is not black and white (no pun intended); it's not something you have or don't have. Privilege is relative, and at one point or another, we all experience privilege through relational and comparative means. The conventionally abled person experiences privilege when they can walk up the stairs. A Black man experiences male privilege when he is asked to speak on behalf of his wife in the grocery store. Gay men like me experience privilege when their stories are more palatable in elementary schools than are those of the transgender population.

Privilege is intersectional and relative.

The intersectionality of privilege doesn't mean that the lack of privilege associated with racial, ethnic, gender, or sexual minority groups should be overlooked. It simply necessitates a greater understanding of it. It requires more storytelling and more conversations around each of our experiences, culminating with suggestions for how we might remove barriers for as many people as possible.

Without a doubt, it's uncomfortable to begin this process. In college, it made me uncomfortable to admit that I had been afforded privileges because I was a White male from an upper-middle-class suburb. I didn't want to admit that my circumstances were partially a product of chance; it scared me to think that my life could and likely would have turned out much differently had I been born in a different place or of a different race.

But it was important that I came to terms with it. It is important for *all* of us to unpack privilege, not so we carry around guilt or shame in relation to it but so we can do something productive with it. This enhanced awareness of privilege and the intersectionality of identity has made me inextinguishably curious, constantly wanting to find out more about my students, their experiences, and their stories. It's helped me continuously develop my understanding of equitable classroom practices, finding solace in the fact that I am going to spend extra time helping my female students of color see that they, too, can be mathematicians and engineers (if they want), because the society they live in does such a poor job of showing them that this is possible.

But most of all, it's helped me see when to step up and advocate for myself and when to step back and pass the mic to others. Every year now, I come out to my students—and not as a political act, intended to rock the boat and make others uncomfortable, but because it's *necessary* to shape the collective conscious of the future. I do so in a way that counteracts the emotional baggage that too many adults carry around in relation to sex and sexuality; I do so in a way that Zaretta Hammond (2014) might say is *selectively vulnerable*, meaning I choose to share specific parts of my identity, humanizing myself to connect with my students, meanwhile advocating for my minority group to remove the barriers and biases that often encourage LGBTQ folks to stay closeted. But it all began with unpacking my privilege and my own identity.

TEACH AND LEARN WITH VULNERABILITY

The first time I came out to students was in my fourth year of teaching, not too long after the "controversial lesson incident" that defined my final year teaching in public school. It was one of the hardest things I ever had to do.

The very idea of coming out to young children planted a fear so deep inside of me that I couldn't even find the courage to do it on my own terms. I'd spent the previous three and a half years terrified that my students would learn or realize I was gay, tarnishing my reputation or disintegrating my relationships with them.

I was teaching fifth grade at the time. I looped with my students during those years, and as the end of fifth grade approached, I had built impenetrable relationships with them. We knew one another like family, having spent the better part of the previous two years together. As their time in elementary school was winding down, they transformed into apprentice middle school-ers, showing developmental signs of early adolescence. With the recent advent of Instagram, many students had created accounts, despite the fact that they were not yet thirteen. They illicitly began posting pictures of each other on Instagram, matching students as couples without their consent.

The issue was so pervasive and subversive that it warranted a class-wide discussion. I ended the discussion by requesting they come see me in private if they knew anything more about the situation. Shortly thereafter, two of my students, Lana and Mara, came to me because they did in fact have some information. It wasn't information about other students, though. It was about me.

"What's up?" I asked.

"Well, we're kind of nervous to talk to you about it," Lana replied, the girls exchanging uncomfortable glances with each other.

"This is a safe environment. Whatever you need to tell me will stay between us," I reassured them.

"Well, it's kind of about you," Mara said. "Kids are saying things about you."

"Oh, really?" I replied to them, smiling, ready for something immature and infantile that I could roll off my shoulders. "What are they saying?"

"They're saying you're . . . *gay*," Mara revealed.

My face felt hot. My palms began to sweat. My long-held fears were coming to life right in front of me, and haunting questions crossed my mind. *Will I be fired? Will parents be upset? Have my students lost respect for me?*

I brought the girls into my colleague's classroom across the hall. It was important to me to have this conversation in front of another adult, given the year's previous events.

"Well, do you know what that word means?" I inquired cautiously. They nodded and told me their definition.

"Okay, yes, that's what it means. And, yeah, I *am* gay, but it's nothing that anyone should be making fun of. It's all about how you say it. Just because someone calls me gay doesn't mean they're saying something bad. It's true. I *am* gay."

It seemed like the girls were expecting me to defend my straightness or perhaps even seek out their friends to reprimand them. But I did no such thing. In fact, I didn't speak a word of it to any of the other students that year, just Lana and Mara.

Funny enough, the conversation ended quite casually. I left them by telling them that sometimes people made fun of things they didn't understand, which I assumed to be the case with the group of students who had targeted me. I think we all anticipated that the situation would be climactic and dramatic, but in reality, it was the opposite—just another moment to learn about one another and connect through our imperfect humanity. It turned out to be simply a matter of fact: their teacher they had grown to love was, in fact, *gay*.

Little did I know that this was only the start of my story as an openly gay teacher—an exposition that would frame the remainder of my career and solidify the importance of telling our stories in schools. For us to rehumanize school cultures—to place equity and humanity at the center of our agenda for personalization—we all must be represented, seen, and heard, able to own our stories and step into our truths.

Since then, I've come out to almost all my students, in some way or another. When I taught kindergarten and first grade, little Nora asked me if I had a girlfriend. I told her no and that I had a boyfriend instead.

"That's weird," she replied.

Truth be told, my heart broke for a second. But through my own journey with identity and intersectionality, I knew better than to take it personally. She was merely a product of her environment, and this was my opportunity to make a change for the better.

"It *is* different," I said. "Why do you think it's weird?"

She sat in silence, unsure what to say.

"I understand. Sometimes when things are different, they seem a little *weird*," I said, all the while knowing this little pumpkin was trying to rectify a heavy internal dissonance. I loved her for doing it so vulnerably and courageously.

She finally interjected, "Well, I just don't like when people make fun of you. I feel bad for you."

I was humbled by her innocence, by her honesty. Even at six years old, she knew people like me were oppressed; she knew I was *different*. The best word she had for it at that very moment was *weird*, victim to nothing more than the linguistic capabilities of a young child and a society that does not talk openly enough about sexuality.

"You know," I replied, "people will always find something to make fun of you for. Some people are just like that. All you can do is remember that a lot of people love you and that people who say mean things are really just sad themselves."

The truth is, I could have led by telling Nora that she hurt my feelings and that she shouldn't use words like *weird* to describe someone like me. But I knew that wouldn't be educative, and I instead chose the more vulnerable path. As the LGBTQ adult in the room, my job was to make the most of this experience, striking a balance between advocating for my minority group and leveraging my privilege as a White male in a position of authority to reshape this part of her inner dialogue.

CULTIVATE AWARENESS AND HUMILITY

Months later, that same kindergarten and first-grade multi-age class was putting on a play. We had begun an adaptation of *Bringing the Rain to Kapiti Plain* for our winter learning exhibition. I'd chosen this as a project to help build reading fluency and to teach about story structure—a class-wide need, easily differentiated by readiness level—meanwhile allowing all to participate in creating a set and props, infusing art into the curriculum.

Bringing the Rain to Kapiti Plain is an African folktale that comes from Kenya, adapted into a children's book by Verna Aardema. In it, the narrator tells the story of Ki-pat and the year a great drought came over Kapiti Plain.

After reading the story and revealing to my students that we'd be turning it into a play, they were all bursting with excitement.

"Can I be Ki-pat?" one student blurted out, begging to be the main character.

"I want to be the eagle!" another one exclaimed.

"Can I be Ki-pat's wife?" another asked.

One child's voice emerged from the sea of voices. A boy with curly blond hair and bright blue eyes looked up at me.

"Well, shouldn't one of the kids with brown skin play Ki-pat?" he asked, so astutely referring to the fact that the main character was African. Although he didn't have the words to expand on his thoughts, he was sending a very clear message that it simply made sense for a person of color to play the role of a character of color.

I am reticent to admit that I did not anticipate this conversation. But I do so to reveal my own vulnerabilities as an educator and to briefly comment on my own experiences with White fragility. In that moment, I was uncomfortable. I was unsure what to do. I didn't want anyone to think I was trying to single kids out based on their race or ethnicity, nor did I want to send a message that Black main characters can come only from Africa. So I did what I do in a lot of these situations, partially to buy me some time but also to process my own feelings.

"What do you all think about that?" I asked. "Turn and talk."

In that moment of respite, I quickly came to. I got in touch with my privilege and the messages of White fragility that I had received growing up—that skin color didn't matter and that if we lived in a world where we didn't address our differences, they would no longer cause conflict.

But our differences do matter. And in discussing them, we can actually feel closer to one another.

I could see it in the twelve pairs of eyes sitting in front of me, in a palette of brown, beige, and bronze visages. To them, this was a matter of fact: to make our play as realistic as possible, it only made sense for the "kids with brown skin" to play the main characters. And as I thought about it more, I pondered just how many opportunities there are for White children to play White roles in schools—and how often White actors are charged with playing characters of color in movies. It became an opportunity not only to teach and act in a socially just manner but also to make it a *privilege* to be Black in our classroom.

These moments are critical to humanizing personalization—and in a way that digital technology could never achieve. These moments reach the depths of our souls and lay permanent fingerprints on our identities. And I don't just mean for the kids, despite the fact that this moment did cultivate an awareness and humility around racial and ethnic representation in the curriculum. While this story of representation in our class play—and the reminder that skin color *does matter*—was a teachable moment for my students, it was a moment for me to learn, too. It gave me an opportunity to partner with them, continue the process of unpacking my privilege, and expand my perception about what socially just teaching and learning look like.

It further instilled a humble reminder that my work as a White educator—this work where I must continue to confront my privilege and overcome my fragility—will never end.

USE CURIOSITY TO HAVE COURAGEOUS CONVERSATIONS

Curiosity and humility are cut from the same cloth. They are brethren, united through their common roots within courage and empathy. To be curious and humble means to be brave and aware enough to admit that someone else may see it differently. As a result, we must instill curiosity within our students, for a two-way path exists between curiosity and humility, strengthening the empathy and courage required to teach and learn through social justice.

It was the first few weeks of school in my third-grade classroom, and we were just getting started on our identity unit. In exploring our identities, we take time to unpack the many parts of our identity, often through an essential question: *What makes you who you are?*

To begin this exploration process, I chose the book *All Are Welcome* by Alexandra Penfold to generate a list of ways people might differ. The book is relatively simple in terms of its word choice and sentence structure, making it an accessible read for all students. Its drawings, on the other hand, are incredibly engaging and rich with detail. In the drawings, we see a number of group identities represented, with various races, ethnicities, religions, genders, and sexualities.

"She looks like she's from a different country," one of my students said of one of the characters, very early into the read-aloud.

"How do you know?" I asked the child.

"Well, she's wearing one of those things, you know, on her head." She gestured toward the screen.

"Oh, you mean a hijab?" I replied.

Another student raised her hand. "But that doesn't mean she's from another country," she said. "It just means she's Muslim."

"Ah," I said. "So you're saying that she might be from the United States but wearing a hijab because it's part of her religion."

To cultivate awareness around race, ethnicity, religion, or any other group identity, we need not always take radical steps and lead students down counterproductive paths of discomfort. While there are moments where discomfort is necessary—such as in moments of outright racism, sexism, homophobia, and the like—simply teaching kids to be curious can help cultivate both an enhanced cultural awareness and an inquisitive humility that teaches them to ask questions instead of making assumptions.

With this strong foundation in the lower elementary grades, we set them up to better understand how assumptions and biases can lead to discrimination in later years. The ultimate goal of cultivating awareness and humility in students is to help them see that we all live in a system where discrimination is ever present—that it exists within all of us. The ultimate goal is to help students see that, to act in opposition to racism, we must know full well that racism, sexism, homophobia, and the like are sewn into the fabric of our society's collective conscious and, therefore, sewn into our inner dialogues without us even being aware of it.

Cultivating this awareness through social justice education helps relieve us of the shame that accompanies this realization—without relieving us of the responsibility to make meaningful change. It replaces shame with sensitivity to the notion that we are all susceptible to a very powerful institutionalized discrimination that makes our classrooms less inclusive and far more impersonal places to learn. Most important, it instills within us the realization that we are all responsible for correcting it, not only through antibias and antidiscrimination practices in classrooms but also by redefining what it means to experience success within the classroom.

REDEFINE SUCCESS IN YOUR CLASSROOM

When I first started teaching with one-to-one technology, I quickly became obsessed with the flipped classroom. My strategy for differentiation in mathematics became dependent on it. Each night, my students would access the classroom website and watch instructional videos that corresponded with math journal pages. They would complete the math journal pages by watching a video, and when they came in the next morning for math, I would give them an entry slip to determine how close they were to mastery.

For the students who demonstrated mastery, I had enrichment activities available, and for those who seemed as though they needed just a bit more guided practice, I had extra skill practice on hand. For students who seemed to have misconceptions, I planned to work with them in small groups.

It goes without saying that it was an immense amount of work to create this variation of activities every day. What's more, I experienced some of the very same by-products of this level of individualization that we've explored throughout the book. There were fewer points of convergence in the classroom, with groups of children working on different activities. Likewise, my classroom ended up becoming tracked. Generally speaking, a specific subset of students would consistently receive enrichment while a pretty reliable subset of other students would receive small-group intervention with me, which more often than not became didactic and rote.

Hindsight has granted me the wisdom to understand why this was happening. It's because my definition of success was reductive and linear. I presumed that, for all students to get what they needed in the classroom, I had to break the curriculum into pieces and provide those pieces in a predetermined order to reliably help my students reach grade-level proficiency. I know now that these various skills are neither orthogonal nor mutually exclusive; they are concomitant, working together in a nonlinear fashion. This also explains why my groupings were relatively consistent. Students who succeed in math oftentimes have strong visuospatial and executive functioning skills, aiding them in more efficiently abstracting mathematics concepts and demonstrating a superficial mastery of content.

While I noticed, generally speaking, that my students' scores on standardized assessments were strong, it's hard to say whether or not it was due to these flipped classroom practices. I was teaching in a high-achieving school district, in a community that spent a great deal of time outside of school building a schema within their children that helped them play by the rules of our education system. That's not to discount their strengths and achievements—because there were many. My point is that I strongly doubt that these extra steps I took to individualize the curriculum contributed to their success in school in the long-term; it was, instead, the culture of learning that was built into the community that set so many of these children up for success. For them, it was simply a way of life to read lots of books, to be curious about numbers, and to share about themselves through writing.

I didn't know it then, but what I was doing wasn't differentiation. At the heart of differentiated instruction lie equity and inclusion, and the steps

I was taking to meet the needs of individual children was more likely to create divides between my students than it was to bring them together around a rigorous academic curriculum.

At the heart of differentiation lie equity and justice.

I did this not out of ill intent or in an explicit effort to widen the achievement gap; I did this because my perspective was so narrowed. It was so colored by the achievement culture in which I'd grown up—in which my own success had been constructed. As a result, it caused me to define success in such a reductive and linear fashion—like boxes I needed to check off. To me, success was mastery of the content, as measured by the assessments I'd used to gauge mastery. I was a victim to Campbell's Law, and those assessments and the narrow metrics I used impacted the way I taught the students.

I'm not saying that we shouldn't keep measuring success in reading, writing, mathematics, the sciences, and the arts in our curriculum—and I'm not saying we shouldn't use valid and reliable assessments to gauge academic progress. We absolutely should. I'm simply saying that our modern perspective on education has discolored and distorted the true purpose of these content areas. We too often see these literacies in a utilitarian manner; we use them as fuel for our own cultural and economic hegemony, and we forget that they originated as ways for human beings to connect with one another. The printed word, mathematics, the sciences, and the arts are—at their most basic levels— literacies that humans have used for thousands of years to interact with and understand the surrounding world. It is these literacies that have helped the human race evolve and expand beyond the constraints of our tiny blue planet. And similar to how the exploitation of Earth's natural resources could very well lead to our demise, the exploitation of these core human literacies and the education system at large could very well lead to our demise as a society.

It doesn't have to be that way, though. Through intentionality, self-awareness, and a bit of vulnerability, we *can* change our mindset. We can move away from this exploitation of education for economic and cultural hegemony, and we can reconnect with the humanity that exists within teaching and learning to afford equitable and just learning experiences to all students.

RESTORING EQUITY AND RECONNECTING WITH HUMANITY

I'll leave you with one more story.

Meg had always struggled in math. Her parents shared this with me, and I noticed it within my first few weeks of working with her. What's more, when we'd work on math tasks, she would frequently shut down. She would sit at her desk, staring off into the distance with her arms crossed, unwilling to even attempt to solve the problem.

Meg's identity matters here, as it does in all situations. Meg was not only a girl but a girl of color. Girls of color are often excluded from the typical archetype of a mathematician, which is why it's so important to note. Despite recent cinematic portrayals of Katherine Johnson (*Hidden Figures*) and Alan Turing (*The Imitation Game*), the STEM fields have unequivocally been built in the image of the straight, cisgender White male. And while there is a recent push to diversify these fields, to a large degree these biases remain.

It made sense why Meg struggled to integrate into our culture of mathematics, despite the fact that I was leveraging the many practices I share in this book. I was using *complex instruction*, choosing math tasks that I knew were accessible to all students, regardless of math knowledge; I had very intentionally built a classroom culture that was fostering agency, awareness, and autonomy; I was using the flexible frame to build my units and assessments so I could reliably gather enough academic data to understand student misconceptions; and I was humanizing my instruction by creating lots of space for dialogue, discourse, and points of convergence.

Meg saw herself within neither the curriculum nor the mathematical culture of the classroom. This stemmed from the experiences she brought with her. Without a doubt, she'd experienced the world in a way that excluded her from mathematics. She struggled to leverage it to understand the world around her and instead had been using it as a compliance tool to help her do what her teachers said, often relying on flawed procedural knowledge that would only frustrate her more.

In the days of my flipped classroom, I would have worked with her in small groups consistently and perhaps even modified her curriculum. Mainstream thinking on personalized learning might have even encouraged me to match her with first-grade-level content as a third-grader, further isolating her from her peers and making her feel as though she didn't belong in math culture. But this methodology would have acted in opposition to differentiation, despite the fact that many synonymize differentiation and individualization. We must remember that at the heart of differentiation lie equity and justice. When equity and justice are actualized together, children get what they need, and the barriers that prevent them from accessing the curriculum are removed.

No, the solution was not to regress into first-grade content and individualize Meg's curriculum. The solution was, instead, to give Meg the tools to access the class's curriculum, meanwhile integrating her into small-group work that did not track or stigmatize her. It was a slow and patient process, one that did not happen overnight.

It turned out it didn't start with understanding her only academically. It started with better understanding Meg as a human being, her academics contextualized by her identity and humanity. Meg was incredibly sensitive, able to pick up on tender emotions in stories and respond to them in a way that demonstrated her unique ability to make connections to her own life experiences and other stories she'd read. She was funny, trying to make her friends laugh whenever she could. She also had a way of articulating her creativity, her wit, and her sensitivity, which she was able to convey through a well-developed oral vocabulary. But Meg struggled with regulating her emotions and opening herself up to situations and experiences that had once caused her pain. Math was one of those situations.

It was essential for me not only to know this about Meg but to walk the fine line between honoring the experiences that had shaped her identity and drawing appropriate boundaries that would help her productively struggle in the classroom. This entailed frequent breaks, where she would use a regulatory tool (like a stress ball) to calm down when she was feeling overwhelmed; this meant that she would use concrete manipulatives such as base-ten blocks and colored tiles when adding, subtracting, multiplying, and dividing; this meant that we'd do far more reflecting on the process by which she learned math than on the product of her work.

"I'm so proud of all of the hard work you did today," I would say to Meg. "Today, you jumped right in and tried something, even though I know you weren't sure if it was going to lead you to an answer."

For Meg, I knew success would look entirely different than for many of the other children in the classroom. My hopes and dreams for Meg were to have her approach math with increased confidence, to cultivate an awareness within her around the tools she could use to access grade-level curriculum, to open her back up to the uncertainty and vulnerability that often accompanies solving complex math problems, and to move her from *dependence* on her teachers and friends to *independence* and resilience when interacting with mathematics.

It's counterintuitive and ironic, but so many of our issues with achievement relate to the metrics we use to measure success. These metrics dilute our practices and force us to be exclusionary without even realizing it. Through measuring the success of our schools and our classrooms *only* through cold, hard academics, we've managed to lose sight of the necessary human components that exist in all our schools. While these cannot be measured quantitatively, they can be observed and felt through empathetic human interactions driven by curiosity, humility, and vulnerability.

Meg's and my successes were not predicated on rigidly controlling and predicting her academic outcomes. They were not progress-monitored daily, having her reflect on the number she got correct in a contained period of time. Meg's and my successes were, instead, enriched by the relationship she and I built over our time together. Sometimes she pushed and I pulled back. Sometimes I pushed and held a boundary, relying on the trust and positive rapport she and I had developed to get her to take a risk and open up. Together, we both relied on the collective conscious of the classroom, one that infused vulnerability, risk-taking, and mistake-making into its every fiber; we leveraged small-group experiences to provide a more intimate setting for Meg to make mistakes with friends and learn through their experiences; we nurtured each other's inner dialogues through moments when both Meg and I felt the sting of failure; we smiled and hugged when Meg called deep on her courage, took a risk, and was able to share a method with the class and contribute to the collective conscious of the classroom.

It didn't take quite as long as I thought it would to break through to Meg's inner dialogue—to help her begin the process of overcoming her patterns of impenetrability and underdeveloped resilience. Just three months into the school year, Meg came up to me bursting with excitement.

"I really love math now!" she said, a smile beaming on her face.

"I am so happy for you!" I replied, knowing just how hard Meg had worked to overcome her obstacles in math. "I know you wouldn't have said that when the school year started. What do you think changed?"

"I don't get really overwhelmed anymore," she said to me. "I just jump in and try something."

The reality of all this is that Meg likely continued to experience her challenges after she left my classroom. It's always three steps forward and one step back with goals like this. But the point here is that her *mindset* began to change. She went from feeling disempowered and excluded from mathematics to stepping into her own agency. The remainder of that school year was filled with ups and downs, with Meg stumbling and falling back into old patterns, but our relationship and her connectedness to the classroom were always there to pick her back up, to give her the encouragement she needed to keep trying, and to remind her that she belonged there with us, no matter what.

Helping Meg was not a matter of plug and play, as technology-driven personalized learning initiatives would have you believe. Helping Meg was a matter of *partnership*—of not only trying to impart some wisdom and knowledge on her but of learning *with* and *from* her, for she was ultimately the keeper and educator of her own experience. She was the only one who knew what it was like to be her. For me as an educator, this necessitated an understanding of Meg's identity as intersectional and unique, identical to no other; it required me to approach our interactions with curiosity, vulnerability, and empathy. It required me to see her—and to believe her.

AN AGE OF EMPATHY

In his book *The Empathic Civilization*, best-selling author and social and economic theorist Jeremy Rifkin (2009) posits that humanity is headed into a categorically different era of existence—that "the Age of Reason is being eclipsed by the Age of Empathy." Much like we've explored in this book, advancements in technology have made an increased global connectedness possible, diversifying a collective conscious that is now more global than it has ever been. It is this way because the barriers of time and space that once limited our connectedness are now being taken down through digital means.

While this may be true, our ability to digitally reach across the world and communicate with one another entails an enhanced awareness of what is right next to us. We must take these technological advancements in stride and remind ourselves that just because we *can* doesn't mean we always *should*. And if sometimes we *should* leverage the benefits of digital technology, it should *not* be at the expense of the people and relationships right next to us. We must in essence strike a balance between reaching out to the global collective and taking care of the ones we are with.

As we foray further into the twenty-first century, barreling forth at what feels like an ever-increasing speed, with more political and cultural uncertainty than most of us have ever experienced in our lifetimes, it's important we keep stories like Meg's at the center of what we do. We are so swept up in reaching across the globe, connecting with as many followers as we can through social media, and preserving a sense of American exceptionalism that I'm not quite sure ever existed that we're forgetting about the people who are right next to us. In our classrooms, this means that many are forgetting the human beings who breathe life into our classrooms—our students.

We have forgotten that "the most important thing is to do good for the one who is standing by your side" and to remove the barriers that exist for those in our classrooms who are otherwise unable to access an equitable and just education. We have forgotten that "the most important one is the one you are with," not the technology elites, policymakers, or administrators who are encouraging us to be something we're not. But most of all, we've lost sight of the fact that "there is only one important time, and that time is now" (Muth, 2002).

The students in our classrooms only get to be kids once. There is only one time in their lives to cultivate positive and productive relationships around the human condition of learning; there is only one time to turn away from the screen and turn toward the sentient human beings that fill our classrooms; there *is only one time* to reclaim our classrooms, our pedagogy, and what it means for learning to be utterly *personal*.

That time is now.

SECTION III
EQUITY

Implications for Humanized Personalization

Advocating for a sense of belonging is critical to humanizing personalization. We can achieve this through inclusive practices such as

- leveraging complex instruction to encourage heterogeneous groups of students;
- using competency-based assessment practices to deliver feedback and structure learning;
- ensuring equitable representation in children's literature;
- explicitly teaching about racism, sexism, and homophobia;
- removing gender markers in our classrooms;
- acknowledging sexuality as an integral part of the human condition; and
- limiting the use of web-based, adaptive technologies.

When we do incorporate technology into our classrooms, we should allow the following questions to guide our decision-making:

- Does the technology minimize the complexity of making learning personal and meaningful?
- Does the technology maximize the individual power and potential of individuals?

- Does the technology reimagine learning experiences?

- Does the technology preserve or enhance human connection in the classroom?

If the answer to the last question is ever no, then we should think twice before using the tool.

At the heart of humanized personalization lie equity and justice for all students who enter our classrooms. Technology-driven personalized learning fulfills needs of perceived scarcity, grounded in White fragility and privilege. We can teach with equity and justice in mind by

- unpacking our identities and our privilege,

- teaching and learning with vulnerability,

- cultivating awareness and humility,

- using curiosity to have courageous conversations, and

- redefining success in our classrooms.

REFERENCES

INTRODUCTION

Brown, B. (2015). *Daring greatly: How the courage to be vulnerable transforms the way we live, love, parent, and lead.* London, UK: Penguin Books.

Dewey, J. (1938). *Experience and education.* New York, NY: Macmillan.

Fitzgerald, F. S. (2017, October 6). The crack-up. *Esquire.* Retrieved from https://www.esquire.com/lifestyle/a4310/the-crack-up/ (Original work published 1936)

CHAPTER 1

Bray, B., & McClaskey, K. (2014). *Make learning personal.* Thousand Oaks, CA: Corwin.

Bray, B., & McClaskey, K. (2017). *How to personalize learning.* Thousand Oaks, CA: Corwin.

Gladwell, M. (2013). *David and Goliath: Underdogs, misfits, and the art of battling giants.* New York, NY: Turtleback Books.

Hammond, Z. (2014). *Culturally responsive teaching and the brain.* Thousand Oaks, CA: Corwin.

Hattie, J. (2008). *Visible learning.* New York, NY: Routledge.

National Commission on Excellence in Education. (1983). *A nation at risk: The imperative for educational reform—A report to the nation and the secretary of education, United States Department of Education.* Washington, DC: Author.

Nottingham, J. (2017). *The learning challenge.* Thousand Oaks, CA: Corwin.

Pink, D. (2009). *Drive: The surprising truth about what motivates us.* New York, NY: Riverhead Books.

Tomlinson, C. A. (1999). *The differentiated classroom.* Alexandria, VA: Association for Supervision and Curriculum Development.

Yerkes, R. M., & Dodson, J. D. (1908). The relation of strength of stimulus to rapidity of habit formation. *Journal of Comparative Neurology and Psychology, 18,* 459–482.

CHAPTER 2

Boaler, J. (2015). *Mathematical mindsets.* San Francisco, CA: Jossey-Bass.

Calkins, L. (1986). *The art of teaching writing.* Portsmouth, NH: Heinemann.

Durkheim, E. (1893). *The division of labour in society.* New York, NY: Free Press.

Pierson, R. (2013). Every kid needs a champion. *TED: Ideas Worth Spreading.* Retrieved from https://www.ted.com/talks/rita_pierson_every_kid_needs_a_champion?language=en

CHAPTER 3

Tomlinson, C. A. (1999). *The differentiated classroom.* Alexandria, VA: Association for Supervision and Curriculum Development.

CHAPTER 4

Dewey, J. (1938). *Experience and education.* New York, NY: Macmillan.

Hyerle, D. (1995). *Thinking Maps: Tools for learning.* Troy, MI: Innovative Learning Group.

Piaget, J., & Cook, M. T. (1952). *The origins of intelligence in children.* New York, NY: International University Press.

Pink, D. (2009). *Drive: The surprising truth about what motivates us.* New York, NY: Riverhead Books.

Schlechty, P. (2001). *Shaking up the schoolhouse.* San Francisco, CA: Jossey-Bass.

Wertsch, J. (1991). *Voices of the mind: Sociocultural approach to mediated action.* Cambridge, MA: Harvard University Press.

CHAPTER 5

George, D. S. (2016, November 13). How mindfulness practices are changing an inner-city school. *Washington Post.* Retrieved from https://www.washingtonpost.com/local/education/how-mindfulness-practices-are-changing-an-inner-city-school/2016/11/13/7b4a274a-a833-11e6-ba59-a7d93165c6d4_story.html

Hammond, Z. (2014). *Culturally responsive teaching and the brain.* Thousand Oaks, CA: Corwin.

Keene, E., & Zimmermann, S. (2007). *Mosaic of thought: The power of comprehension strategy instruction* (2nd ed.). Portsmouth, NH: Heinemann.

Kuypers, L. (2011). *Zones of Regulation: A curriculum designed to foster self-regulation and emotional control.* Santa Clara, CA: Social Thinking.

Langer, E. (1989). *Mindfulness.* Reading, MA: Addison-Wesley.

Langer, E. (1997). *The power of mindful learning.* Boston, MA: Da Capo Press.

Madrigal, S., & Garcia Winner, M. (2008). *Superflex . . . a superhero social thinking curriculum.* Santa Clara, CA: Social Thinking.

Pink, D. (2009). *Drive: The surprising truth about what motivates us.* New York, NY: Riverhead Books.

Wiggins, G., & McTighe, J. (1998). *Understanding by design.* Alexandria, VA: Association for Supervision and Curriculum Development.

CHAPTER 6

Baumrind, D. (1967). Child care practices anteceding three patterns of preschool behavior. *Genetic Psychology Monographs, 75*(1), 43–88.

Brown, B. (2010). The power of vulnerability. *TED.* Retrieved from https://www.ted.com/talks/brene_brown_on_vulnerability?language=en

Dewey, J. (1938). *Experience and education.* New York, NY: Macmillan.

Garcia Winner, M. (2002). *Thinking about you thinking about me.* Santa Clara, CA: Social Thinking.

Garcia Winner, M. (2008). *Think social! A social thinking curriculum for school-age students.* Santa Clara, CA: Think Social Publishing.

Hammond, Z. (2014). *Culturally responsive teaching and the brain.* Thousand Oaks, CA: Corwin.

Hattie, J. (2008). *Visible learning.* New York, NY: Routledge.

Hyerle, D. (1995). *Thinking Maps: Tools for learning*. Troy, MI: Innovative Learning Group.

Pink, D. (2009). *Drive: The surprising truth about what motivates us*. New York, NY: Riverhead Books.

Responsive Classroom. (2015). *The first six weeks of school* (2nd ed.). Turner Falls, MA: Center for Responsive Schools.

CHAPTER 7

DuFour, R., DuFour, R., Eaker, R., & Many, T. (2010). *Learning by doing: A handbook for professional learning communities at work—A practical guide for PLC teams and leadership* (2nd ed.). Bloomington, IN: Solution Tree.

Fisher, D., Frey, N., Almarode, J., Flories, K., & Nagel, D. (2019). *PLC+: Better decisions and greater impact by design*. Thousand Oaks, CA: Corwin.

Lachat, M. (1999). *Standards, equity, and cultural diversity*. Providence, RI: LAB at Brown University.

Organisation for Economic Co-operation and Development. (2008, January). Ten steps to equity in education. *Policy Brief*. Retrieved from https://www.oecd.org/education/school/39989494.pdf

Pane, J. F., Steiner, E. D., Baird, M. D., Hamilton, L. S., & Pane, J. D. (2017). *Informing progress: Insights on personalized learning implementation and effects*. Santa Monica, CA: RAND Corporation. Retrieved from https://www.rand.org/pubs/research_reports/RR2042.html

Robinson, M. (2017, November 21). Tech billionaires spent $170 million on a new kind of school—now classrooms are shrinking and some parents say their kids are 'guinea pigs.' *Business Insider*. Retrieved from https://www.businessinsider.com/altschool-why-parents-leaving-2017-11

Wiggins, G., & McTighe, J. (1998). *Understanding by design*. Alexandria, VA: Association for Supervision and Curriculum Development.

CHAPTER 8

Brown, B. (2010a). *The gifts of imperfection: Let go of who you think you're supposed to be and embrace who you are*. Center City, MI: Hazelden.

Brown, B. (2010b). The power of vulnerability. *TED*. Retrieved from https://www.ted.com/talks/brene_brown_on_vulnerability?language=en

Campbell, D. T. (1979). Assessing the impact of planned social change. *Evaluation and Program Planning, 2*(1), 67–90.

Chappuis, J. (2009). *Seven strategies of assessment for learning*. London, UK: Pearson.

DuFour, R., DuFour, R., Eaker, R., & Many, T. (2010). *Learning by doing: A handbook for professional learning communities at work—A practical guide for PLC teams and leadership* (2nd ed.). Bloomington, IN: Solution Tree.

Hammond, Z. (2014). *Culturally responsive teaching and the brain*. Thousand Oaks, CA: Corwin.

McTighe, J., & Wiggins, G. (1998). *Understanding by design*. Alexandria, VA: Association for Supervision and Curriculum Development.

Moll, L., Amanti, C., Neff, D., & Gonzalez, N. (1992). Funds of knowledge for teaching: Using a qualitative approach to connect homes and classrooms. *Qualitative Issues in Educational Research, 31*(2), 132–141.

National Commission on Excellence in Education. (1983). *A nation at risk: The imperative for educational reform—A report to the nation and the secretary of education, United States Department of Education.* Washington, DC: Author.

Pane, J. F., Steiner, E. D., Baird, M. D., Hamilton, L. S., & Pane, J. D. (2017). *Informing progress: Insights on personalized learning implementation and effects.* Santa Monica, CA: RAND Corporation. Retrieved from https://www.rand.org/pubs/research_reports/RR2042.html

Ravitch, D. (2016). *The death and life of the great American school system* (3rd ed.). Philadelphia, PA: Basic Books.

CHAPTER 9

Boaler, J. (2015). *Mathematical mindsets.* San Francisco, CA: Jossey-Bass.

Brooks, D. (2012). *The social animal: The hidden sources of love, character, and achievement.* New York, NY: Random House Trade Paperbacks.

Cohen, E., & Lotan, R. (Eds.). (1997). *Working for equity in heterogeneous classrooms: Sociological theory in practice.* New York, NY: Teachers College Press.

Danielson, C. (2007). *Enhancing professional practice: A framework for teaching* (2nd ed.). Richmond, VA: Association for Supervision and Curriculum Development.

Hattie, J. (2008). *Visible learning.* New York, NY: Routledge.

International Baccalaureate. (2014). *MYP: From principles to practice.* Cardiff, UK: Author. Retrieved from https://www.spps.org/site/handlers/filedownload.ashx?moduleinstanceid=38342&dataid=21191&FileName=arts_guide_2014.pdf

Kuypers, L. (2011). *Zones of Regulation: A curriculum designed to foster self-regulation and emotional control.* Santa Clara, CA: Social Thinking.

Madrigal, S., & Garcia Winner, M. (2008). *Superflex . . . a superhero social thinking curriculum.* Santa Clara, CA: Social Thinking.

McTighe, J., & Wiggins, G. (2005). *Understanding by design.* Richmond, VA: Association for Supervision and Curriculum Development.

Pink, D. (2009). *Drive: The surprising truth about what motivates us.* New York, NY: Riverhead Books.

Potts, W. (1984). The chorus-line hypothesis of manoeuvre coordination in avian flocks. *Nature, 309,* 344–345.

Radakov, D. V. (1973). *Schooling in the ecology of fish.* New York, NY: John Wiley & Sons.

Responsive Classroom. (2015). *The first six weeks of school* (2nd ed.). Turner Falls, MA: Center for Responsive Schools.

Ritchhart, R., Church, M., & Morrison, K. (2011). *Making thinking visible: How to promote engagement, understanding, and independence for all learners.* San Francisco, CA: Jossey-Bass.

Serravallo, J. (2010). *Teaching reading in small groups: Differentiated instruction for building strategic, independent readers.* Portsmouth, NH: Heinemann.

Zwiers, J., O'Hara, S., & Pritchard, R. (2014). Conversing to fortify literacy, language, and learning. *Voices From the Middle, 22*(1), 10–14.

CHAPTER 10

Aronsen, D., & Mazmuder, B. (2007). Intergenerational economic mobility in the United States. *Journal of Human Resources, 43*(1), 139–172.

Bowers, P. N., Kirby, J. R., & Deacon, S. H. (2010). The effects of morphological instruction on literacy skills: A systematic review of the literature. *Review of Educational Research, 80*(2), 144–179. https://doi.org/10.3102/0034654309359353

Brown, B. (2010). The power of vulnerability. *TED*. Retrieved from https://www.ted.com/talks/brene_brown_on_vulnerability?language=en

Brown, B. (2015). *Daring greatly: How the courage to be vulnerable transforms the way we live, love, parent, and lead.* London, UK: Penguin Books.

Hattie, J. (2008). *Visible learning.* New York, NY: Routledge.

Organisation for Economic Co-operation and Development. (2015). *21st century learning: research, innovation, and policy.* Paris: Author. Retrieved from http://www.oecd.org/site/educeri21st/40554299.pdf

Pane, J. F. (2018, October). Strategies for implementing personalized learning while evidence and resources are underdeveloped. *Perspective.* Santa Monica, CA: RAND Corporation. Retrieved from https://www.rand.org/content/dam/rand/pubs/perspectives/PE300/PE314/RAND_PE314.pdf

Pane, J. F., Steiner, E. D., Baird, M. D., Hamilton, L. S., & Pane, J. D. (2017). *Informing progress: Insights on personalized learning implementation and effects.* Santa Monica, CA: RAND Corporation. Retrieved from https://www.rand.org/pubs/research_reports/RR2042.html

Steenbergen-Hu, S., & Cooper, H. (2013). A meta-analysis of the effectiveness of intelligent tutoring systems on K–12 students' mathematical learning. *Journal of Educational Psychology, 105*(4), 970–987.

Wilkinson, R. (2011). How economic inequality harms societies. *TED*. Retrieved from https://www.ted.com/talks/richard_wilkinson?language=en

CHAPTER 11

Barrett, P., Zhang, Y., Davies, F., & Barrett, L. (2015, February). *Clever classrooms.* Manchester, UK: University of Salford Manchester. Retrieved from https://www.salford.ac.uk/cleverclassrooms/1503-Salford-Uni-Report-DIGITAL.pdf

Duane, D. (2018, June 28). How the startup mentality failed kids in San Francisco. *Wired.* Retrieved from https://www.wired.com/story/willie-brown-middle-school-startup-mentality-failed/

Hammond, Z. (2014). *Culturally responsive teaching and the brain.* Thousand Oaks, CA: Corwin.

Martin, E. (2018, June 28). In San Francisco, households earning $117,000 qualify as 'low income.' *CNBC.* Retrieved from https://www.cnbc.com/2018/06/28/families-earning-117000-qualify-as-low-income-in-san-francisco.html

Puentedura, R. (2015, October 24). SAMR: A brief introduction. Retrieved from http://hippasus.com/rrpweblog/archives/2015/10/SAMR_ABriefIntro.pdf

Rifkin, J. (2009). *The empathic civilization: The race to global consciousness in a world in crisis.* New York, NY: Penguin.

Solon, O. (2017, November 9). Ex-Facebook president Sean Parker: Site made to exploit human 'vulnerability'. *The Guardian*. Retrieved from https://www.theguardian.com/technology/2017/nov/09/facebook-sean-parker-vulnerability-brain-psychology

CHAPTER 12

Centers for Disease Control and Prevention. (2016). Sexual identity, sex of sexual contacts, and health-related behaviors among students in grades 9–12—United States and selected sites, 2015. *MMWR Surveillance Summaries, 65*(9). Retrieved from https://www.cdc.gov/mmwr/volumes/65/ss/pdfs/ss6509.pdf

DiAngelo, R. (2011). White fragility. *International Journal of Critical Pedagogy, 3*(2), 54–70.

DiAngelo, R. (2018). *White fragility: Why it's so hard for White people to talk about racism.* Boston, MA: Beacon Press.

Hammond, Z. (2014). *Culturally responsive teaching and the brain.* Thousand Oaks, CA: Corwin.

Hanson, J. (2014, January 6). The science of snowflakes. *It's okay to be smart.* Retrieved from https://www.youtube.com/watch?v=fUot7XSX8uA&feature=youtu.be

Muth, J. J. (2002). *The three questions.* New York, NY: Scholastic Press.

Pane, J. (2018). Strategies for implementing personalized learning while evidence and resources are underdeveloped. *Perspective.* Santa Monica, CA: RAND Corporation. Retrieved from https://www.rand.org/content/dam/rand/pubs/perspectives/PE300/PE314/RAND_PE314.pdf

Pane, J. F., Steiner, E. D., Baird, M. D., Hamilton, L. S., & Pane, J. D. (2017). *Informing progress: Insights on personalized learning implementation and effects.* Santa Monica, CA: RAND Corporation. Retrieved from https://www.rand.org/pubs/research_reports/RR2042.html

Rifkin, J. (2009). *The empathic civilization: The race to global consciousness in a world in crisis.* New York, NY: Penguin.

Robin DiAngelo on White people's 'fragility.' (2018, August 18). *Weekend Edition Saturday.* NPR. Retrieved from https://www.npr.org/2018/08/18/639822895/robin-diangelo-on-white-peoples-fragility

U.S. Census. (2018). Vintage 2017 population estimates. Retrieved from https://www.census.gov/content/dam/Census/library/visualizations/2018/comm/diverse-nation.pdf

VanderVeen, A. (2014, August 10). Personalization and the 2 sigma problem. *EdSurge.* Retrieved from https://www.edsurge.com/news/2014-08-10-personalization-and-the-2-sigma-problem

INDEX

A SAGE Publishing Company

Helping educators make the greatest impact

CORWIN HAS ONE MISSION: to enhance education through intentional professional learning.

We build long-term relationships with our authors, educators, clients, and associations who partner with us to develop and continuously improve the best evidence-based practices that establish and support lifelong learning.

Solutions YOU WANT | Experts YOU TRUST | Results YOU NEED

EVENTS

>>> **INSTITUTES**

Corwin Institutes provide large regional events where educators collaborate with peers and learn from industry experts. Prepare to be recharged and motivated!

corwin.com/institutes

ON-SITE PD

>>> **ON-SITE PROFESSIONAL LEARNING**

Corwin on-site PD is delivered through high-energy keynotes, practical workshops, and custom coaching services designed to support knowledge development and implementation.

corwin.com/pd

>>> **PROFESSIONAL DEVELOPMENT RESOURCE CENTER**

The PD Resource Center provides school and district PD facilitators with the tools and resources needed to deliver effective PD.

corwin.com/pdrc

ONLINE

>>> **ADVANCE**

Designed for K–12 teachers, Advance offers a range of online learning options that can qualify for graduate-level credit and apply toward license renewal.

corwin.com/advance

Contact a PD Advisor at (800) 831-6640 or visit www.corwin.com for more information